The Berlin of George Grosz
Drawings, Watercolours and Prints, 1912–1930

Royal Academy of Arts, London
20 March–8 June 1997

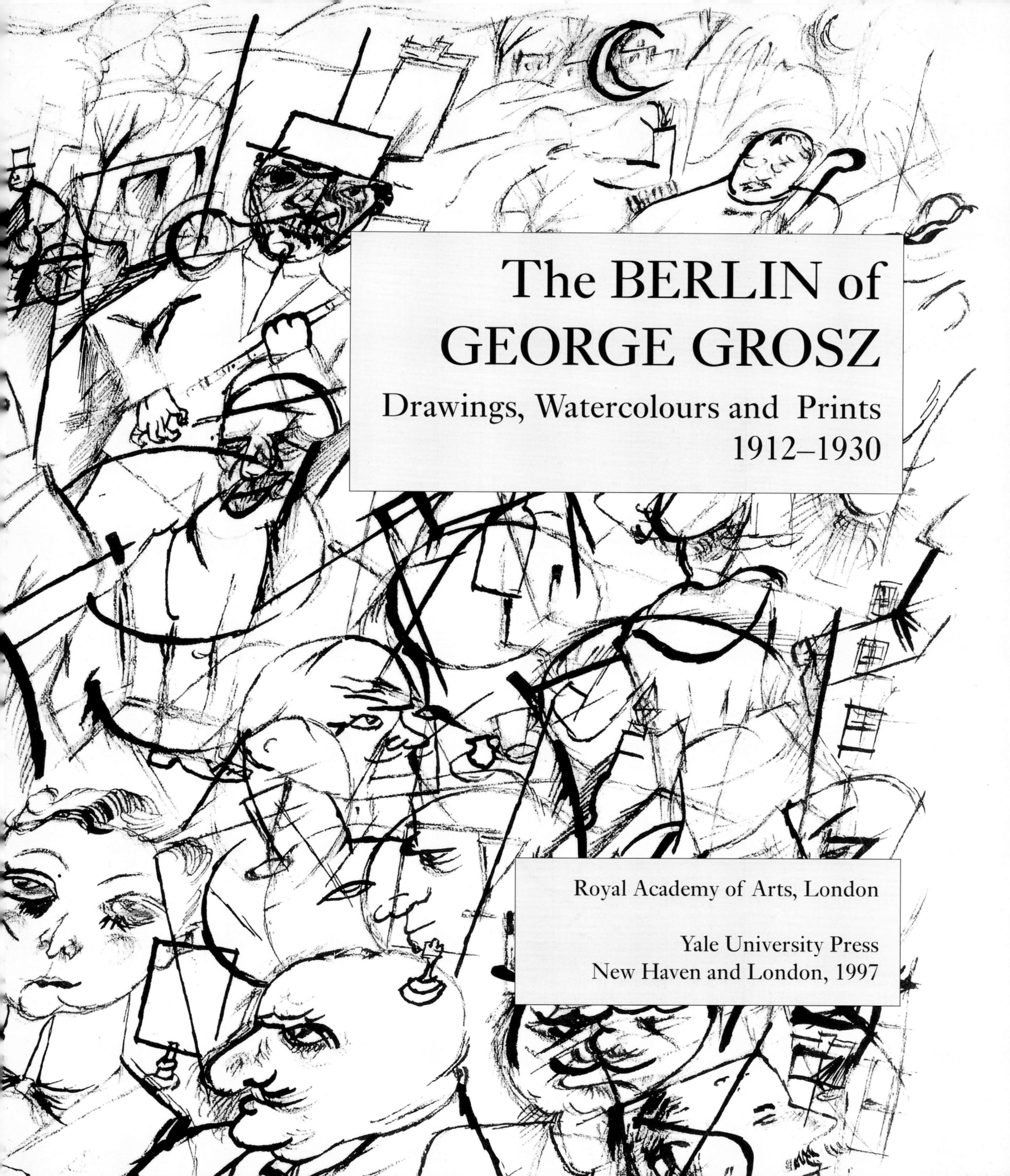

The BERLIN of GEORGE GROSZ

Drawings, Watercolours and Prints
1912–1930

Royal Academy of Arts, London

Yale University Press
New Haven and London, 1997

First published on the occasion of the exhibition
'The Berlin of George Grosz: Drawings, Watercolours and Prints, 1912-1930'
Royal Academy of Arts, London, 20 March–8 June 1997

Supported by  Auswärtiges Amt, Bonn

The Royal Academy of Arts is grateful to Her Majesty's Government for its help in agreeing to indemnify the exhibition under the National Heritage Act 1980, and to the Museums and Galleries Commission for its help in arranging this indemnity.

Copyright © 1997 Royal Academy of Arts, London

All rights reserved. This book may not be reproduced, in whole or in part, in any form (beyond that permitted by Sections 107 and 108 of the U.S. Copyright Law and except by reviewers for the public press), without written permission from the publishers.

Library of Congress Catalog Card Number 97-60164
ISBN 0-300-07206-6 (hard cover)
ISBN 0-300-07211-2 (paperback)

Exhibition Curator: Frank Whitford
Exhibitions Secretary: Norman Rosenthal
Exhibition Organiser and Curatorial Assistant: Emeline Max
Exhibition Assistant: Sam Oakley

Text Editor: Antony Wood
Photographic and Copyright Coordinator: Miranda Bennion
Editorial Coordinator: Sophie Lawrence

Designed by Sally Salvesen
Typeset by SX Composing DTP, Rayleigh, Essex
Printed in Italy

Cover illustrations: *Diamond Profiteers in the Café Kaiserhof*, 1920 (Sammlung Karsch/Nierendorf, Berlin); *Sunny Country*, c. 1920 (Theodore B. Donson Ltd, New York)

Frontispiece: *People in a Café*, 1917 (Trustees of the British Museum, London)

CONTENTS

President's Foreword	vii
Acknowledgements	viii
Lenders to the Exhibition	ix
Editorial note	xi
THE MANY FACES OF GEORGE GROSZ *Frank Whitford*	1
WEIMAR POLITICS AND GEORGE GROSZ *Christopher Clark*	21
GROSZ THROUGH THE EYES OF HIS CONTEMPORARIES	28
GROSZ AS AN ART THEORIST	32
CATALOGUE	41
Chronology	197
Bibliography	202
Index	205
Photographic Credits	208
Friends of the Royal Academy	209
Royal Academy Trust	209
Sponsors of Past Exhibitions	211

PRESIDENT'S FOREWORD

George Grosz is one of the most significant German artists and inventive draftsmen of this century. This exhibition covers the years Grosz spent in Berlin – 1912 to 1930 – during which his work reflected with often uncomfortable accuracy the moral decay and political turbulence of the German capital. Though many of Grosz's drawings are politically inspired and satirical, this exhibition shows that there is much more to him than this: the amused observer of middle-class life; the moral arbiter; the artistic innovator; the prophet who sensed what was to come. He was an enormously varied artist who was as capable of making an outrageously avant-garde statement as he was of respecting the great tradition. Given the unparalleled contribution of British artists to satirical drawing, it is regrettable that his extraordinarily original work is not better known in the United Kingdom. This is the first major show of Grosz's work to be held in Britain for over a quarter of a century, and we trust that it will restore him to his rightful status in this country, equal to that of his great contemporaries Max Beckmann and Otto Dix.

We are greatly indebted to Frank Whitford, a specialist in twentieth-century German art and one-time professional cartoonist, for selecting the exhibition, which was first suggested by Norman Rosenthal, and also for writing much of the catalogue. The exhibition would not have been possible without the help and advice of many people. Above all, we would like to thank Peter M. Grosz, the artist's elder son and his wife, Lilian, for their encouragement, unflagging enthusiasm and unfailing practical help. We are equally grateful for the support of the German Foreign Office, Bonn, without which this exhibition could not have been realised. Finally, our warmest thanks go to the many lenders, both private and public. Through their generosity we are able to show many important works by George Grosz in Britain for the first time.

Sir Philip Dowson CBE
President, Royal Academy of Arts

ACKNOWLEDGEMENTS

The organisers would like to thank the following people who have contributed to the organisation of the exhibition and the preparation of the catalogue in many different ways:

Petra Albrecht
Lutz Becker
Eugen Blume
Camilla Boodle
Richard A. Cohn
Roberta Kimmel Cohn
Margaret Dong
Alexander Dückers
Gregory J. Eades
Richard L. Feigen
Sabine Fischer
Dorota Folga-Januszewska
Simonetta Fraquelli
Ulrike Gauss
Peter and Lilian Grosz
Martin and Rachel Grosz
Ralph Jentsch
Jane Kallir
Eberhard W. Kornfeld
Roland März
Jörn Merkert
Rozita Moamem
Achim Moeller
Freya Mülhaupt
Elke Ostländer
The late Marjorie Proops
Phyllis Rosenzweig
Margit Rowell
Marie Santos
Emma Sarjant
Peter-Klaus Schuster
Mahboubeh Soufer
Irmgard Spencker
Gudrun Schmidt

LENDERS TO THE EXHIBITION

Austria
Vienna, Leopold Museum, Privatstiftung

Germany
Berlin, Berlinische Galerie, Landesmuseum für Moderne Kunst Photographie und Architektur
Berlin, Staatliche Museen zu Berlin, Kupferstichkabinett
Berlin, Stiftung Archiv der Akademie der Künste, Kunstsammlung
Berlin, Stiftung Stadtmuseum
Berlin, Sammlung Karsch/Nierendorf, Berlin
Berlin, Galerie Pels-Leusden
Cologne, Museum Ludwig
Darmstadt, Hessisches Landesmuseum
Düsseldorf, Graphische Sammlung Kunstmuseum
Hannover, Sprengel Museum
Leipzig, Deutsches Buch- und Schriftmuseum der Deutschen Bücherei
Ludwigshafen a. Rh., Wilhelm-Hack-Museum
Marbach am Neckar, Schiller-Nationalmuseum, Deutsches Literaturarchiv
Stuttgart, Graphische Sammlung der Staatsgalerie Stuttgart

Great Britain
Yorick Blumenfeld
Cambridge, The Syndics of the Fitzwilliam Museum, Cambridge
Edinburgh, Scottish National Gallery of Modern Art
Robin Garton Ltd, Devizes, Wiltshire
Leicester, Leicestershire Museums, Arts and Records Service
London, Henry Boxer Gallery
London, The Trustees of the British Museum
London, Tate Gallery
Collection of Roy and Jenny Wright

Poland
Warsaw, The National Museum in Warsaw

SWITZERLAND
Basel, Öffentliche Kunstsammlung, Kupferstichkabinett
Bern, Collection E.W.K.
Zurich, Claudius Ochsner

UNITED STATES
Brooklyn, The Brooklyn Museum
Cambridge, Busch-Reisinger Museum, Harvard University Art Museums
Cambridge, Fogg Art Museum, Harvard University Art Museums
Dr and Mrs George Dean
New York, The Metropolitan Museum of Art
New York, The Museum of Modern Art
New York, Richard A. Cohn Ltd
New York, Theodore B. Donson Ltd
New York, Richard L. Feigen & Co.
New York, Achim Moeller Fine Art
New York, Soufer Gallery
Washington, Hirshhorn Museum and Sculpture Garden, Smithsonian Institution

and those lenders who wish to remain anonymous

EDITORIAL NOTE

Dimensions are given in centimetres, height before width.

There is no *catalogue raisonné* of Grosz's drawings, and their titles often vary from one publication to another. Unless otherwise stated, the titles given here and their English versions are those most commonly used. The German and English titles of Grosz's prints follow the *catalogue raisonné* by Alexander Dückers, *George Grosz, Das druckgraphische Werk*, Frankfurt a.M., Berlin and Vienna, 1979.

All works included in the Exhibition are referred to by a catalogue number; works not exhibited but reproduced in the catalogue are referred to by a figure number.

The catalogue entries and the chronology are by Frank Whitford. All translations are the author's own, unless otherwise stated.

The abbreviations for frequently cited literature are listed at the beginning of the bibliography.

1. George Grosz as a sex murderer with Eva Peter in the studio, *c.* 1920. This one of several photographs probably taken by Grosz himself using a delayed exposure. He and his wife posed as attacker and victim in his studio The sex murderer was one of several identities he liked playfully or ironically to assume.

THE MANY FACES OF GEORGE GROSZ

Frank Whitford

Contradictions

Towards the end of the 1920s a 'Guide to Dissolute Berlin' – *Führer durch das lasterhafte Berlin* – was published in Leipzig. Written by Curt Moreck, it provided information about male and female prostitution in the capital and laconically described the cafés, nightclubs and bathhouses where, it claimed, every imaginable sexual fantasy could be realized. The pocket-sized guide included details of, for example, the Mikado on the Puttkamerstrasse where transvestites could be observed dancing in full fig; the Verona-Diele on the Kleiststrasse where lesbians congregated; and the Voo-Doo, Bürger-Casino and Monte-Casino, just three of the innumerable meeting-places for homosexual men.

Between the wars such establishments did much to establish Berlin's international reputation as the bawdiest, most licentious city in Europe. Its cabaret acts were outrageously explicit. Its brothels were well publicised. The tables in its dance-halls were furnished with telephones to permit assignations between customers who had never met. In its clubs, pubs and doorways girls, rent boys and entire pharmacopoeias of drugs, especially cocaine, could be had for less than the price of a decent dinner.

Moreck's prurient publication was illustrated with paintings and drawings by Jeanne Mammen, Christian Schad and George Grosz, artists known for their vivid depictions of the capital's night life. Grosz's drawings, less sensational than the others, were originally made for a quite different purpose and had been previously published elsewhere. But their inclusion in the book speaks volumes about Grosz's contemporary reputation: he was almost universally regarded as the most perceptive and accurate reporter of the seamy side of German metropolitan life.

Grosz is still chiefly seen in the same way. His drawings and watercolours seem to give off the putrid whiff of the social decadence and political corruption of the Weimar Republic. Like Christopher Isherwood's Berlin stories about Mr Norris and Sally Bowles, they have made an essential and indelible contribution to our picture of what the German capital was like at a turbulent and fateful point in its history. Grosz's art provides a panoramic, multi-faceted view of German society between the collapse of the monarchy in 1918 and Hitler's coming to power fourteen years later.

When a film based on Isherwood's stories was produced in 1955 Grosz was commissioned to design the sets.[1] He was the obvious choice to evoke the seedy atmosphere of Berlin during the rise of the Nazis. Yet Grosz's designs were disappointing. Tentative, bland, and undistinguished, they entirely lack the conviction of his earlier work. There are several reasons for this. By 1954 Grosz had been living in the USA for more than twenty years and pre-war Berlin was a distant memory. More importantly, he had become a quite different artist, long since grown weary of his popular reputation as the most accurate chronicler of decadent Berlin. He accepted the film commission only for the sake of the money; but his art was considerably more varied, extensive and complex than was commonly imagined.

In America Grosz had become a painter of apocalyptic visions, of teeming cityscapes and depopulated nature. He worked as an illustrator, too, in a style so different from his earlier work that it might be that of another artist entirely. In Germany Grosz's art had been even more various. He made humorous sketches, drawings of entertainers, vagrants, criminals and drunks, and political cartoons with an uncompromisingly radical message. Inspired by Expressionism and Futurism, he painted city streets in chaos, exploding with rioting mobs or crowded with pimps, prostitutes and gangsters. He produced ambitious compositions in which allegory is combined with satire. He made Dadaist photomontages, and for a time used his ruler, projector and pen to create mechanistic images in a near-anonymous manner. He painted naturalistic portraits in sharp detail and close focus, erotic female nudes, decorative still-lifes, and undemanding landscapes.

In Berlin Grosz observed the milieu in which he moved like a patrolling shark with an eye that was amused and entertained as often as it was remorselessly critical. While exposing the hypocrisy and double standards of middle-class behaviour, his drawings betray sympathy as often as disgust and condemnation. He secretly identified with those he attacked and found those he pretended to support unappealing. He was a Communist who disliked the proletariat, a child of poor parents who acquired bourgeois ambitions, a political radical who came to be alarmed by extremes of every kind. He was a leading member of the artistic avant-garde who remained sceptical of its claims and pretensions. Although most of his own art was fiercely original, his tastes were conservative, even reactionary. Who was George Grosz really?

Identities

Grosz's art was complex and contradictory and so was the man who made it. Like many of the heroes and villains in the penny dreadfuls he liked reading as a boy, he was a man of many disguises. One of his favourite activities was dressing up and striking poses for the camera. In one photograph he appears as an American gangster, a fedora on his head and a cocked pistol in his hand. In another he lurks with a knife behind a full-length mirror while his wife, seemingly unaware of his imminent assault, preens herself in a one-piece bathing costume (fig.1).

Grosz loved pretending. Opening his door to callers he had never met, he would often introduce himself as Herr Grosz's butler, regretting his master's temporary absence. For some time the walls of his studio were hung with camera portraits of such celebrities as Edison and Henry Ford, each of them furnished with a forged signature and personal dedication. Before World War I he would regularly appear at his favourite café with his face powdered and rouged, wearing a fashionably tailored suit, spats and patent leather shoes, and sporting a Malacca cane, its ivory pommel carved into the shape of a skull.

But there was more to these false identities than a desire to attract attention or a liking for practical jokes. Grosz lived the parts he played and convinced others of their authenticity. This was the case in 1916 when, at a party for artists and intellectuals, he assumed the identity of a businessman from neutral Holland eager to make a quick profit from the war. It was all so simple, the immaculately groomed guest told his increasingly dismayed audience of bohemian pacifists and republicans. His plan was to employ limbless war veterans in the manufacture of ashtrays and other useful household items, each engraved with a patriotic slogan, from salvaged shrapnel and spent artillery shells. The act was effective, its irony, when the truth was revealed, devastating.[2]

The various personae Grosz assumed, from the dandy to the Dutch businessman with the sex murderer in between, were more than characters in an elaborate charade. They were projections of contradictory parts of himself. Grosz knew it and made it clear in a letter of 1915 written at a critical moment in his life: he had recently been released from the army on medical grounds. 'I am terribly lonely', he admitted,

> or rather alone with my *Doppelgänger*, phantoms in whose forms I give reality to particular dreams, ideas, desires etc. I can wrest 3 other people out of my inner imaginings, and I believe in these imaginary pseudonyms myself. Gradually three clearly distinguished types have emerged. 1. Grosz. 2. Count Ehrenfried, the nonchalant aristocrat with manicured fingernails intent only on cultivating himself, in a word the exclusive aristocratic individualist. 3. The physician Dr William King Thomas who provides the more American, practical and materialistic balance within the host figure of Grosz himself.[3]

Further phantoms were announced in signatures on letters, drawings, prints and the covers of sketchbooks: Count Bessler-Orffyre, Ritter von Thorn, Georges le Boeuf, Böff, Graf Ehrenfried, Lord Hatton Dixon, and Edgar A. Hussler. Not all of them were invented. Thorn was the small town where Grosz had spent part of his youth, Ehrenfried was his middle name, while Bessler-Orffyre was a fraudster who claimed to have discovered the secret of perpetual motion. Thomas William King was a ship-owner who in 1875 blew up one of his vessels at Bremerhaven, killing most of the people on board, for the insurance money. Grosz clearly felt a special affinity with him. Somehow he managed to acquire his death mask.

Strictly speaking, even the name George Grosz was a pseudonym, the anglicised version of what appeared on his baptismal certificate. The change from Georg Gross, which he made around 1916, was initially part of a larger stratagem: the desire to pass himself off as an American. At the height of the war (which the USA had not yet joined) he began to wear clothes tailored in the American style and, although still anything but a master of the language, would ostentatiously pretend to converse in something like English with friends on the street. He told everyone he met that he liked to attend boxing matches, loved jazz and played the banjo, all then almost exclusively American or Anglo-Saxon activities – as was the habit of smoking a pipe which he adopted.

George Grosz the American was one of the most convincing and enduring of all the roles he played. At the beginning of his career several critics drew attention to his German-American background as a contributory factor in his artistic development. And towards the end of his career the role became reality. In 1932 he finally visited the USA for the first time, and in 1938, having been stripped of his German citizenship, legally became an American.

So who was George Grosz? The question is as difficult for us to answer as it was for Grosz himself. Like Walt Whitman whom he liked to quote, he was large and contained multitudes. He was each of his many *Doppelgänger* in turn and sometimes several of them together. The phantoms that populated his imagination brought both loneliness and despair, and in his repeated attempts, increasingly assisted by alcohol during his later years, to flee from himself, he was running away from all of them.

Most of the Berlin Dadaists gave themselves nicknames. Raoul Hausmann was 'Dadasoph', his girlfriend Hannah Hoech 'Dadasophin', and Johannes Baader 'Oberdada'. Grosz was called 'Propagandada' and had visiting cards printed accordingly. On the back were printed the words *Wie denke ich morgen?*, What will my opinion be tomorrow? It was more than a joke. It was Grosz's problem – although also one of the strengths of his art – that he was never sure what he would be thinking next or who he was.

2. *In the Robbers' Den. A guest who has been given a sleeping draught is robbed. Mr Angstmeier's dream*, 1908, pencil and wash. George Grosz Estate.

Childhood

Grosz grew up not in Berlin, where he was born in July 1893, but in Stolp, a small town in eastern Pomerania not far from the Baltic. He spent much of his childhood feeding his imagination on a rich diet of luridly illustrated pulp fiction, the adventure stories of Karl May and James Fenimore Cooper's novels about the trappers and Indians of colonial north America. His heroes were Old Shatterhand, Winnetou, Leather-Stocking, Chingachgook and Texas Jack, and several Sherlock Holmes imitations weekly left a trail of blood across the badly printed pages of his books and magazines. He copied the illustrations and made others for stories of his own (fig. 2). This was the first art he saw and it was popular and trivial.

A little later his imagination was set racing by trivial art of a different kind. When funfairs and circuses (some with freak shows) made their annual visits to Stolp Grosz always went to see them, open-eyed at the garishly coloured paintings decorating the booths and stands and fascinated by the bold lettering. He was even more impressed by the illusionistic cycloramas exhibited in tents which gave a convincing impression of celebrated battles, natural catastrophes and other dramatic events.

An enthusiasm for the bloodthirsty and grotesque never left him. Nor did a liking for the sentimental and popular academic art which he discovered in books and on the walls of the army officers' mess where his mother worked as a cook. He was above all impressed by the work of Eduard Grützner, a specialist in paintings of plump monks and carousing cardinals.

Grosz's artistic preferences were shared by every small-town German of basic education and average taste. They became far more sophisticated later but he never lost his early liking for whatever was popular and skilfully executed. Towards the end of his life in America he professed his admiration for the illustrator Norman Rockwell, a kind of Grützner in Yankee dress, although Rockwell's ability to make money probably had as much to do with Grosz's enthusiasm as his prodigious powers of narrative and description.

If Grosz's taste was conformist, little else about him was. At school he was a rebel, and his refusal to treat his teachers with the exaggerated respect expected in an authoritarian society led to his expulsion. Given a slap by a trainee teacher, Grosz hit him back and was expelled. The punishment was severe. Prevented from taking the examination that would have qualified him to begin working towards a professional career, he was seemingly condemned to a future of manual labour.

His talent for drawing, honed by hours of copying illustrations in books, saved him from such a fate. The school art master, clearly something of a nonconformist himself, advised Grosz to become a painter and helped him prepare for the entrance examination to one of Germany's most distinguished art schools, the Art Academy in Dresden.

In 1909 he became a student there, drawing from plaster casts and life, and learning the principles of composition in the Academy's impressive buildings overlooking the Elbe. He said he wanted to paint battle scenes and other historical subjects although he realised that it would be difficult to make money from them, at least initially. So he developed the double strategy that served him well for the rest of his career. He would support himself as a serious artist by selling drawings and cartoons to popular magazines. Moderate success came remarkably quickly. In 1910 the first of his sketches was published in *Ulk*, the comic supplement of the *Berliner Tageblatt*.

A year later he left Dresden with a diploma and arrived in Berlin to continue his studies at the School of Arts and Crafts. He was nineteen, in the capital for the first time in a decade, hungry for experience and determined to make his name. He was neither the first nor the last young artist to realise that success would probably depend as much on a talent for self-advertisement as on genuinely artistic gifts. So he cultivated an image as a dandy and displayed himself at the cafés frequented by journalists and other opinion-makers. At the same time he got to know Berlin, walking its streets by day and night, filling countless sketchbooks with his impressions of its buildings and people.

In Pre-War Berlin

It was in the German capital that Grosz lived for the next twenty-two years, made his name, and died after more than two decades in America. Although he came to hate what it stood for, he loved the city with a passion. Still rapidly expanding, it seemed to contain the entire world in microcosm, to offer every conceivable kind of human experience, and to be inhabited by every imaginable type of human being.

In 1911 Berlin had been the German capital for only forty years. Already dominant in industry and technology, it had only recently become the nation's pre-eminent intellectual and cultural centre. Its continuing growth and increasing distinction added to the excitement of living there. 'In Berlin people were progressive . . . there was wonderful theatre, a gigantic circus, cabarets and revues. Beer palaces as big as railway concourses, wine palaces which occupied four floors, six-day [bicycle] races, futuristic exhibitions, international tango competitions. . .That was Berlin when I arrived there.'[4]

Most of the city's architecture was depressingly humdrum. Most people lived in great grey apartment blocks whose façades masked a progression of increasingly dismal rear courtyards. Even Berlin's grander representative buildings were intimidating, severe in their neoclassicism or oppressive in the cluttered ornamention of their neobaroque. But there were also vast department stores, huge luxury hotels and low dives both picturesque and sinister. The people were energetic, abrasive, and had a – frequently witty – answer to everything. Berlin was famous for its *Tempo*, the breakneck speed at which everything seemed to move, and its *Luft*, the bracing air which kept everyone on his toes even after a hard night's drinking.

Grosz enjoyed the spectacle of it all, the opulence and poverty, the glitter and grime. He was poor but cultivated the image of a dandified idler, leaving his room in the southwestern suburb of Südende to take the train to the centre where he would stroll along the Kurfürstendamm and Tauentzienstrasse, haughtily eyeing the crowds.

But he worked, too, not only at the School of Arts and Crafts but wherever he found himself, transferring his impressions directly into sketchbooks and working them up in more elaborate drawings. His impressions of Südende were especially vivid. A relatively underprivileged district on the furthermost limits of the city, it was mostly inhabited by petty clerks, industrial labourers and the unemployed. The ceaseless construction work there made Berlin's inexorable expansion dramatically obvious.

Grosz drew the building sites and the workers employed on them. He drew the blank-faced apartment blocks and the people he encountered on the street: men on the way to their factories, vagrants and alcoholics. In this he was following in the footsteps of the popular artist and quintessential Berliner Heinrich Zille (1858–1929), who specialised in cartoons of working-class families indomitably coping with the problems of everyday life (fig. 3). But where Zille was anecdotal and sentimental, Grosz's approach to urban subjects was essentially that of a realist with a liking for drama and exaggeration.

He also found the drama (and the glamour) he craved in cabarets and circuses where he sketched singers, musicians, clowns, acrobats and tightrope-walkers. His graphic style became looser, more vivid and spontaneous as he abandoned a soft pencil in favour of pen and ink often supplemented by watercolour washes and coloured crayons.

In the city centre he became a regular at the Café des Westens, the preferred haunt of the Expressionists (and, improbably, the place where Rupert Brooke wrote *The Old Vicarage, Granchester* in 1912). Thanks to the grandiose postures that were habitually struck there, it became known as the *Café Grössenwahn* – Café Megalomania.

Expressionism then dominated the avant-garde in all the German arts. It celebrated the self and employed extreme distortions of reality to convey exaggerated emotions. Grosz soon came to know several Expressionist writers, among them the eccentric poet Else Lasker-Schüler, one of his earliest admirers. He was impressed by the style for a time, especially by its violent and otherwise sensational subject-matter. In his drawings suburban streets and domestic interiors increasingly became the settings of brawls, savage murders and suicides. Direct observation was replaced by dark, grotesque imaginings indebted as much to Edgar Allan Poe and his German-speaking disciples Hanns Heinz Ewers and Gustav Meyrinck as to any of the Expressionists.

Grosz was also affected by Italian Futurist painting which was introduced into Germany in April 1912 at Der Sturm, the gallery owned by Lasker-Schüler's husband, the art dealer Herwarth Walden. The following year Walden staged another show which placed special emphasis on both Futurism and Expressionism and left a deep impression on Grosz's mind.

He was to borrow heavily from Futurism in both his paintings and drawings; but first Grosz's progress was interrupted by war. In November 1914, still a student and unsure of the direction he wished his art to take, he volunteered for the army.

At War

Most of those who volunteered were enthusiastic and fired with anticipation. Grosz was not one of them: he chose to go simply because he knew his conscription was imminent. He reluctantly joined a conflict which he thought senseless and unnecessary. Fortunately for him his regiment was not immediately ordered to the front and, more luckily still, he soon found himself in a military hospital with a severe sinus infection. After an operation in May 1915 he was declared unfit and sent home.

He had seen nothing of battle and his encounter with the Prussian military mind had been brief. His army experience was nevertheless long and disturbing enough to change him thoroughly – or rather to bring the bleakly pessimistic side of his personality to the fore. Returning to Berlin, he found the city

> cold and grey. The frenzied activity of the cabarets and bars contrasted unnervingly with

3. Heinrich Zille, *Moving House with the Brown Sofa*, 1900, black and coloured chalks. Stiftung Preussischer Kulturbesitz, Kupferstichkabinett.

the dark, murky and unheated places where people lived. The same soldiers who sang, danced and hung drunkenly on the arms of prostitutes could later be seen, ill-tempered, laden with parcels and still muddy from grave-digging duty, marching through the streets from one railway station to the next. How right Swedenborg was, I thought, when he said that Heaven and Hell exist here on earth side by side.[5]

For the moment there was no trace of Heaven at all.

As yet Grosz was not politically engaged. His attitude to the War and Germany's part in it was ill-defined, shaped less by his brain than his emotions. Everything disgusted him. He hated the authorities who, like the trainee teacher in Stolp, had done their best to bend his will to theirs. He loathed humanity in general and Germans in particular. Significantly, it was the way people looked more than their beliefs that brought him to the boil.

> Every day my hatred of Germany is fuelled by the impossible ugliness of the unaesthetic (yes indeed!) and bad, entirely bad dress of the most German of her citizens. . . I'll put it down here for you: 'I do not feel related to this mishmash of a people'. . . What do I see? . . . only unkempt, fat, deformed, incredibly ugly men and (above all) women, degenerate creatures (although a fat, red, plump, lazy man is here considered to be a 'stately gentleman'), with bad juices (from beer) and hips that are too fat and short. . .[6]

The letter concludes with a quotation from Zola: 'Hatred is holy'.

Although far from politically active, Grosz was nevertheless pulled into the orbit of those who were. In 1915 and 1916 his still unpolitical drawings were published in *Die Aktion*, the Expressionist, pacifist and republican journal; and from 1916 he began to collaborate with Wieland Herzfelde, a young writer of the radical left whom he first met (and outraged) while pretending to be the businessman from Holland.

Herzfelde, who published a journal of his own, was the first to give Grosz's drawings real exposure. He also encouraged Grosz's literary talent by printing his poetry. Above all, Herzfelde gave shape and direction to the artist's ill-defined ideas about the reasons for the War, the nature of German society and the solutions to its ills. But before their collaboration could flourish Grosz was mobilised for a second time.

By 1917 the War was going badly for Germany and men already released from duty on medical grounds were being called up again. Grosz was among them, and although his second introduction to military life was almost as short as his first, it was much more agonising. The circumstances of his service and demobilisation remain unclear. There are stories about his refusing to obey an order, about a court martial sentencing him to be shot by firing squad, but about these things the military records are silent. This much seems certain, however: conscripted on 4 January, he was admitted to a field hospital the following day, and on 23 February transferred to a military mental asylum.

In hospital he used drawing as a safety valve for his boiling resentment, sketching 'what I disliked about my surroundings: the beastly faces of my comrades, the malicious cripples, arrogant officers, lecherous nurses, etc. There was no particular point to these drawings; at first I made them . . . simply to record the laughable and grotesque world of the busy, deadly little ants around me. . .'[7] Released in March, Grosz was finally discharged as permanently unfit on 20 May after convincing army doctors that he was mad.

The War continued for almost five months and when it ended Grosz was neither taken by surprise, nor, of course, disappointed. But he was depressed by the fact that 'people had suffered and endured it for years, that no one had listened to the few voices raised against the mass slaughter.'[8] His transformation into a political radical and artist dedicated to revolutionary change was almost complete. He had already begun to turn the hell Berlin and the world had become into pictures.

The Political Animal

During the war Grosz began to paint in oils. Until then he had made almost no use of the medium and now taught himself the technique which for him involved the extensive use of underpainting and glazing. In a letter of December 1917 he revealed that he was painting a large picture of Hell – a *Gin Lane* of grotesque corpses and lunatics; there's a lot going on – Old Nick himself is riding on the slanting coffin through the picture out towards the left; on the right a young man is throwing up, vomiting on the canvas all the beautiful illusions of youth. . . A teeming multitude of possessed human beasts – I am totally convinced that this epoch is sailing on down to its own destruction – our sullied paradise. . . just think: wherever you step smells of shit.[9]

Widmung an Oskar Panizza (Dedicated to Oskar Panizza)[10] was finished six months later (fig. 4). The characters it portrays include flag waving chauvinists, bemedalled generals and a priest. In the bottom left-hand corner three hideous figures symbolise alcoholism, syphilis and plague. The entire fragmented scene is lit by a glowing red suggestive of both blood and conflagration.

Grosz later explained that the painting was a 'protest against humanity gone mad'[11] but its message is not as unambiguous as this makes it sound. Grosz's reference to Hogarth's *Gin Lane* in his letter suggests a satirical and moral purpose, but this apocalyptic vision is presented with as much relish as fear, and it is difficult to decide whether Grosz was guided chiefly by disgust and foreboding or by the perverse pleasure he took in depicting horror and violence.

There is no doubting his intentions in another painting completed in 1918, however. *Deutschland, ein Wintermärchen* (Germany, a Winter's Tale), its title taken from a satirical poem by Heinrich Heine, again shows a collapsing world populated by representative social types (fig. 5). While an apprehensive soldier finishes his meal in the centre of this chaotic scene, a priest, a general and a nationalistic schoolmaster holding a copy of Goethe's works function as pillars of society supporting the rickety structure above. In the bottom left-hand corner Grosz shows himself in profile, the red spot on his temple symbolising the anger with which he surveys the mess and the men and institutions that made it. Packed with fragmentary details and seemingly unrelated events, the painting is reminiscent of collage. Indeed, there are collaged elements in it: real newspaper clippings and ration coupons litter the table in the centre.

Finished while the November revolution was raging in Berlin, *Germany, a Winter's Tale* marked Grosz's emergence as a full-blooded political satirist. Together with *Dedicated to Oskar Panizza*, it also announced his arrival as a brilliant and original painter in the forefront of the avant-garde. In the dynamic angularity of their jostling, superimposed forms, both compositions owe much to Futurism; but there is more that is entirely foreign to it. The style makes a message explicit, projects a view of the city at total variance with that of the Futurists. It is the location not of utopia but of a jungle. Emotional thrills may be had but they are perverse and terrifying. Limitless energies are generated there, not by factories and power stations as in the Futurist city, but by rapacious, mindless or calculating beasts hell-bent on their own and the city's destruction.

The city in chaos, destroyed by mobs of marauding lunatics, is also the subject of numerous drawings made during the War. In them the fighting retreats to the home front where the brutality of the acts depicted is emphasised by a consciously primitive style derived from graffiti.

As a student in Dresden, Grosz imagined a career as a painter financially supported by sales of drawings to magazines. This was the course he now took. Paintings like *Dedicated to Oskar Panizza* were anything but commercial, but Wieland Herzfelde's business sense as a publisher ensured that Grosz would be able to make money from his drawings. In the first issue of the journal *Die Neue Jugend* (New Youth), Herzfelde's first publishing venture, signed prints of the Grosz drawings that appeared there were advertised for sale. Enough of them were bought to encourage Herzfelde to produce a portfolio of reproductions not in one but several variously priced editions. This, the *Erste George Grosz-Mappe* (First George Grosz Portfolio), consisted of nine lithographs and appeared in the spring of 1917. It was followed in the autumn by the *Kleine Grosz Mappe* (Little Grosz Portfolio), twenty lithographs of a smaller size.

These and most of the subsequent publications of Grosz's drawings in portfolios and books were the products of a cleverly commercial idea. The most expensive editions,

4. *Dedicated to Oskar Panizza*, 1917–18, oil on canvas. Staatsgalerie Stuttgart.

5. *Germany, A Winter's Tale*, oil on canvas. Present whereabouts unknown.

6. George Grosz and John Heartfield, Advertisement for the *Little George Grosz Portfolio*, 1917.

intended for collectors, were strictly limited and consisted of signed prints on heavy paper. The cheapest, which usually appeared in large numbers, were unsigned and on stock that was little better than newsprint. The rich therefore subsidised those for whom Grosz's work was increasingly intended.

The collector's editions, however, were not quite what they seemed. The portfolios contained not original graphics but cheap lithographic reproductions, some of which were impressed with a border to make them look like etchings. Many were used again and again in a variety of publications.

Indeed, Grosz was not really a printmaker at all. Apart from some early drypoints, a single wood-engraving and lithographs pulled from drawings made on stone, he never produced what are properly described as original graphics, images specifically conceived to exploit the peculiarities of and be reproduced by means of a particular technique. Almost all of his prints were photo-mechanical reproductions of drawings. Grosz considered the polite art trade corrupt and did not think of himself as a conventional artist in any case. He wanted his work to be seen by and to influence as many people as possible, and knew that publication, in whatever form, was the best way to achieve this. As he once replied to questions put to him by a literary magazine: 'I love newspapers even though I do not regard them uncritically. For the propagation of ideas newspapers are of course considerably better than books because many more people read newspapers.'[12]

As interesting as the *Little Grosz Portfolio* itself is the advertisement for it, published in place of an issue of *New Youth* that, having fallen foul of the military censors, was banned (fig. 6).

The advertisement was made up of stock typographical decorations and old blocks distributed between slugs of text printed at angles in a confusing variety of founts and sizes. As a piece of graphic design it was startlingly original, defied all existing conventions, and eventually became very influential. It was the work of Grosz and Herzfelde's brother Helmut who, annoyed by the government's anti-British propaganda (and especially the often repeated slogan *Gott strafe England!* – May God punish England!) – had anglicised his name and was now generally known as John Heartfield.

Heartfield was a talented artist but, impressed (and depressed) by Grosz's far superior gifts as a draftsman, gave up drawing almost completely to concentrate on graphic design. He and Grosz were also among the first to use an entirely new technique, called photomontage, which involved assembling parts of photographs to create a new synthetic image seemingly produced by a camera. Together and separately, Heartfield and Grosz made photomontages which reveal their shared sense of the ridiculous and their cynical view of society. Their attitudes made them susceptible to the subversive ideas which, emanating from Zurich and arriving in Berlin late in the War, had been given the infantile name of Dada.

The Lunacy of the Sane

Dada was many things. In its original form it was an incoherent cry uttered by refugees from the belligerent countries who had found physical but not mental sanctuary in neutral Switzerland. Since the barbarous war was being waged by supposedly rational people in the name of culture and civilisation, the Dadaists argued that what was commonly thought to be sane was lunatic, and that true sanity therefore had the appearance of madness. Since conventional notions of education and culture had been powerless to prevent the War – were, indeed, among its causes – they ought to be turned on their head. Seemingly irrational and offensive acts were therefore designed to attack every form of polite and high culture and shock the public out of its complacent acceptance of all received values and behaviour. From Zurich where it began, Dada spread to several European cities, arriving in Berlin in 1917. It was taken there by the future psychiatrist Richard Huelsenbeck who had decided to return to his native Germany before the hostilities were over.

Berlin, demoralised, starving and volatile, was ripe for subversion. Huelsenbeck quickly found allies, Grosz among them. He, Herzfelde, Heartfield and others gave the irreverent nonsense of Dada a political edge; and Dada gave that aspect of Grosz's personality that had always delighted in irony, japes and playacting an opportunity to unfold. As the Dutch merchant episode had already shown, Grosz's liking for loaded practical jokes made him especially receptive to Dadaist ideas. Moreover, his vision, presented in numerous drawings and paintings, of a world ruled by lunatics, anticipated Dada in several ways, not least in his use of graffiti and other forms of naïve art as stylistic sources.

The Berlin Dadaists (who also included the artists Raoul Hausmann and Hannah Hoech and the writers Franz Jung and Walter Mehring) published magazines and staged outrageous performances. Grosz contributed to them all, making photomontages and drawings and appearing on stage, dancing and declaiming his poems and stories. One of his performances – in February 1918 – consisted of an obscene tap-dance during which he pretended to relieve himself against a painting by Lovis Corinth (an important contemporary artist) while shouting '*Kunst ist Scheisse*' – 'Art is shit' – and reassuring his audience that urine made 'the best varnish'. Another act consisted of a 'race between a sewing machine and a typewriter', the one operated by Grosz, the other by Walter Mehring. These provocative cabaret turns attracted crowds of bemused and noisy Berliners and reports of Dadaist activities filled countless columns in the press. Many people saw the Dadaists' point. After all, their feigned insanity seemed rational by comparison with the improbable realities of the War.

Berlin Dada, which had begun before the end of the War and the beginning of the November Revolution, gathered speed and urgency in 1919. For Grosz, Heartfield and Herzfelde (who were now closely collaborating), the most important battle had just begun. All three were now members of the German Communist Party and admirers of Soviet Russia. They wanted not only a new society but also revenge on those associated with the monarchist, military and capitalist régime. They saw that it had not been swept aside but continued to exist under literally changed colours. The black, white and red of the empire had been replaced by the republican black, red and gold; the Kaiser had abdicated and gone into exile in Holland; but the influence of the royalists and nationalists had not been curbed. The legal system had not been reformed; the power of the Church was still undiminished; the economy was in ruins; but the social inequalities were as huge as ever. They were also more visible, dramatised by the hideously maimed veterans begging on the streets while vulgar war profiteers ostentatiously spent their dubiously acquired fortunes.

Against this background Wieland Herzfelde founded the Malik Verlag, a publishing house dedicated to left-wing propaganda. During the Weimar Republic it became the most successful undertaking of its kind and developed an impressive list of politically inspired fiction and non-fiction. At first it concentrated on creating a series of satirical journals and broadsheets so critical and outspoken that most were quickly banned. Grosz was involved in all of them as contributor or editor. The first, prohibited after a single issue, was *Jedermann sein eigner Fussball*, best translated as 'Kick yourself before someone else does'. It was followed by *Die Pleite* (Bankruptcy), *Der blutige Ernst* (Bloody Earnest), *Der Gegner* (The Opponent) and *Der Knüppel* (The Cudgel). The titles alone are enough to give an idea of their contents.

Grosz, their most visible and brilliant contributor, now emerged as a political cartoonist, rivalling Daumier in the force of his ideas, the clarity of his imagery and the effectiveness of his line. In the first issue of *Die Pleite*, for example, he showed Ebert, the president of the new republic, as an overweight bourgeois wearing a crown, enthroned in an armchair and waited on by a lackey (cat. 152). The message was obvious: the Kaiser and everything he represented lived on in the awkward form of a one-time saddle-maker. In subsequent issues Grosz exposed the bloody deeds of the Freikorps and attacked the military, industrialists, judges and priests with unparalleled viciousness and relish.

Grosz's work for *Die Pleite* and the other Malik publications made him famous. It also brought him many enemies, especially and inevitably from among the ranks of his victims, as an exhibition which he helped to organise demonstrated.

This was *The First International Dada Fair*, staged in the summer of 1920 in two rooms of the Burchard Gallery which usually specialised in Oriental art (fig. 7). The exhibition, which turned out to be both the climax and the conclusion of Dadaism in Berlin, was startlingly unconventional. The framed paintings, collages and prints were hung on the walls in a confusing way and interspersed with printer's proofs, posters and placards, most bearing incomprehensible slogans: 'Take Dada Seriously, It's Worth It!'; 'Dilettantes, Revolt Against Art!';

7. Exhibitors at the Opening of *The First International Dada Fair*, Berlin, 1920. Grosz is in the centre wearing a hat.

8. *The New Man*, 1920, pen, ink and watercolour. Present whereabouts unknown.

The Many Faces of George Grosz 9

'Art is Dead, Long Live the Machine Art of Tatlin!' and so on.

Many artists contributed to the exhibition. Hannah Hoech showed her large photomontage, *Schnitt mit dem Kuchenmesser . . .* (Cut with the Cake-Knife, Dada through the last Weimar German Beer Belly Cultural Epoch), and Otto Dix, Max Ernst, Raoul Hausmann and Georg Scholz were among those represented. There was also an assemblage made by John Heartfield and Rudolf Schlichter entitled *Preussischer Erzengel* (Prussian Archangel), and suspended from the ceiling. It was a dummy dressed in army officer's uniform with a pig's head; a card hanging from its trousers explained: 'In order to understand this work of art go on a daily twelve-hour exercise on the Tempelhof Field with full backpack and equipped for manoeuvres.'

Grosz was one of the major contributors to *The First International Dada Fair*. He exhibited a variety of photomontages, drawings, watercolours and oils, among them *Germany, a Winter's Tale*. Also on view (and for sale) was his recently published portfolio of prints attacking the military, *Gott mit Uns* (May God Be With Us). It was both this and the *Prussian Archangel* that fell foul of the authorities. Grosz, his publisher Herzfelde, Schlichter, Heartfield, the owner of the gallery Otto Burchard, and Johannes Baader, self-styled 'Supreme Dada', were accused of bringing the military into disrepute and taken to court. Thanks to the intervention of a number of respected art historians only Grosz and Herzfelde were found guilty and were fined 300 and 600 marks respectively. The lithographic plates for *May God Be With Us* were also confiscated. It was by no means the last time that Grosz appeared in court.

One of those who testified on behalf of the defendants was no less a figure than Edwin Redslob, government advisor on the arts, and another was P. F. Schmidt, director of Dresden's municipal collections. Schmidt assured the court that Dada was 'the reaction against all unpleasant contemporary manifestations. A major weapon in the fight against them was satire and humour.'[13] The imprimatur of such experts gave Dada legitimacy as an art form and thus emasculated its subversive power. But it had done its work by demonstrating the effectiveness of satire to dismay, offend and persuade.

Significantly, not only Dada's enemies were outraged by the exhibition. So were many of its supposed allies on the radical left. Gertrud Alexander, cultural editor of the Communist Party newspaper *Die Rote Fahne* (The Red Flag), attacked the Dada Fair as 'a collection of perversities'. 'A worker-revolutionary', she went on, 'does not find it necessary, as Dada does, to destroy works of art in order to escape from the bourgeois state, for a worker-revolutionary is not bourgeois. The Dadaists are, however.'[14]

When applied to Grosz's work, this criticism was at least partly true, for it isolated by implication the contradictions at the heart of his intentions. He was more of an anarchist than a communist and too much of an individual to follow any collectivist party line.

The Year of the Robots

In Grosz's personal and creative life 1920 was a more important year than most. He married; he had his first one-man exhibition – at Hans Goltz's Galerie Neue Kunst in Munich; and his art changed direction briefly but radically.

His wife was Eva Peter whom he had known since his days at the Berlin School of Arts and Crafts where both were students. She was artistically gifted (two of her works were exhibited at the Dada Fair), strikingly attractive, and shared Grosz's sense of humour if not his political views. Her sexual appeal, obvious in the many drawings and photographs he made of her (to say nothing of his erotic letters), was considerable and enduring. Eva, whom Grosz always referred to as 'Maud' or 'Daum', was less interested in politics than he, and from the first was wary of some of his activist friends, Herzfelde and Heartfield above all.

The marriage was to become one of the factors in Grosz's decision to loosen his ties with the Communist Party several years later. The one-man exhibition, and the earlier contract with a dealer which produced it, were clear immediate signs of the artist's wavering sympathies, showing that he was prepared to do business with the commercial system he claimed to despise and wanted to be seen as a conventional artist.

Grosz's work, however, continued to admit no compromise for some time. Indeed, in a series of oils and watercolours executed in 1920, he attempted to create a new style which was inspired by politics in an original way, different to that of his satirical drawings. It was intended to reflect a positive view of a modern, technological and mass society and to employ an instantly legible pictorial language.

These paintings are like nothing Grosz had created before. They are, with a few revealing exceptions, devoid of satire and caricature and show faceless people like lay figures in bare rooms or empty streets hemmed in by houses and factories with blank façades. Their style – sharp outlines drawn with a pen, ruler and protractor and filled in with unmodulated washes of mostly pale colour – is bland and almost anonymous, an impression heightened by the use of a rubber stamp instead of a signature. The commercially manufactured stamp includes the artist's address and the words 'constructed in 1920 by George Grosz'.

Russian Constructivism was in fact a source of the new style. Another was the *pittura metafisica* of Giorgio de Chirico and Carlo Carrà who located dummy-like figures in dream-like architectural environments. Grosz admitted to his debt in an essay, *Zu meinen neuen Bildern* (On My New Paintings; see pages 35–6), while pointing out that he did not at all share the Italians' interest in the poetic and mysterious.

With its references to 'the masses', 'sobriety and clarity' and 'the true classless culture', *On My New Paintings* leaves little doubt about the aim of these 'constructions', which is also made clear by some of their titles. *The Gymnast* and *The Boxer* are examples of *The New Man* who trains his body with punchbags, Indian clubs and other apparatus, while keeping his brain in trim by studying architectural plans and technical drawings (fig. 8). Thus perfected, he is eligible for the new, utopian, collectivist and classless society which, driven by science and technology, can confront the future with confidence. These works were no doubt a response to that aspect of Grosz's personality expressed through the imaginary Dr William King Thomas who provided the artist with 'the more American and practical materialistic balance'[15] necessary to keep his other personae in check.

The other personae nevertheless continued to interrupt and interfere. They make their presence felt in the paintings' ambiguities and contradictions. The utopia they describe is chilling: regimented, standardised, normed and shaped by soulless machines. There is no room for individuality or dissent. The new man survives only as a precisely programmed robot.

9. *Cycling and Weightlifting*, 1920, pen, ink and watercolour. Present whereabouts unknown.

10. *Republican Automata*, 1920, pen, ink and watercolour. The Museum of Modern Art, New York.

11. *Grey Day*, 1921, oil on canvas. Stiftung Preussischer Kulturbesitz, Nationalgalerie, Berlin.

That Grosz could create such pictures only by suppressing an important part of himself is made plain by a series of contemporary works in the same dry style which have a quite different message. In *Republikanische Automaten* (Republican Automata, 1920), for example, the robots are, far more appropriately, jingoistic, flag-waving nationalists (fig. 10); and in *Grauer Tag* (Grey Day, 1921), the soulless brick and concrete environment provides a stage set on which types representative of the existing, flawed society appear (fig. 11). A cross-eyed, scar-faced 'Official for the Relief of War-Wounded' (the title under which the painting was once exhibited) takes no interest in the armless ex-soldier limping past.

Grosz was aware of the contradictions inherent in his new style. He not only abandoned it after a few months, he also gave up oils altogether for four years, returning exclusively to drawings and watercolours devoted to satire and social comment. As he put it in 1922:

> The so-called new figuration has no value for us today. The return to classical French painting, Poussin, Ingres and Corot, is a bad Biedermeier fashion. It seems that intellectual reaction is now following the political one. . . Another kind of figuration appears to lie in journalism, in the journalistic artist with access to the rotary presses who draws the day's events . . . this line of development will put him together with technical artists and industrial and commercial painters – with the constructivist draftsman and the inventor and engineer.[16]

On My New Paintings was one of several essays about art written by Grosz in 1920. In them he emerged as an important theorist, addressing issues to which he would return intermittently during the following years. Extracts from the most representative of them are included in this catalogue (see pages 32–40), and they will not be discussed here. Suffice it to say that the main elements in Grosz's artistic philosophy at that time were: a belief that all art is intentionally or unwittingly committed to a particular class and therefore politically loaded; a conviction that the art of the past is irrelevant to the working class and a factor in its continuing enslavement; and a contempt for art that is in any way subjective or autobiographical.

Many of these views were too extreme even for the Communist Party. Condemning the vitriolic essay *Der Kunstlump* (The Art Scab, 1920), in which Grosz and Heartfield attacked the Expressionist painter Oskar Kokoschka and his allegedly reactionary ideas, *The Red Flag* took the authors to task for asserting 'that the dusty works of Rembrandt and Rubens no longer have any significance for the worker'.[17] In general, however, the party approved of the propaganda Grosz was providing. *The Red Flag* celebrated the 'satirical genius' the like of which 'Germany has never previously seen' and, referring to Grosz's recently published collection of drawings *Das Gesicht der herrschenden Klasse* (The Face of the Ruling Class), said that it 'created an archive which gives a better historical picture than a thousand files of documents'.[18]

Sneaking Disillusion

The Face of the Ruling Class, a book containing fifty-five 'political drawings' was one of two collections of Grosz's drawings published in 1921. The second, *Im Schatten* (In The Shadows), is a portfolio of nine lithographs. Both works contain much recycled material most of which employs conventions, above all the revealing juxtaposition of opposites, that had become familiar in Grosz's work. The rich confront the poor; tricksters and black marketeers are brought together with honest labourers; haughty army officers appear beside maimed veterans; workers trudge wearily to their factories while industrialists ogle the money and jewels piled before them. Among these types representative of a polarised society, those embodying evil are more distinctive and interesting than those with whom we are intended to sympathise. The bosses have individual characteristics while those they exploit are generalised and clichéd, mere stereotypes.

Grosz was by no means the first artist to find evil easier to depict than good. But there is a suspicion, shared by several of his contemporaries, that his drawings of industrialists and profiteers are so vivid because, unlike the masses, they were people with whom he was able to identify. They were also, as Bert Brecht pointed out, more engaging as subjects.

The Many Faces of George Grosz

What the bourgeoisie hold against proletarians is their bad complexion. I fancy that what made you, George Grosz, an enemy of the bourgeois was their physiognomy... I don't believe, Grosz, that overwhelming compassion for the exploited or anger against the exploiter one day filled you with an irresistible desire to get something about this down on paper. I think drawing was something you enjoyed, and people's physiognomies so many pretexts for it. I imagine you becoming aware one day of a sudden overwhelming love for a particular type of face as a marvellous opportunity for you to amuse yourself. It was *The Face of the Ruling Class* ... the type you adore as subject-matter you are bound to detest as a member of the public. Politically you regard the bourgeoisie as your enemy not because you are a proletarian but because you are an artist.[19]

This was perceptive, for the doubts, here gently expressed, about Grosz's political commitment were shared by the artist himself. He was unable to identify with the masses because a major part of his contradictory self had little more than contempt for them. At the same time he was coming to recognise his own features in those he satirised.

In 1922 Grosz's political allegiance was severely tested. The Communist, the admirer of the Soviet Union, travelled to the peasants' and workers' paradise for the first time. The purpose of the visit, encouraged by the Soviet authorities, was to illustrate a propagandistic book to be written by the Danish author Martin Andersen-Nexø who accompanied Grosz on the trip. The artist had every reason to expect a warm welcome since his work was well-known and widely admired in the Soviet Union. His and Andersen-Nexø's travels took six months in all, and what Grosz saw of Russia shocked and depressed him. Arriving in Murmansk, they were arrested as spies and, once released, confronted by evidence of privation and hunger which, Grosz concluded, were exacerbated by the very bureaucracy entrusted with their alleviation. The members of the Politbureau, including Lenin, to whom Grosz was introduced, failed to make an impression. And constant arguments with Andersen-Nexø, whose convictions held firm throughout, contributed to Grosz's disillusion. His illustrations were never published.

It still took some time for him to loosen his ties to the Party, however. Although he ceased to pay his subscription in 1923, he continued to publish drawings in *The Red Flag*, and in 1924 even became chairman of the Association of German Communist Artists which issued a manifesto entirely loyal to the party line.

For several years Grosz's work betrayed little of his serious doubts about Communism. He continued to allow the Malik Press to publish anthologies of his drawings, two of which, *Abrechnung folgt!* (The Reckoning is Coming!) and *Ecce Homo*, appeared in 1923. Both followed the by now expected pattern in their extensive use of material previously used elsewhere, but *Ecce Homo* was unlike any of Grosz's earlier anthologies in several ways. It consisted of one hundred offset lithographs, sixteen of which were reproduced in full colour, and ten thousand copies – an enormously high edition – were published as variously priced portfolios and books. Very few of the images include specific political references. Almost all portray aspects of middle-class life in a satirical and moralising manner. Many are erotic or otherwise sexually explicit. Naked women are lecherously surveyed by drunken men with their flies undone; prostitutes parade on streets, naked beneath their lifted skirts; orgies take place in restaurants and private rooms.

Ecce Homo portrays the moral collapse of Germany as reflected in scenes from the lives and dreams of its average citizens. But in contrast to earlier publications the anthology has nothing to say about the causes of the German condition. In spite of their obvious exaggerations and the voyeuristic relish with which they are portrayed, the images are presented simply as the truth.

That was how they were regarded by many who saw and admired them at the time. As Hannah Arendt remembered, Grosz's 'cartoons seemed to us not satires but realistic reportage: we knew these types; they were all around us'.[20] And Stefan Zweig confirmed the extent of the moral collapse *Ecce Homo* describes:

Berlin transformed itself into the Babel of the world. Bars, amusement parks, pubs shot up like mushrooms ... made-up boys with artificial waistlines promenaded along the Kurfürstendamm – and not only professionals. Every high school pupil wanted to make some money, and in the darkened bars one could see high public officials and financiers courting drunken sailors without shame. Even the Rome of Suentonius had not known orgies like Berlin's transvestite balls... Amid the general collapse of values a kind of insanity took hold of precisely those middle-class circles which had hitherto been unshakable in their order. Young ladies proudly boasted that they were perverted; to be suspected of virginity at the age of sixteen would have been considered a disgrace in every school in Berlin.[21]

Ecce Homo made an immediate and powerful impact, and not just on those who, like Grosz, viewed their fellow Germans with alarm and distaste. Grosz was verbally and physically attacked so often that he applied (successfully) to the police for a pistol licence. He was also taken to court. After fifty-two images from the portfolio were confiscated because of their allegedly pornographic subject-matter, Grosz and his co-publishers Wieland Herzfelde and Julian Gumperz were found guilty of making and distributing sexually explicit images. Each was fined 500 marks.

During the trial (which extended into the following year), the presiding judge said that he failed to see why the artist had felt it necessary to place so much emphasis on the description of genitalia. Grosz replied: 'I see things as I have described them. If I look at the majority of people I don't see beauty or attractive features... In my opinion the depictions of the most ugly things which appear in these works and which, it might be assumed, will alienate some people, have an important educative function.'[22] Although much of Grosz's testimony is heavily ironic, he was serious enough about the 'educative function' of his work, more serious indeed than he was about its possible effect as political propaganda.

In the words of Uwe M. Schneede, 'Grosz had once again undergone a thorough transformation. If between 1918 and 1919 the misanthrope had become a fighter in the class struggle, not very much later the fighter became a moralist.'[23]

The Immutability of Life

In 1923 Grosz signed a contract with Alfred Flechtheim, one of Germany's most successful dealers in contemporary art. Known for the celebrated French painters on his books, Braque and Léger among them, he represented very few Germans, so his interest in Grosz was a measure of the artist's growing renown. It was also evidence that Grosz might be able to make a good living from his painting – Flechtheim had no time for the unsuccessful.

Once again Grosz's drawing underwent a dramatic change. While continuing to work mostly in pen and ink, he began to use a soft pencil in a series of closely observed and detailed studies of landscapes and people. The titles identify some of the sitters as unemployed and menial labourers; they are not representative social types, however, but clearly distinguished individuals. The style is also consciously traditional, revealing an increasing interest in Cranach, Dürer and other earlier German Masters.

A less obvious change was also evident in Grosz's more characteristic work. In 1925 another collection of drawings was published, *Der Spiesser-Spiegel* (The Philistine's Mirror). It was published not by Herzfelde but the Dresden house of Carl Reissner, and its tone is noticeably different from that of Grosz's previous collections. Although it is critical of middle-class pretensions and vices and includes a few drawings that would not look out of place in *Ecce Homo*, the dominant atmosphere is one of wry amusement and gently-poked fun.

The Philistine's Mirror was the first publication of Grosz's work with which Wieland Herzfelde had nothing to do. Their collaboration had by no means ended, but Grosz now recognised that money could be made from more popular work intended for a wider public. So he began regularly to submit drawings to such mass circulation magazines as the *Illustrierte Blatt* for which he also produced light-hearted, illustrated articles about such uncontroversial subjects as the Paul Whiteman Band and bullfights in Provence. He did the same for *Der Querschnitt* (The Cross-Section), the journal published by Flechtheim.

This change in attitude was caused not only by disillusionment with the left. It also reflected an improvement in the German economy, and by 1925 the political situation had

also stabilised. By now Grosz, married and about to become a father (his first son, Peter, was born in May 1926), was above all interested in security. At the age of thirty and within sight of middle age, he began to feel the tug of the conservative side of his personality.

The naturalistic pencil drawings show it. And they prepared the way for oil paintings in the same spare, seemingly objective and tradition-conscious style. After a gap of more than four years Grosz took out his easel again to make portraits: of himself and, among others, Wieland Herzfelde, the writer Walter Mehring, and the boxer Max Schmeling who had recently become the German heavyweight champion and would eventually hold the world title (fig. 12).

Like the related drawings, these paintings reveal Grosz's growing interest in traditional subjects and methods. 'I'm studying technique intensively,' he wrote to his friend Mark Neven DuMont, 'trying a mixed technique. First tempera and then oil glazes – à la van Eyck. I prepare the canvas myself. Make, after the fashion of the old paint chemists, emulsions of egg, linseed oil, varnish, vinegar and oil of cloves – and experiment. The portrait interests me, I'm working on several. . .'[24] It was a major shift. The artist who only a few years before was in favour of destroying the contents of every museum was now trying to paint like an Old Master. His work was now also being acquired by and shown in major public galleries.

One of the best of Grosz's portraits is of the poet Max Herrmann-Neisse who was a close friend (fig. 13). It was one of several paintings by Grosz included in an important exhibition staged in 1925 at the Mannheim Kunsthalle, *Die Neue Sachlichkeit* (The New Objectivity), subtitled 'German Painting Since Expressionism'. This exhibition revealed that German art had changed direction in recent years. Many of the most interesting painters, it argued, were now chiefly interested in the sober, precise and instantly legible depiction of what they saw rather than felt or imagined. The exhibition was in fact considerably more varied than this makes it seem. The works by Grosz on show included not only the portrait of Hermann-Neisse but also *Dedicated to Oskar Panizza* and *Germany, a Winter's Tale*.

That Grosz had neither forgotten nor suppressed the feelings that inspired those political paintings is made clear by his return to contemporary allegory. In 1926 he produced two more of them: *Stützen der Gesellschaft* (Pillars of Society) and *Sonnenfinsternis* (Eclipse of the Sun). The first rehearses the message and much of the imagery of *Germany, a Winter's Tale*, while the second (fig. 14) identifies Germany's problems by means of readily interpreted symbols. The old warrior Hindenburg, now German President, is in conference with a group

12. *The Boxer Max Schmeling*, 1926, oil on canvas. Axel Springer Verlag, Berlin.

13. *Portrait of the Writer Max Hermann-Neisse*, 1925, oil on canvas. Städtische Kunsthalle, Mannheim.

14. *Eclipse of the Sun*, 1926, oil on canvas. Heckscher Museum, Huntington, New York.

The Many Faces of George Grosz 15

of capitalists, one of whom is offering him weapons and a railway engine. Meanwhile a blinkered donkey – the German public – feeds on the popular press and a prisoner rots beneath the bars of an oubliette. In the background the sun is being totally obscured by the dollar on which the German economy, soon to be ruined again by the New York stock market crash, depended.

These two works are the finest examples of what Grosz described as 'modern history painting', and they testify to his continuing determination to teach and moralise in the manner of Hogarth and the English caricaturists he so admired. Yet he also felt the tug of rival sympathies, especially since such works were difficult to sell and Flechtheim's demands for more obviously commercial paintings were urgent and unremitting.

In 1927 Grosz spent more than six months on the French Riviera. He clearly felt that by distancing himself from Berlin he would find it easier to discover new and more appealing motifs. His plan was 'to paint a series of "saleable" landscapes here – i.e. in such a way that offensive subjects are excluded. If I sell, I'll then get to work on the big paintings I like, à la *Eclipse of the Sun* or *Pillars of Society*. Courbet also did this. He painted Lake Geneva on numerous occasions for those able to pay.'[25]

15. *Landscape near Point Rouge, Marseille,* 1927, oil on canvas. Private collection, USA.

The small landscapes and still-lifes that Grosz produced in the South of France are different from anything that he had done before (fig. 15). They are consciously picturesque and well-mannered; they are even a little dull. They have no obvious content. But they are still accomplished and in any case did not satisfy him for long: 'I am not a particular friend of motifs', he wrote to Otto Schmalhausen from Marseille.[26] Nor did they satisfy Flechtheim who eventually cancelled his contract with the words 'You can draw a little but you can't paint at all'.[27]

That was manifestly untrue. It was rather that the feeling for beauty and nature which had always been present but held back had finally surfaced. What is more, Grosz's determination to produce a few potboilers did not prevent him from working in his more familiar manner. In 1928 the seventeen drawings published, once again by Herzfelde, under the title *Hintergrund* (Background), demonstrated that the old combative Grosz was still present and still in fighting form.

Originally made as studies for stage designs (see cat. 128), these drawings are among the most vicious attacks on the military, judiciary and the church Grosz ever made, and they offended many. Three of the drawings, including an image of the crucified Christ wearing a gasmask and army boots, were declared blasphemous and involved Grosz and Herzfelde in yet another well-publicised trial (see cat. 131). It ran on, the appeals and counter-appeals mounting, until November 1931 when Grosz was finally acquitted.

By then another publication had shown how various Grosz's work had become and how quickly he could alter its tone and intention. The collection of drawings that appeared in 1930 was by and large even more benign than *The Philistine's Mirror*. Titled *Über alles die Liebe* (Love Above All), it provides intimate glimpses into contemporary middle-class life. Maids assist women at their toilet; people dance in cafés and walk in parks. There is more affection than scorn but, as Grosz made clear in his preface:

> The subject here is interpersonal relations. Fine, but don't expect my drawings to illustrate any run-of-the-mill lovers' idyll. Realist that I am, I use my pen and brush primarily for taking down what I see and observe, and that is generally unromantic, sober and not very dreamy . . . I raise my hand and hail the eternal human law . . . and the cheerful good-for-nothing immutability of life!

Between Two Worlds

In 1931 Grosz wrote an essay with a revealing title: *Unter anderem ein Wort für deutsche Tradition* (*Among Other Things a Word in Favour of German Tradition*). 'We are certainly living at a transitional time', he said, 'All convictions have gradually become dubious and begun to totter, and outdated liberalism is wreathed in the glow of evening. . . Everywhere there is a decisive reaction against what was generally valid the day before yesterday. The

Right and Left are dividing ever more clearly in preparation for the final struggle for power... How fast it is happening! After the War – I believed – no one would ever think about uniforms, standing to attention and so on, again.'[28]

These are the words of a disillusioned man who had come to recognise the similarities between the methods and dogma of the left and right. The Communists and Nazis were equally totalitarian; the only difference between them was in the colour of the uniforms their bully-boys wore and the fact that it was the Nazis were winning 'the final struggle for power'. In 1930, to Grosz's alarm, they became the second largest party in the Reichstag.

Grosz had perceived the threat Hitler represented long before, at a time when most people thought of him as little more than a joke (see cat. 107). But Grosz's prescience and his opposition had been pointless: Hitler endured. Grosz even came to suspect that his art, intended to ridicule, weaken and undermine, had achieved the opposite effect; paradoxically, by drawing attention to the Nazis, it had made them better known. This was not a view shared by the Nazis themselves. They gave him a prominent place on their blacklist, and took every opportunity to intimidate him. 'For example, I found one of those iron bars outside my studio, and, written on a label attached to it: "This is for you, you Jewish swine, if you keep going on like this!"'[29] It was no wonder that Grosz considered leaving Germany before it was too late. In 1932 he readily accepted an invitation to teach at a summer school organised by the Art Students' League in New York. The contract was only for three months, but it would give him the opportunity to see how he took to life in North America and perhaps stay there permanently.

He adapted quickly. From the moment he landed on 3 July 1932 until he left New York on 6 October his enthusiasm did not wane. Overwhelmed by the scale of Manhattan and its teeming life, he filled many sketchbooks with drawings of shopfronts, neon advertisements, ice machines, hot dog vendors, policemen and shoeshine boys. Even the signs of unemployment and poverty, results of the continuing depression, failed to dampen his mood.

While in New York Grosz taught not only at the Art Students' League but also at a private school which he founded together with the painter Maurice Sterne and the dealer Israel Ber Neumann. This, the promise of more teaching at the Art Students' League, and evidence that there was a market for his work in the USA gave him reason to believe that he would be able to support himself and his family if he managed to get the necessary permission to return.

This he did, departing for America again on 12 January 1933, little more than a fortnight before Hitler was appointed German Chancellor. Eva went with him – she would collect their two young sons within the year. For the moment they remained with an aunt and, unlike their father, were not in danger.

Grosz was determined to conform, to become a typical American as quickly as he could. He never thought of himself as an exile, and since he turned his back on Germany before he was obliged to, he was right. For the first time in his life the role he was playing was real. Ironically, it was that of a solid middle-class citizen, anxious about the education of his children, acquisitive and concerned about financial security: precisely the type of man who had previously been one of the main targets of his satire.

In America, unlike Germany, artists who worked for a mass public were not looked down on. Grosz admired the illustrators of popular magazines, and did his best to become one himself. He acquired US citizenship as soon as he could, and envied the speed with which his sons acclimatised. Thanks to his income from the Art Students' League and sales of his work he was able before long to buy a house and a car (unlike Eva, he never learned to drive it).

This is not to say that Grosz's American persona extinguished all the others. Grosz the Berliner remained, dwelling on the fate that might have befallen him, worrying about his mother and his wife's family, gloomy about the war he knew was imminent, cutting reports about events in Europe from newspapers and sticking them into his diary. He kept in touch with friends by letter, too, fulminating against the Nazis and the German intellectuals unable or unwilling to oppose them.

Grosz the American and Grosz the German were uneasy neighbours, however, and, as so often, irony proved the best means of reconciling them, if only partially. This is revealed by a story – reminiscent of that concerning the businessman from Holland – about an event in

The Many Faces of George Grosz

16. *New York Harbor*, 1936, watercolour. The Metropolitan Museum of Art, New York.

1934 told by Erwin Piscator, the Communist theatre director for whom Grosz had designed costumes and sets in Berlin:

> Grosz sits together with a group of antifascists in New York as the news arrives that [the writer] Erich Mühsam has been murdered in a concentration camp. Inexpressible sadness, pain seize the group. Suddenly Grosz remonstrates with the others. 'You're being sentimental. The whole thing is laughable. A person like Mühsam ought to have reckoned with such a fate. In any case art doesn't have the least thing to do with politics'. All those present are disappointed, outraged, unable to explain Grosz's words. Some time later a friend visits George Grosz in his studio and asks, 'Well, what have you been doing lately?' 'Have a look. There are a few things over there in the corner.' The visitor opens some portfolios where he finds some fifteen drawings on the subject of Mühsam's death, among the best things Grosz had done for years. The spark that was already almost extinguished was glowing again.[30]

Some of those drawings appeared in *Interregnum*, a portfolio of prints published by the Black Sun Press in 1936, and they do indeed possess much of Grosz's familiar fire and anger. But by then he knew they would not change anything and was not surprised when very few copies of *Interregnum* were sold. It confirmed him in his view that the kind of work he used to produce in Germany was unsuitable for an American audience and compounded his despair.

His art mirrored the two worlds he precariously inhabited. On the one hand he painted the street life and spectacle of Manhattan (fig. 16) and the empty, windswept dunes of Cape Cod; on the other, apocalyptic visions of death and destruction which expressed his anguish at what was happening in the world beyond America. He painted himself, his face registering defeat, sitting in a smouldering ruin and as a lonely windswept figure trudging through mud beneath a threatening sky. But he also drew and painted nature, immersing himself in one kind of reality in order to find refuge from another.

The end of the War brought no respite. His mother had been killed during a bombing raid, Germany was in ruins. In *The Pit* (1946, Wichita Art Museum, Kansas) Grosz evoked a terrifying vision of Hell reminiscent of Bosch and Bruegel, and in a series of oils, watercolours and drawings he showed himself as an emaciated, ghostly figure without hope painting nothing but holes.

Grosz had always enjoyed alcohol but his drinking became excessive after the War and his health declined. He became irritable and secretive, and Eva's concern led her to believe that a return to Germany and familiar surroundings might improve his state of mind. She had never been able to share his determination to become an American and had never entirely settled. But Grosz resisted her pleas to return home. He secretly felt the tug of Berlin, too, but to yield to it would be to admit that he had not become as completely assimilated as he pretended to be. Yet he also knew that a move to Berlin might solve his financial problems: for some time his work had not been selling well. From Germany he received repeated signals that he would be welcomed with open arms should he decide to settle there.

He was prevailed upon to make two visits to Germany, in 1951 and 1954, both of which depressed him. During the latter he was the subject of a perceptive cover story in the news magazine *Der Spiegel*.

> It seems almost impossible to recognise . . . in Grosz the man who once possessed satirical skill and intellectual distinction. And in conversation with Grosz it is equally difficult to rediscover the great caricaturist of earlier days. . . The respectable-looking, seemingly self-satisfied and chubby man – 'I'm a German-American, a conformist' – with the crafty eyes, apple cheeks and ruddy face of an old-age pensioner – did this man really ever paint all those hate-filled, silently screaming, relentlessly provocative pictures which made the name George Grosz famous?[31]

A third visit four years later, however, was happier. Grosz then rediscovered many of the simple pleasures Berlin had to offer, especially its restaurants and bars, and took pleasure in the evidence of his fame. He was invited to become a member of the Akademie der Künste, the Academy of Arts, and was delighted when the National Gallery acquired one of his masterpieces, *Stützen der Gesellschaft* (Pillars of Society). Berlin clearly wanted him, and the pull it exerted became irresistible.

To Eva's delight, Grosz decided to return permanently to the city of his birth. They sold their house in Huntington, wrote their wills, and in May 1958 moved into the flat on the Savignyplatz which had once belonged to Eva's parents, and which was full of happy memories for them both. It was also in the liveliest district of West Berlin, close to the Kurfürstendamm and its many attractions.

Berlin

In 1958, before returning to Germany, Grosz produced a small number of works that, both original and funny, looked back to his Dada period and forward to the techniques and subject-matter of Pop Art. They are coloured photomontages made up of details of illustrations and advertisements culled from glossy American and German magazines. They make extensive use of food, especially processed meat, in close-up, and draw attention to the way commercial art manipulates the emotions with the aid of romanticised imagery. Free from the black despair that characterises so much of Grosz's other American work, with a lightness of touch and wayward wit, they are among the best things Grosz ever did, effectively satirising not only the idols of the American consumerist society but also its exaggerated respect for the heroes of contemporary art. Grosz even pokes fun at himself and his American fantasies. Indeed, the late photomontages can be seen as his ironic farewell to America, as 'the last brilliant testament to his failure to realise a life-long dream of becoming a good American instead of a demoralised German', and may also reveal that Grosz 'at last realised that his protracted love affair with America was a kind of clowning.'[32]

17. *George Grosz, The Clown of New York*, 1957, collage. George Grosz Estate.

In one of these photomontages (fig. 17) Grosz put his own head disguised by clown's make-up on the ample body of a burlesque dancer who, clutching a bottle of whisky, stands in front of a panorama of Manhattan by night. But if he is an artiste acting out yet another role, so are other contemporary artists: Chagall (whose folksy fantasies Grosz could never stand) appears in another of these photomontages turning into the chicken he is painting. In other photomontages of this impressive series, slices of Spam and frankfurters speared on forks sport eyes and mouths like creatures from a dispeptic nightmare; and a group of well-scrubbed American schoolgirls contemplates a table laden with offal and alarmingly enlarged human fingers, the nails painted bright red, during a domestic science lesson. As though calling his entire career into question, Grosz even used details from reproductions of two of his own paintings – *Widmung an Oskar Panizza* (Dedicated to Oskar Panizza) and *The Pit* – as the basis for one of these photomontages about food. They were virtually the last works he ever produced.

After his final return to Germany, where he arrived on 28 May 1959, Grosz abandoned art almost entirely. On his arrival in West Berlin, since the airlift of 1948 virtually an island surrounded by the Red Army and the East German military, he was lionised by the government, the Academy of Arts and the press. Unlike Wieland Herzfelde, John Heartfield and Bert Brecht who had moved to the Soviet Zone, he had chosen to settle in the last redoubt of freedom, and the propaganda value of his move was incalculable, especially since he was German by birth and American by nationality.

He could not have been unaware of some symbolic gestures. When he arrived in his hotel room he was met by several bottles of pink champagne suitably cooled, a cleverly ironic touch which amused the former Marxist. And the studio he was offered turned out to have belonged previously to Hitler's favourite sculptor Arno Breker. On the Chausseestrasse, encountering a group of women talking in Berlin dialect, emotion got the better of him and he burst into tears.[33]

Eventually Grosz might well have become disillusioned with Berlin, but there was not enough time left for him to feel deflated. Soon after midnight on 5 July – a fortnight after his arrival and three weeks before his sixty-sixth birthday – he spent the evening drinking with friends as was his custom. As soon as he arrived home he collapsed at the foot of the stairs to his flat. He never regained consciousness and about five hours later he was dead.

Grosz was buried in the city where he was born and with which he and his art will always be associated. For all the manifest quality of his American work, he will be chiefly remembered for the paintings – and above all the drawings – he produced in Berlin during the most turbulent epoch in its history. Whether provoked by political conviction, hatred or the desire to depict the foibles and pretensions of those about him, his art transcends the place, period and circumstances in which it was made. It is both timeless and universal because his true subject was mankind itself.

The day after Grosz's death, his old friend Walter Mehring noted in his diary that all the obituaries had said that he had returned home. But, Mehring added, Grosz had never had a homeland 'outside his studio. And inside it were as many homelands as the rapidly changing moods of this multiply split personality.'[34]

It was with that split personality that we began; but in spite of the many disguises Grosz assumed during his career, he resolutely remained his own man, as proudly independent of dogma as of fashion – a complex individual fired by dissent. We admire the brilliance of his drawing and the merciless accuracy of his observation. But we should also celebrate the unyielding independence of his spirit. In this century such a quality has been all too rare.

1. *I Am a Camera* (1955), a British production directed by Henry Cornelius and starring Julie Harris and Laurence Harvey. The screenplay was based on a play by John van Druten, itself derived from Isherwood's stories. The play was later adapted as both a musical and the film *Cabaret*. Grosz came to London to work on the designs, lodging at White's Hotel for part of September and November 1954. One of the designs, probably for Sally Bowles's bedroom, is owned by the Leicester Museum (see Barry Herbert and Alisdair Hinshelwood, *The Expressionist Revolution in German Art, 1911–1933*, Leicester, 1978, p. 65).
2. The revealing episode is recounted by one of those present in Wieland Herzfelde, 'Ein Kaufmann aus Holland', in *Immergrün*, Berlin, 1969, pp. 164–81.
3. Letter to Robert Bell, end of September 1915, Knust, 1979, pp. 30–31.
4. *Autobiography*, 1974, p. 94.
5. *Autobiography*, 1974, p. 102.
6. Undated letter (1916/17) to Robert Bell, in Knust, 1979, pp. 42–3.
7. *Autobiography*, 1974, pp. 113–14.
8. *Autobiography*, 1974, p. 114.
9. Letter to Otto Schmalhausen, 15 December 1917, Knust, 1979, pp. 56–7.
10. Oskar Panizza (1853–1921) was a specialist in mental disorders, an anarchist and playwright who in 1895 wrote a violently anti-clerical play *Das Liebeskonzil* (The Council of Love), in which popes take part in orgies and God and the Virgin Mary are ridiculed. Panizza was imprisoned for blasphemy and later spent twelve years in a lunatic asylum. He was, needless to say, one of Grosz's heroes.
11. In a curriculum vitae written for Grosz's own trial in 1930, quoted after cat. Berlin 1994, p. 329.
12. 'Reportage und Dichtung. Eine Rundfrage', *Die literarische Welt*, No. 2, 1926, quoted after Uwe M. Schneede (ed.), *George Grosz, Leben und Werk*, Stuttgart, 1975, p. 70.
13. N. N., 'Die Auswüchse der Dada-Messe', *Berliner Tageblatt*, 21 April 1921, quoted after Helen Adkins, 'Erste Internationale Dada-Messe', in cat. *Stationen der Moderne*, Berlinische Galerie, Berlin, 1988, p. 167.
14. *Die Rote Fahne*, 27 July 1920.
15. See note 3 above.
16. George Grosz, 'Ein Neuer Naturalismus? – Eine Rundfrage', *Das Kunstblatt*, Vol. 6, 1922, pp. 382–3.
17. Gertrud Alexander, *Die Rote Fahne*, 9 June 1920.
18. *Die Rote Fahne*, 17 May 1921.
19. 'Conversation with George Grosz' from the preface to *Drums in the Night*, 1924(?), trs. John Willett, quoted after John Willett and Ralph Mannheim (eds), *Bertolt Brecht: Collected Plays*, I, London, 1970, pp. 395–6.
20. Quoted after Beth Irwin Lewis, 1971, p. 8.
21. Stefan Zweig, *The World of Yesterday*, London, 1953, p. 287.
22. Transcript of the *Ecce Homo* trial in *Das Tagebuch*, 23 February 1924, quoted after Uwe M. Schneede, *George Grosz, Leben und Werk*, Stuttgart, 1975, p. 86.
23. Uwe M. Schneede, *George Grosz, Der Künstler in seiner Gesellschaft*, Cologne, 1975, p. 146.
24. Letter of 23 November 1926, in *George Grosz, Teurer Makkaroni! Briefe an Mark Neven DuMont 1922–1959*, Berlin, 1992, p. 92.
25. Letter to Otto Schmalhausen, 27 May 1927, in Knust, 1979, p. 101.
26. Letter of May 1927, quoted after Hess, 1974, p. 148.
27. Letter to Herbert Fiedler, 18 February 1937, quoted after Hess, 1974, p. 151.
28. George Grosz, 'Unter anderem ein Wort für deutsche Tradition', *Das Kunstblatt*, March 1931, quoted after exhib. cat. Berlin 1994, p. 546.
29. Interview, 1954, quoted after Fischer, 1976, p. 104.
30. Erwin Piscator, 'Einiges über George Grosz', in exh. cat. *George Grosz 1893-1959*, Akademie der Künste, Berlin, 1962, p. 9.
31. 'Ein grosses Nein', anonymous article in *Der Spiegel*, Hamburg, 30 June 1954, pp. 26–30.
32. Robert Melville, 'The Bastard from Berlin', in *The Sunday Times Magazine*, 4 November 1973, p. 65.
33. Related to the author on 13 April 1977 by Walther Huder, the Academy of Arts official concerned.
34. Walter Mehring, *Berlin Dada*, Zurich, 1959, p. 84.

WEIMAR POLITICS AND GEORGE GROSZ

C̲h̲r̲i̲s̲t̲o̲p̲h̲e̲r̲ C̲l̲a̲r̲k̲

The revolution that gave birth to the Weimar Republic was equivocal from the very beginning. On Saturday 9 November 1918, the Republic was proclaimed not once but twice. At around two o'clock in the afternoon, Philipp Scheidemann, speaking for the Majority and Independent Social Democrats (SPD and USPD) who had only that morning formed a provisional government, announced to cheering crowds from the balcony of the Reichstag building in Berlin that 'the old rotten order, the monarchy, has collapsed. Long live the new! Long live the German Republic!' Only hours later on the balcony of the Berlin Palace, Karl Liebknecht, one of the leaders of the revolutionary Spartacus League, proclaimed to cheering crowds a 'free, Socialist Republic of Germany'.

For Friedrich Ebert and Philipp Scheidemann, the moderate Social Democrats who dominated the 'Council of People's Plenipotentiaries', as the new government called itself, the foundation of a German Republic meant an orderly transfer of power from the now defunct monarchical régime to a German parliament elected on a universal suffrage and underwritten by a liberal, democratic constitution. It was a process that had already begun in October, when the old constitution was altered to enhance the role of parliament and curtail the powers of the monarchical executive. Ebert saw his task in the peaceful further development of these initiatives through a democratically elected national body of representatives and in cooperation with the various 'bourgeois parties' that had worked with the SPD in opposition during the war years. For the revolutionary Spartacists who were subsequently to found the German Communist Party (KPD), by contrast, the foundation of a new republic would be meaningless unless it were accompanied by the establishment of a dictatorship of the proletariat: 'the wresting by degrees of all capital from the bourgeoisie', the 'centralisation of all instruments of production in the hands of the state', the constitution of the proletariat as the new 'ruling class'.[1] The realisation of these goals could be achieved only by class war. After all, as one Spartacist programme announced in late November 1918: 'the imperialism of all countries knows only one right – the profit of capital; it knows only one language – the sword; it knows only one method – violence.'[2] In the light of such radical demands, the liberal parliamentary aspirations of Ebert, Scheidemann and their colleagues were doomed to seem little more than 'a fig-leaf for the decent veiling of a counter-revolutionary policy' (Rosa Luxemburg).

The revolutionary situation of winter 1918 was thus characterised from the outset by a labile stand-off between two conflicting political visions. To complicate matters, Germany's defeat in the west and the collapse of discipline in her armed forces had produced widespread confusion and upheaval. At the end of October, just as the German constitution was being altered to make way for a parliamentary democracy, the army's attempts to suppress a mutiny of sailors in Kiel harbour gave rise to a wave of strikes and military rebellions that spread across the country like a bushfire, engulfing all the major cities. The German revolution quickly acquired its own novel political organisations – 'councils' elected locally by workers and servicemen across the country to articulate the aspirations of those broad sectors of the population that had withdrawn their allegiance from the monarchical system and its doomed war effort.

In the struggle between the Social Democrats and the extreme left to gain control over this unpredictable state of affairs, the SPD retained two crucial advantages. Unlike the

18. *Pandemonium*, 1915/16, pen and ink. Collection Bernard J. Reis, New York.

19. *Cheers Noske!*, front cover of *Die Pleite*, No. 3, 1920.

Grosz's preoccupation with carnage predated his conversion to Spartacism. The original drawing of *Cheers Noske!* included a baby impaled on the sword.

Communists, the Social Democrats enjoyed mass support among the working population now represented in the hastily-formed 'November councils'. And, more importantly, they could count on the support of the supreme command of the German army, which, having seen which way the wind was blowing, made a formal 'proposal of alliance' to the Ebert government on 10 November. Both factors were to play an important role in the consolidation of a parliamentary republican order under SPD supervision. The SPD used its popular support and superior political know-how to assert control over, and ultimately to neutralise, the workers' and soldiers' councils. And when, in January 1919, the Communists mounted their first concerted attempt to seize power in Berlin, pillaging arsenals, arming bands of radical workers and occupying key buildings and positions in the city, Gustav Noske, the government's provisional minister for military affairs, called in the army to bring an end to the unrest.

'For some days the city was transformed into a lurid and dangerous jungle, a Dadaist nightmare. There was shooting at every corner and it was seldom clear who was shooting at whom. Neighbouring streets were occupied by opposing forces, there were desperate struggles on roofs and in cellars, machine-guns positioned anywhere suddenly struck up fire and then fell silent, squares and streets that had just now been quiet were suddenly filled with running, fleeing pedestrians, groaning wounded and the bodies of the dead.'[3] On 15 January, after an extensive manhunt, the Communist leaders Rosa Luxemburg and Karl Liebknecht were found, arrested and subsequently murdered by members of a Cavalry Guards division stationed at the Hotel Eden.

The violent suppression of the January uprising – in part through privately financed anti-Communist volunteer units known as Freikorps – and the brutal murder of its leaders dealt the Communist left a blow that it was never prepared to forgive. Henceforth the contempt of the Communists for the new republican order made way for implacable hatred; hatred of the reactionary soldiery and of the Social Democrats who had allegedly betrayed the German worker to sign a 'devil's pact' with German militarism.[4]

The violence and revolutionary rhetoric of the 'November Revolution' and the events that followed had an immediate and galvanising effect on Berlin's cultural avant-garde. The last two years of the war had seen a dramatic radicalisation in the political tone of the city's critical artistic and literary intelligentsia. Thanks in part to the medical policy of the German army, which tended to treat those deemed psychologically unfit for service with relative leniency, a loose network of pacifist artists and writers had established itself in Berlin by spring 1917. This was the milieu that generated the activist, utopian brand of Expressionism articulated in Franz Pfempfert's radical journal *Die Aktion* and the pacifist, anti-Expressionist nihilism of early Berlin Dada. The 'July crisis' of German domestic morale in 1917, the October Revolution of the Bolsheviks in Russia, and the subsequent opening of a Soviet embassy in Berlin, all helped to focus and politicise the social and cultural alienation of the radical avant-garde. For many artists, these transformations in the political environment produced a sense of urgency and impending change. At a meeting held in February 1918 in the J. B. Neumann gallery, the poet Richard Huelsenbeck prefaced an evening of poetry readings with the declaration that Dadaism was for 'people with sharpened instincts, who realise that they stand at a historical turning point. Politics are only a step away. Tomorrow it's either a ministry, or martyrdom in the Schlüsselburg [a notorious tsarist political prison].'[5] In the aftermath of the events of October/November 1918, many artists organised themselves in associations modelled on the sailors' and soldiers' councils, distancing themselves from the lofty individualism of traditional art production and urging their colleagues to work with the revolutionary forces in society to forge a new cultural and political order. One of the earliest groups to emerge in this way was the 'November Group', formed in December 1918, which called upon 'all artists who have broken with the old forms of art' to work towards achieving 'the closest possible relationship between the people and art'.[6]

For George Grosz, a contributor to *Die Aktion* and an early participant in Berlin Dada who had been exempted from military service on psychological grounds and spent the final War years in Berlin, the November revolution brought an intoxicating sense of momentousness and occasion: 'To all of us and to me, it seemed as if the gates had opened up and the light was coming through', he later recalled.[7] 'We saw our great new task: committed art in the service of the revolutionary cause.'[8] The 'revolutionary cause' emphatically did not denote the moderate parliamentary course espoused by the SPD. In December 1918, Grosz was among the first wave of Communist Party members, reputedly receiving his party card from the hands of Rosa Luxemburg. His closest allegiance during the later War years had been with the group around Wieland Herzfelde, whose makeshift publishing operation Verlag Neue Jugend produced the first portfolio of Grosz drawings early in 1917. Herzfelde's Malik Verlag, founded clandestinely in an attic on the Kurfürstendamm to publish the *Erste George Grosz-Mappe* (First George Grosz Portfolio, 1917), was to become one of the foremost publishing houses for Communist intellectuals in the Weimar Republic.

In this first portfolio, comprising nine lithographs in all, imaginary 'memories' of New York and the wild west were juxtaposed with desolate urban scenes evoking the Berlin cityscape: peripheral locations peopled with isolated figures (*By the Canal*, *Suburb*) or untidy squares traversed by horse-drawn carts and hurrying pedestrians. There was little overtly political content in these drawings, but they did anticipate many of the preoccupations of Grosz's later work – violence, death, suicide, sex, life in the city as a war of all against all. And they offered striking evidence of Grosz's distinctiveness as a draughtsman. An Expressionist collapsing and distortion of perspectives generated a charged and unstable sense of space which seemed at odds with Grosz's dramatic and two-dimensional deployment of line – cut-out human figures sliding upwards along the paper, flat buildings rising from the streets like incongruous theatre props, razor-sharp lines superimposed on each other like generations of graffiti.

In the aftermath of the events of January 1919, the context in and for which Grosz worked was dramatically politicised. In February 1919 he co-edited *Jedermann sein eigner Fussball* (Everyman His Own Football), a four-sided broadsheet published by Malik which combined Spartacist political commentary with satirical drawings and Dadaist pranks. The lead article was a polemic by Wieland Herzfelde denouncing elections as a reactionary institution on the grounds that the populace had not yet had time to develop 'correct' (i.e. Communist) political views. Page three carried a heavy-handed allegory by Grosz, in which the Catholic centrist minister Erzberger used a Bolshevik bogeyman to frighten the masses into the arms of the church. *Jedermann* sold out its first print run and was immediately banned by the new authorities.

In March 1919 the Communists called a general strike and fighting once again broke out in Berlin. Some fifteen thousand armed Communists and fellow-travellers seized control of police stations and rail terminals. Determined to break the power of the extreme left at all costs, SPD Defence Minister Gustav Noske now brought in 40,000 army and Freikorps troops, who used machine-guns, field artillery, flame throwers and even aerial strafing and bombardment to suppress the rebellion. When the fighting in Berlin came to an end on 16 March some 1200 people were dead. As a known member of the leftist circle around Malik, Grosz was himself at risk at this time and spent several days hiding in the flat of his future mother-in-law on the Savignyplatz. He remarked at the time that the experience had converted him into a convinced Spartacist;[9] certainly it generated one of his most memorable polemical drawings. At the beginning of April, the third issue of *Die Pleite* (Bankruptcy), the successor flysheet to *Jedermann*, carried a full-page Grosz cartoon on its cover. It showed a street littered with corpses, one disembowelled, many mutilated. Standing in the centre foreground, with the heel of his boot pressing on the belly of one of the dead, is the travesty of a Prussian officer, his monocle screwed tightly into his face, his teeth bared in a cramped grimace, his posture ramrod-straight. In his right hand he carries a blood-smeared sword, in his left a raised champagne flute. The caption reads: 'Cheers Noske! – The Proletariat has been disarmed!'

Prost Noske! (fig. 19) was among the earliest of Grosz's drawings to refer to a specific contemporary political event. The 'R' on the officer's helmet presumably denoted the Freikorps 'Reinhard' whose henchmen figured in an article printed in the same flysheet by Herzfelde, though it could also signify 'Reichswehr' (army), or the republic which had sanctioned a murderous assault on the German proletariat. Like many of Grosz's most successful political drawings, 'Cheers Noske!' combined topical reference with more abiding preoccupations; carnage and dismemberment had never been far from the centre of his interest. Indeed, the

20. Max Beckmann, *The Disappointed I*, lithograph, 1922. British Museum, London.

21. . . . *where they go*, from *The Face of the Ruling Class*, Berlin, 1921.

Two views of the ruling class at table. Beckmann's lithograph shows a circle of wealthy Berliners responding to bad news from their conservative newspaper, the *Kreuzzeitung*. The subtlety and individuation of Beckmann's treatment is in marked contrast to Grosz's homogenised parodies of the Weimar 'ruling class'; so is the presence of fully clothed women.

Weimar Politics and George Grosz

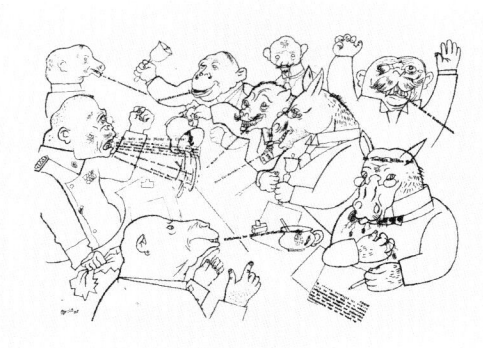

22. *The Voice of the People is the Voice of God*, from *The Face of the Ruling Class*, Berlin, 1921.

The radicalism of Grosz's propaganda required the 'dehumanisation' of the political enemy – literally so in this drawing of 1921, which included collaged fragments from the conservative press. At this time the swastika signified the *völkisch* and nationalist right, rather than the NSDAP in particular.

corpse protruding diagonally into the lower right-hand of the picture-frame, its trousers pulled down to reveal (mutilated?) genitalia, bore close resemblance to one of the murdered male figures strewn across the street in Grosz's *Pandemonium* of 1915/16 (fig. 18).

By contrast with the earlier productions, the most important Malik portfolios of 1920-21, *Gott mit uns* (God Be With Us) and *Das Gesicht der herrschenden Klasse* (The Face of the Ruling Class), bore the subtitles 'Political Album' and 'Political Drawings' respectively. Recurrent themes in the drawings of these years were the conspiratorial alliance between militarism and capital, crass contrasts between the grotesque wealth of an avaricious 'ruling class' and the poverty and resignation of workers or mutilated veterans, and the cruelty of the anti-Communist Freikorps. Some of these scenes did refer to specific events: the Munich skyline that forms the backdrop to *Feierabend* (End of the Day's Work), in which a Freikorps henchman leans against a tree smoking a cigarette beside the battered corpse of one of his victims, indicates that the picture referred to the role played by volunteer units in the suppression of the 'Soviet Republic of Bavaria' in April 1919. But most of Grosz's drawings were tableaux whose function was emblematic or allegorical. It was not unusual for Herzfelde to sharpen their relevance to contemporary developments through the use of captions. An example is the drawing *Stinnes & Cie.* published in *Der Gegner* in 1921, which showed obese industrialists haggling over a bound male figure marked 'Labour'. It was probably Herzfelde who added an explanatory note relating the scene – which contains no recognisable caricature of Hugo Stinnes himself – to a specific remark made by the industrialist and reported by the press. The note was omitted when the drawing was reprinted by Malik in *The Face of the Ruling Class*.

Throughout the early 1920s, political tableaux peopled by indeterminate allegorical figures were interspersed in Grosz's graphic work with grotesque caricatures of prominent Republican political figures: Erzberger, Fehrenbach, Noske, Scheidemann, Hindenburg, Ludendorff and, above all, the tailor's son from Heidelberg and Chairman of the SPD, Reich President Friedrich Ebert. Ebert appears in the Malik books and periodicals as a fat, drunken neo-Kaiser with an addiction to luxury ('By the grace of Money-Bags'), a class traitor in his ill-fitting bourgeois costume ('His Majesty'), as the cuckolded husband of a Republic whose real passion is the military ('Return from the Constitutional Celebrations'), or as a contemptible puppet in the hands of the industrial magnate Hugo Stinnes ('Stinnes and His President'). Perhaps the most striking feature of these caricatures is the way in which political hostility is mediated by a sense of aesthetic revulsion. Ebert is not merely venal, he is fat, ill-shaven, his hands are hairy, his legs bowed, his shoes crude and lumpy. This emphasis on physical imperfection as the index of a corrupt ethos doubtless owed something to the tendency of late Expressionism to articulate political positions in aesthetic terms; we also know that Grosz himself was a vain man who took great care over his clothing and appearance and was attentive to that of others – the autobiography reports that he found it difficult, during an extended interview in Moscow with Lunacharsky, the Soviet Minister of Culture, to take his eyes off the commissar's fine patent leather shoes.[10] But it should be noted that here, as in other areas of his work, Grosz was in tune with a broader anti-Republican sensibility. Slights about the plebeian build and physiognomy of the new president were commonplace in the bourgeois press. On 21 August 1919, the day on which Friedrich Ebert took his oath as Reich President, the right-wing *Tägliche Illustrierte* observed that the new head of state had a 'bloated, short-necked face' and 'folds of fat in the nape of his neck' and added that an odour of leather still hung about his person (Ebert had been trained as a saddler).[11] On the very morning of the ceremony, the *Berliner Illustrirte* and several other papers saw fit to publish a photograph of Ebert and Noske in their bathing trunks. 'The memory of the picture haunted the ceremony', one observer recalled.[12]

Grosz was now a political artist in the fullest sense, coediting various publications for Malik and producing work for a range of Communist and radical journals. He was a keen participant in demonstrations and protest marches. In 1922 he travelled to the Soviet Union, where he met various prominent personalities from the worlds of government and culture. By his own account, he was no longer producing 'art' at all, a concept he now denounced as 'an annulment of human equality', but visual weapons for the revolutionary struggle. In *Der Kunstlump* (The Art Scab), a famous polemical essay he wrote jointly with John Heartfield in

Weimar Politics and George Grosz

1920, Grosz denounced art galleries as symbols of bourgeois hegemony and declared that 'today the cleaning of a gun by a Red soldier is of greater significance than the entire metaphysical output of all the painters'. Grosz and Heartfield observed with approval that a Rubens painting housed in the Dresden State Gallery had been damaged by a bullet fired during a political streetfight: 'With joy we welcome the news that the bullets are whistling through the galleries and palaces, into the masterpieces [...], instead of into the houses of the poor in the working-class neighbourhoods!'[13] Such shrill iconoclasm was not unusual amongst the radicalised post-war intelligentsia – in an article entitled 'The Hole in Rubens's Ham', the radical painter Franz Seiwert called for the 'destruction of idolatrous images' in the name of 'true' (proletarian) art.[14] The Bolshevik poet Mayakovsky remarked in a similar vein that one ought to put Raphael up against a wall and treat him like a White Guard.

Grosz's call for a mobilisation of art in the service of revolution, reiterated in numerous variations during the early 1920s, signalled a transition in his work away from the formal subtlety and psychological intensity of his wartime work towards a flatter, poster-like style in which residual Expressionist features were subordinated to the purposes of propaganda. The synaesthetic simultaneity of multiple impressions in his early drawings of the city increasingly made way for didactic binary compositions juxtaposing wealthy venal manipulators with dishevelled workers and down-and-outers. Occasionally Grosz even resorted to the time-honoured technique of splitting the frame between two incongruous but simultaneous realities as, for example, in *Früh um 5 Uhr* (Five in the Morning) where industrialists cavort with their whores while emaciated proletarians trudge tiredly to work.[15]

In an article he wrote for *Die Aktion* in 1923, the writer Max Hermann-Neisse observed that Grosz 'sees things as one is not supposed to see them in bourgeois Germany: as they are, not as they seem'.[16] With these words Hermann-Neisse inadvertently hinted at a tension central to Grosz's work as an artist: an ambition, on the one hand, to reproduce the specific surfaces of things, the way they 'seem', and a commitment, on the other, to the political 'realities' behind the surface, to the universal themes essential to the purposes of propaganda. Grosz had a keen eye for material detail – the labels on bottles and cigar boxes, the lines of dresses and trousers, the contents of a desk, the fall of a curtain, the alluring glow of the shop window. And yet his best-known drawings and watercolours were never works of observation in any literal sense. His protagonists were ideal types, like the masked characters in a miracle play: the fat capitalist (whose fatness had an unmistakeable social resonance in the hungry working-class quarters of post-war Berlin), the militarist, the lumpen thug of the Freikorps, the decadent venal burgher, the ageing whore. Two things prevented Grosz's morality scenes from collapsing into banality. The first was his ability to deploy keenly-observed detail so that his figures retained just enough material specificity to compensate for what was lost in the process of typification. The second was the artist's sharp awareness – unsurprising, perhaps, in a some-time actor, dandy and poseur – of the performativeness of social roles: posture, cosmetics, accessories, hand movements, the angles of hats and caps, the play of facial muscles. Grosz hinted at the mimetic dimension in his work when he wrote in his autobiography: 'in reality, I myself was everybody I drew, the rich man favoured by fate, stuffing himself and guzzling champagne, as much as the one who stood outside in the pouring rain holding out his hand.'[17]

Grosz remained politically engaged well into the mid-1920s, producing work for a range of radical journals, including the official Communist organ *Die Rote Fahne* (The Red Flag) and the leftist satirical paper *Der Knüppel* (The Cudgel). In 1924 he helped to found and lead the Red Group, the first organisation of Communist artists in the Weimar Republic, whose purpose was to produce art in the service of 'agitation and propaganda'.[18] But his relationship with the Communist party proper remained problematic. The Communists were not impressed by the playful excesses of Berlin Dada, which they denounced as perverse and sensationalist, nor did they endorse the call for an assault on the art galleries. As Gertrud Alexander, the combative cultural editor of *Rote Fahne*, announced in 1920: 'The proletariat will wage this struggle and be victorious without a bourgeois literary clique mounting its superfluous campaign against art and culture.'[19] The Malik circle responded by faulting the Communists for their intolerance of progressive artistic experimentation.[20]

However, even at the height of his career as an agitator-propagandist, when Grosz put formal

23. *God-willed Dependence*, from *The Face of the Ruling Classes*, Berlin, 1921.

24. M.E., *The Wire-Puller*, poster of 1924 for the NSDAP (Nazi Party).

Wirepullers of Left and Right. The Nazi poster is addressed to 'workers of the head and hand'. Communists and Nazis shared a paranoid worldview in which powerful and malevolent conspiratorial élites played a central role.

Weimar Politics and George Grosz

experiments aside, his work lacked a specifically Communist sensibility. It was viciously anti-bourgeois and anti-militarist in the Expressionist tradition, and of course it was anti-capitalist, but it seldom even hinted at the role of the party (an exception was the famous drawing of an imprisoned Communist passing his vote for the KPD through the bars of his cell window) and it neglected to evoke the classless utopian society of the Communist future. Grosz's workers were never the supercharged mobilised 'masses' of the KPD posters, but ragged groups of individuals, disaggregated and entropic like the urban crowds in his early drawings. It was a negative vision that drew on Grosz's misanthropy and pessimism. Moreover, his work incessantly returned to motifs that bore little if any relation to the class struggle. Foremost among these were his obsessive depictions of women. Some three-quarters of the drawings in the album *Ecce Homo* of 1923 depict erotic scenes involving women in a state of partial or complete nudity. Throughout the drawings of the early twenties, women figure as sexual predators shamelessly naked beneath their clothes, masochists receiving punishment, victims of rape-murder, and even detached pairs of buttocks floating across the picture plane. Grosz claimed at an obscenity trial relating to *Ecce Homo* in 1924 that these motifs derived from his critique of the bourgeoisie and its perverse sexuality, but this rationalisation should be treated with scepticism. An ambivalently-charged preoccupation with women and the erotic runs through much of the art of the period, and these themes have been persuasively linked with contemporary anxieties about social and sexual hygiene and the introduction of female suffrage which many men found so unsettling.[21]

Around 1923–4, for reasons that remain unclear (the autobiography is painfully evasive and disingenuous on the question of his political allegiances), Grosz ceased to pay his party membership dues. In any case, the centralisation of the KPD from 1925 under its new leader Ernst Thälmann resulted in stricter and more dogmatic policing of cultural activity, making the party a less congenial ally for independent artists. Characteristic of the changed mood was a resolution adopted by the agitprop section at the tenth Party Congress of 1925, which found fault with Grosz's drawings for expressing a 'merely anarchistic critique of the decomposition of bourgeois society, without embodying our Communist critique and ideology'.[22]

At about this time, as many analysts have observed, the intensity of Grosz's political commitment appears to have waned. He had been working with the commercial dealer Flechtheim since 1923 and was beginning to receive lucrative commissions from the quality bourgeois journals. He was into his thirties and would soon have two children to provide for. The Republic had stabilised itself after the inflationary episode of 1922–3, and the upper middle classes were beginning to take a friendly interest in the maverick *Bürgerschreck* who had vilified their manners and habitat with a pen dipped in gall. There were occasional explosions of polemical prose, but the few political drawings Grosz did produce in the late 1920s failed to achieve the force and quality of the earlier pieces, and there is evidence to suggest that he approached these commissions with little enthusiasm.[23] The drawings in portfolios such as *Spiesser-Spiegel* (The Philistine's Mirror, 1925) and *Das neue Gesicht der herrschenden Klasse* (The New Face of the Ruling Class, 1930) were void of polemical content – café scenes, gentle vignettes, fashionable strollers, film stills from the panorama of urban life.

In the light of the horrors that followed the formation of a Hitler government in January 1933, it is perhaps understandable that Grosz has been celebrated as the unflinching chronicler of a sick and immoral society.[24] The same claim was frequently made by his left-wing contemporaries. Kurt Tucholsky declared that he knew of no one who had so completely grasped the modern face of the holders of power 'right down to the last claret-coloured broken vein'. Grosz even described himself as a 'natural scientist' of Weimar society; in the later 1920s he liked to pose as a 'warner', one finger raised, hinting at trouble ahead. But we should not forget that in the years of his most effective activity as a political artist Grosz was an implacable enemy of the first German democracy, not only of its militarists and industrialists, but also of its socialist politicians, its elections and union leaders. The 'faces' he drew in the service of his struggle against a young and unstable republic were brilliant inventions. They were designed to persuade the leftist worker or intellectual that the enemy was inhuman, that he deserved nothing but hatred and destruction, that there could be no hope of reconciliation. They were part of that 'dehumanisation of the enemy' (fig. 22) that so poisoned the tone of Weimar politics.[25] In this sense, perhaps, it is legitimate to speak of a 'negative solidarity' between the extreme left and the extreme right, in propaganda as in politics. It is not difficult, in retrospect, to discern the cousinhood between the obese industrialist who pulled the strings in Grosz's paranoid vision of German society (fig. 23) and the ubiquitous 'Jewish capitalist' of National Socialist propaganda (fig. 24).

1. Rosa Luxemburg, 'Foundation of the Communist Party', *Die rote Fahne*, 31 December 1918.
2. 'Outines for the German Workers' and Soldiers' Councils', *Die rote Fahne*, 26 November 1918.
3. Hagen Schulze, *Weimar. Deutschland 1917–1933*, Berlin, 1982, p. 180.
4. Annemarie Lange, *Berlin in der Weimarer Republik*, Berlin/GDR, 1987, pp. 47, 198–9.
5. Cited in John Willett, *The New Sobriety 1917–1933. Art and Politics in the Weimar Republic*, London, 1978, p. 33.
6. November Group Circular, 13 December 1918 (Berlin, 1918) in Anton Kaes, Martin Jay and Edward Dimendberg, *The Weimar Republic Sourcebook*, Berkeley and Los Angeles, 1994, p. 477.
7. Cited from an autobiographical essay of 1928 in Beth Irwin Lewis, *George Grosz. Art and Politics in the Weimar Republic*, 2nd ed., Princeton, NJ, 1991, p. 66.
8. George Grosz and Wieland Herzfelde, *Die Kunst ist in Gefahr* (1925), cited in Uwe M. Schneede, *George Grosz. Life and Work*, London, 1979, p. 74.
9. Remark to Harry Count Kessler cited in Lewis, *George Grosz*, p. 75.
10. George Grosz, *A Small Yes and a Big No*, trans. A. J. Pomerans, London and New York, 1982, p. 142.
11. Cited in Schulze, *Weimar*, p. 207.
12. Count Harry Kessler, Diary entry of 21 August 1919, in Kaes, Jay and Dimendberg, *Sourcebook*, p. 51.
13. George Grosz and John Heartfield, 'The Art Scab' (1920) in Kaes, Jay and Dimendberg, *Sourcebook*, pp. 483–6.
14. Harald Maier-Metz, *Expressionismus – Dada Agitprop. Zur Entwicklung des Malik-Kreises in Berlin 1912–1924*, Frankfurt/Main, 1984, p. 299.
15. See John Czaplicka, 'Pictures of a City at Work, Berlin, circa 1890–1930: Visual Reflections on Social Structures and Technology in the Modern Urban Construct', in Charles W. Haxthausen and Heidrun Suhr (eds), *Berlin: Culture and Metropolis*, Minneapolis, MN, 1991, pp. 4–36; here p. 25.
16. Cited in Ivo Kranzfelder, *George Grosz 1893–1959*, Cologne, 1994, p. 69.
17. Cited in Schneede, *George Grosz*, p. 84.
18. Maier-Metz, *Dada*, p. 396.
19. G. Alexander, 'Dada', *Die rote Fahne* 3, cited in Maier-Metz, *Dada*, p. 271.
20. See e.g. Wieland Herzfelde, 'Gesellschaft, Künstler und Kommunismus' Part II, *Der Gegner*, Vol. 2, No. 6, 1920/21 (repr. Leipzig, 1979), p. 196.
21. On these aspects of Grosz's work, see esp. Beth Irwin Lewis, 'Lustmord: Into the windows of the Metropolis', in Haxthausen and Suhr (eds), *Berlin: Culture and Metropolis*, pp. 111–40; Kathrin Hoffmann-Curtius, '"Wenn Blicke töten könnten", oder: Der Künstler als Selbstmörder', in Ines Lindner (ed.), *Blick-Wechsel: Konstruktion von Männlichkeit und Weiblichkeit in Kunst und Kunstgeschichte*, Berlin, 1989, pp. 369–93; Maria Tatar, *Lustmord. Sexual Murder in Weimar Germany*, Princeton, 1995, pp. 98–131.
22. Cited in Maier-Metz, *Dada*, p. 398.
23. Lewis, *George Grosz*, p. 191.
24. See eg. Uwe M. Schneede, 'Infernalischer Wirklichkeitsspuk', in Serge Sabarsky (ed.), *George Grosz. Die Berliner Jahre*, Hamburg, 1986, pp. 27–33; here p. 29.
25. G. L. Mosse, *Fallen Soldiers. Reshaping the Memory of the World Wars*, Oxford, 1990, p. 172.

GROSZ THROUGH THE EYES OF HIS CONTEMPORARIES

Walter Mehring

Somewhen around 1912 in the . . . Café 'Megalomania' a fop with a white powdered face attracted the attention of the individuals who frequented the place. This was because of his padded check jacket, his bowler hat and his small walking stick with which every now and again he would make fencing movements into the empty air. He usually sat right at the front on the terrace, cheekily staring at everyone walking past, rudely eyeing them up and down from the partings in their hair to their socks and boots. He seemed to be someone who worked in a circus or a music hall. Was he a clown looking for work? An acrobatic dancer? Or the agent of small time artistes?

    Walter Mehring, *Berlin Dada*, Giessen, 1983, p. 27

Erwin Blumenfeld

One night in 1915 I went, slightly merry, to the urinal on Potsdamer Platz. A young dandy entered from the opposite side, put his monocle in his eye, opened his black and white checked trousers and traced my profile in one fell swoop on the wall in so masterly a fashion that I could not help exclaiming in admiration. We became friends.

    Erwin Blumenfeld, *Durch tausendjährige Zeit*, Winterthur, 1976, p. 105

Wieland Herzfelde

I got to know him in 1915 . . . in the flat of the painter Ludwig Meidner. I was surprised by . . . the 'normal' appearance of this young gentleman. . . He looked as if he had stepped out of a fashion magazine. . . His ash blond hair was perfectly cut, his parting as sharp as the creases in the knickerbockers hitched up above his knees. The ruddy face with the sharp profile and blue, sceptical eyes might have been that of a German army officer. And yet . . . the smart grey suit which, devoid of a single speck of dust, hugged the muscular body somewhat too tightly, the silk tie, tightly tied into a small knot on the starched shirt, the blue-black, almost transparent socks stretched over the calves . . . the new, thick soled, ornamental brogues – this man obviously loved them all and would never have exchanged them for any kind of uniform at any price. But what was extraordinary about him was that he did not give the impression of a gigolo or someone mad about fashion. . . His eyes were those of a marksman taking aim, and his mouth had a bitterness about it that was only slightly softened by the powder on his cleanly shaven, powerful chin.

    Wieland Herzfelde, 'Ein Kaufmann aus Holland', *Pass Auf! Hier kommt Grosz,
    Bilder, Rhythmen und Gesänge 1915–18*, Wieland Herzfelde and Hans Marquardt
    (eds), Leipzig, 1981, pp. 65–6.

Hans Sahl

He was wearing a bowler, monocle and green cravat when I once met him in Munich after the war. It was at a Munch exhibition, and he was making the visitors despair as they respectfully walked around. Right at the entrance he called out, 'Come quickly – this is where art's destruction begins!' After that, standing in front of the famous portraits, he spoke an inimitable monologue on the subject of the master's regrettable ignorance of gentlemen's tailoring. 'A great painter must also be a great tailor. He must know how to make shirts, gloves, ties and walking sticks! Look at this foot. It's not a shoe but a smoothing iron!'

Hans Sahl, 'George Grosz oder die Vertreibung aus dem Paradies', in Karl Riha (ed.), *George Grosz – Hans Sahl: So long mit Händedruck. Briefe und Dokumente*, Hamburg, 1993, pp. 19f.

Paul Westheim

His studio was in Südende. An attic room whose extreme modesty made the furnishing and decoration seem the more fantastic – they were completely in the Red Indian style. You believed you were entering the wigwam of a Sioux chief. Wonderfully boyish. On the walls hung tomahawks, clubs, buffalo-skin shields – whether they were real or painted, I can't remember. Nor can I recall whether scalps were dangling there as well. Between them were photographs, manifestos and epigrams of the sort that later decorated the Dada exhibition. Among other things was a large photograph of Edison . . . on which Grosz had written the dedication: 'To dear George Grosz. Thomas A. Edison.' The entire arrangement gave a foretaste of Dada. We squatted in the middle of this wigwam . . . on low stools . . . drinking not fire water but tea, and we smoked not a pipe of peace but, alas, German war-standard tobacco.

Whenever I visited Grosz in his studio in later years its appearance was somewhat different. Very businesslike, entirely like a workshop, even a little like an official Prussian office, at least as far as the immaculate organisation was concerned. I was above all impressed by a table with pigeon-holes on it. Each compartment was labelled with a small drawing depicting the contents: string, drawing pins, pencils, charcoal, etc. As precise and lucid as George Grosz's drawings.

Paul Westheim, 'Erinnerungen an George Grosz', in *Weltkunst*, Vol.32, No.22, November 1962, p.16

Count Harry Kessler

18 November 1917
In Grosz there is a kind of demon. I think rather highly of him. . . All the new art coming out of Berlin is especially remarkable. . . It is big city art, a hypertense concentration of impressions which cumulates in simultaneity. It is brutally realistic but like a fairy tale at the same time – like the big city itself – things turn red as though illuminated by spotlights. They are distorted and then disappear in the glow. It is a highly nervous, cerebral, illusionistic art, and thus most intimately related to musical hall; to the cinema, too. . . It is art like flash photography exuding the perfume of vice and perversion like every big city street at night.

Count Harry Kessler, *The Diaries of a Cosmopolitan, 1918–37*, trans. and ed. Charles Kessler, London, 1971, pp. 187–8

Wieland Herzfelde

At about this time [1917] Grosz and Heartfield also worked for the cabaret *Schall und Rauch* (Noise and Smoke). They designed programmes and made a number of grotesque puppets. . . In the summer of 1917 Heartfield became a director of scientific documentary films at the Military Pictorial Office, the predecessor of the Universal Film Company, known as UFA. . . [His and Grosz's] new ideas led to the establishment of an animated film department. Grosz made drawings which Heartfield turned into two-dimensional figures with movable limbs for an animated film, as far as I know the first ever in Germany. Titled *Pierre in Saint Nazarre*, the film was meant to poke fun at American plans to invade allied France while glorifying the imperial German army and in particular Big Bertha – the 42-cm-calibre gun manufactured by Krupp... When the film was finally finished it was turned down. By then the Americans had landed, and Grosz had drawn not them but our own soldiers in such a way that they provoked disgust.

      Wieland Herzfelde, 'George Grosz, John Heartfield, Erwin Piscator, Dada und die Folgen – oder die Macht der Freundschaft', in *Sinn und Form*, Vol. 23 (1971), No. 6, pp. 1242–4

COUNT HARRY KESSLER

Wednesday, 3 February 1919
In the morning I visited George Grosz... He wants to become the German Hogarth, deliberately realistic and didactic; to preach, improve and reform. Art for art's sake does not interest him at all... He is really a Bolshevist in the guise of a painter. He loathes painting and the pointlessness of painting as practised so far, yet by means of it wants to achieve something quite new, or, more accurately, something that it used to achieve (through Hogarth or religious art), but which got lost in the nineteenth century. He is reactionary and revolutionary in one, a symbol of the times. Intellectually his thought processes are in part rudimentary and easily demolished.

      Kessler, 1971, p. 62

RICHARD HUELSENBECK

Every evening Grosz sat in the Kempinski [Hotel] with bottles of wine and good food (as far as it could then be had for money) in front of him. And Grosz told me of his ambitions. I clearly remember him speaking about the magnificent snobbery of the English artist Aubrey Beardsley, his numerous suits, shoes and ties, and about the servant who would wait on him with paints and pens. This was the idol of a man who at the same time was flirting with the proletariat and was prepared to accept the political consequences.

      Richard Huelsenbeck in *Neue Zürcher Zeitung*, 14 July 1959

EDUARD PLIETZSCH

The young George Grosz went so far as to eliminate from his artist's workshop everything even remotely reminiscent of a painter's studio. Visitors were meant to think that they found themselves in the office of a smart American businesman. There was a typewriter, a card index file containing clearly labelled records of the pictures completed so far, and other office equipment. Grosz would have dearly loved to have an American till as well, to produce, by pulling a lever, a receipt for every promptly delivered painting... At that time Grosz was making compositions with scissors and paste in a purely mechanical way – his photomontages. If he occasionally resorted to brushes and palette again, he never wrote his signature. He would apply a business stamp bearing his address and telephone number.

      Eduard Plietzsch, *... heiter ist die Kunst*, Gütersloh, 1955, p. 82

COUNT HARRY KESSLER

Friday, 7 July 1922
The devotion of [Grosz's] art exclusively to the depiction of the repulsiveness of bourgeois philistinism is, so to speak, merely the counterpart to some sort of secret ideal of beauty that he conceals as though it were a badge of shame. In his drawings he harasses with fanatical

hatred the antithesis to this ideal, which he protects from public gaze like something sacred. His whole art is a campaign of extermination against what is irreconcilable with his secret 'lady love'. Instead of singing her praises like a troubador, he does battle against her opponents with unsparing fury like a dedicated knight. Only in his colours does he ever let his secret ideal show through. His is an excessively sensitive nature which turns outrageously brutal by reason of its sensibility, and he has the talent for delineating this brutality creatively.

    Kessler, 1971, pp.187–8

HANS RICHTER

He trained daily with a punchbag because it was not enough simply to skewer the philistine with a pencil or pen – one had to be physically ready to hit him in the gob. On the street with his hat and cane he looked like the romanticised image of the American gangster, a type he admired...

    Hans Richter, *Begegnungen von Dada bis heute*, Cologne, 1973, pp. 97–8

OTTO GRIEBEL

[Grosz] had altered his artistic approach in line with Constructivism and inspired by the formal language of the Italian Chirico, but with the difference that Grosz was much more sober in his choice of subject and expressive means. As long as Grosz was drawing political satires he liked to wear a striped convict's suit in the studio. Now he preferred to proceed like a technician, using geometric instruments at an adjustable drawing board, working everything through with schematic precision... While I was with Grosz on another occasion he was visited by a foreigner interested in his work. But he kept him waiting for quite a long time in another room while we continued talking. 'You should make a note of this', my eccentrically inclined friend said, 'these people have more time and money than we do. One shouldn't receive them immediately. He must learn to be patient. It's better that way and also more advantageous for business.'

    Otto Griebel, *Ich war ein Mann der Strasse*, Halle and Leipzig, 1986, p. 134

MAX SCHMELING

Since he had questioned me about my profession so directly on previous occasions, I now found the courage to put some questions to him. 'Tell me, Mr Grosz, why do all the people in your drawings have thick skulls, bald heads, roughly stitched scars on their faces and fat bellies? I never encounter people like that...' 'That's the point', he said, 'I'm not a portraitist in the traditional sense. I'm not at all interested in the real Frau Meier, the real commercial counsellor Müller or the real master butcher Lehmann... What I try to portray ... is what drives such people: the rapacity of Frau Meier, the vanity of Herr Müller and the brutality of Herr Lehmann. I've always been more interested in types than individuals.'

    Max Schmeling, *Erinnerungen*, Frankfurt am Main, Berlin and Vienna, 1977, paperback edition, pp. 91–2

KURT TUCHOLSKY

Whenever he draws a man in a suit and silly pince-nez then the following are present: the body of the man shining through the suit ... illuminating ... his entire life. We know instantly which books he reads, how he voted at the elections, his acquaintances, the pubs he uses... Grosz includes the aura of the man in his drawings, precisely what only a tiny minority of actors understand how to do on stage.

    Kurt Tucholsky writing as Peter Panter in *Die Weltbühne*, No. 50, 1930, p. 862

GROSZ AS AN ART THEORIST

George Grosz possessed formidable literary skills. His letters range from the vividly descriptive to the devastatingly satirical, and his autobiography may be unreliable but it remains one of the most entertaining ever written by an artist. His verse (most of which defies translation) is also irrepressibly energetic and inventive. But Grosz wrote theoretical essays, too, and they are among the most important of their period, a memorable mixture of argument and invective. For the most part written between 1920 and 1925, they reveal his artistic development almost as clearly as his paintings and drawings. In the theories the radical activist comes gradually to reject dogma and respect tradition. Most of the following extracts appear here in English for the first time.

DER KUNSTLUMP
The Art Scab

Written with John Heartfield and first published in *Der Gegner* (Vol. 1, Nos 10–12, 1919–21), this essay is a vitriolic attack on 'formalist' art, art exclusively concerned with aesthetic values. Grosz's first published theoretical statement, it was prompted by an open letter to the inhabitants of Dresden from the Expressionist painter Oskar Kokoschka, then a Professor at the Dresden Academy of Art. During the general strike following the Kapp Putsch of 1920 there was a battle between the army and demonstrators in Dresden. The result was 59 deaths, more than 150 wounded, and a bullet hole in Rubens's *Bathsheba at the Well*, one of the glories of Dresden's matchless collection of Old Masters. Deploring the accident, Kokoschka urged the populace to remember that great art is apolitical and timeless: the 'most sacred treasures' of humanity should be protected and preserved at all costs; they were far more important for future generations than any contemporary political squabble. *The Art Scab* sought to demolish this assertion.

Although both Grosz and Heartfield were already members of the German Communist Party, the official party line diverged from their extreme views. The reaction of Johannes R. Becher, the Communist poet (and later Cultural Minister of the GDR), was typical: 'I read the filthy article . . . against Kokoschka with disgust and loathing . . . he has more proletarian feeling in the tips of his fingers than these chaps have in their entire dessicated bodies' (quoted after Rosamunde Neugebauer, Gräfin von der Schulenburg, *George Grosz, Macht und Ohnmacht satirischer Kunst*, Berlin, 1993, p. 52).

What is art to the working man?

When he has to toil hour upon hour to meet his most basic needs; when he chafes at the desperate predicament to which he sees his comrades, his family, all his fellow fighters, reduced by the bloodsuckers and bloated toads of the bourgeoisie – and when he begrudges every minute not spent in freeing this world from the filthy clutches of the capitalist system . . .

What is art to the working man? In the face of all these horrifying truths, art seeks to lead him into an ideal world where they do not apply; it strives to divert him from revolutionary action, to make him forget the crimes of the rich, and to hoodwink him into believing in the bourgeois notion of a world of order and tranquillity. Art thus delivers him up, defenceless, to the talons that rend his flesh – instead of spurring him on to join battle with these dogs.

What are poets and thinkers to the working man, if they can see all that chokes his very life and yet feel no obligation to join in the fight against his exploiters? And what good is art to the workers? Have painters ever put into their paintings the ideas appropriate to the workers' fight for freedom – the ideas that teach them to cast off the yoke of a thousand years of oppression? Have they?

In the face of all this infamy, they have painted the world in a comforting light. The beauties of nature; forest, birdsong and setting sun! Do they show that the forest is in the filthy clutches of the profiteer, who declares mile upon mile of it to be his private property, under his sole control; who fells it when he wants money to burn, but fences it round to keep the frostbitten poor from gathering firewood.

Oh, but art is apolitical! Just look! . . .

This is why works of visual art preach emotional and intellectual escapism: away from the intolerable state of this world, up to the moon and the stars, up to heaven, leaving this world to the machine-guns of democracy – which are, after all, expressly designed to help the poor man on his way to a better world beyond. That is why we find a milksop like Rainer Maria Rilke, the kept poet of perfumed loafers, writing: 'Poverty is a great glory from within' (*Book of Hours*).

Workers! . . . When they refer you to art, when they start shouting 'Art for the People', they are trying to fool you into believing that this is a treasure that you own jointly with your tormentors – a treasure for whose sake you must cease the most justified struggle the world has ever seen. Once again, they mean to use 'spiritual' values to make you docile – this time by giving you a sense of your own insignificance in the presence of the miraculous achievements of the human mind and spirit.

Fraud! Fraud!

A sordid imposture!

No, the place for art is in the museums, for petty bourgeois tourists to goggle at. Art belongs in the palaces of the killers. In front of their wall safes.

Even when dressed up as Art, Culture, Country, and all the rest, the 'most sacred treasures' are none other than the output of productive human labour; and when the call goes out to fight for them, what gentlemen like Oskar Kokoschka (or Kaiser Wilhelm II, for that matter) really mean is that you should fight to keep these most sacred treasures where they are, in the hands of owners who habitually treat them as objects of speculation. Those who really want to protect 'the poor people of the future' from being 'robbed of their most sacred treasures' would be glad if – unlike Kokoschka, the cultural blimp, who holds out the prospect of a punitive raid on our art galleries by the Entente – we were to follow the example of the city of Vienna and sell those paintings to the Entente to buy food for the undernourished coming generation. That would do more for the 'poor people of the future' than the opportunity to stand in front of intact masterpieces on legs warped and bent by rickets. In the long run, this act of cultural oblivion would be more appreciated by the German people than jam on the ration for Rembrandt's sake . . .

Cleaning just one Red soldier's rifle now means more than the metaphysical work of all the painters put together. The terms 'art' and 'artist' are bourgeois inventions; their place in the State can only be on the side of the ruling caste, i.e., the bourgeoisie.

The title 'artist' is an insult.

The term 'art' is a negation of human equality.

To worship the artist is to worship oneself.

The artist never stands higher than his milieu, or than the society that gives him approval. For his little brain does not produce the ideas contained in his work: it processes (like a sausage machine) the world-view of his public . . .

We are delighted to see bullets whistling into galleries and palaces, into the masterpieces of the Rubenses of this world, rather than into the houses of the poor in the proletarian districts!

We are delighted when the open war between capital and labour is fought out on the home territory of the infamous culture and art that has always served to crush the poor; the art that uplifts the bourgeois every Sunday afternoon and gives him the peace of mind to resume his skin trade, his exploitation, on Monday morning!

STATT EINER BIOGRAPHIE
Instead of an Autobiography

> Parts of this text first appeared in *Der Gegner* (Vol. 2, No. 3, 1920–21) before it was published in 1921 in its entirety. It continues the argument outlined in *The Art Scab* although its tone is less anarchic. Grosz here urges every artist to take a political stance and attacks the idea that 'revolutionary', avant-garde styles can express revolutionary political attitudes. But the most important section is the last in which Grosz denies that facts about the artist's own life and personality in any way aid an interpretation of his work.

Art today depends on the bourgeoisie and dies with it. Perhaps unintentionally, the painter acts as a banknote factory, an equity machine, used by the rich exploiter and pseudo-aesthete to invest his money more or less lucratively while allowing him to appear in his own eyes and in those of society as a patron of the arts. To many, art is also an escape from this 'squalid' world of ours on to a better and cleaner plane: the lunar paradise of the imagination, where there is no partisan strife and no civil war. The cult of individualism and personality that painters and writers encourage – with varying degrees of charlatanism, according to talent – is a matter for the art market. The more the personality looks like a 'genius', the more the profit.

How does the artist today rise within the bourgeoisie?

By fraud!

Mostly living a proletarian life to start with, in a filthy studio, striving with unwitting but impressive skill to 'rise' by conforming to expectations, the artist soon finds some influential bigwig who will be the 'making' of him – that is, pave his way on to the capitalist market. At some point his path crosses that of a patron, who steals his entire output in return for a hundred marks a month; or he falls into the clutches of the dealer, who can make the bourgeois customer want absolutely anything. All this of course requires a solid grounding in spiritual ideas, as dictated by the current business climate. To this end, roll out all the old trappings of pious fraud: God and the Saints, plenty of cosmos and metaphysics, and some hefty blasts on the Trump of Eternity. Behind the scenes, cynical deals are done with the insiders ('O Organist, where thou art not, the flutes they all fall silent!'). In public, the priestly gesture of the Patron of Culture. That is what the system requires – and business is good.

Whether inflated or crushed, the artists themselves derive their privileged status from their own inability to cope with the world – with Life – and are largely cretinised, dragged along in the wake of the great reactionary spiritual fraud. They imagine themselves 'creators', far superior – at the very least – to the average philistine who takes it on himself to laugh at the profundities of Picasso and Company. But these artists' own 'creations' precisely reflect the structure of the so-called spirit of culture: they are mindless, fact-hostile and irrelevant to the struggle. Go to their exhibitions and look at the ideas that blaze forth from the walls! This age of ours is so idyllic, don't you think, so lush with violins, so utterly right for Gothic saints, or Negro village belles, or cosmic inspirations! 'Reality is so hideous! All that racket upsets our sensitive souls.'

Or just look at those to whom the present age is sheer torment. Riven with convulsions, oppressed – it seems – by their own overwhelming visions. Wasted pallor, that's what we need: plenty of Gothic and Greco, not forgetting Egypt! Behold great Grünewald – or Cézanne, so proud of his medals, or Henri Rousseau, dear old dumb Douanier! Revel in that sainted simplicity – everything these days is so bleak, so cold, so empty. And today's revolution is so prosaic, with no resonance, no élan! (Isn't it just a wage dispute? Nothing sacred about that!) These people have quite forgotten their own divine origins.

It is a mistake to suppose that, if a man paints spinning tops, or cubes, or deep psychic entanglements, this necessarily makes him a revolutionary – by comparison with, say, Hans Makart. Just take Makart: he was a painter of the bourgeoisie. He painted their longings, their ideas, their history. But what about yourselves? Are you any more than the wretched lackeys of the bourgeoisie? Your snobbish ideas, your original thoughts – who supplies them?

Do you work for the proletariat, which will be the bearer of the culture that is to come? Do you make any effort to encounter and absorb the mental world of the proletariat, and to sustain it in the teeth of the exploiters and the oppressors? – Surely that ought to be within your capabilities! Do you never wonder whether it is not high time to give up mother-of-pearl inlays for good and all? You claim to be timeless; you claim that you stand above all party strife – guardians of your own inner ivory tower. You claim to work for Humanity: and where is Humanity? Your creative detachment, your abstract babble of timelessness – what is it but an absurd and futile speculation on eternity? *Your brushes and pens, which ought to be weapons, are hollow wisps of straw.* Get out and about, make the effort, come out of your seclusion, let the ideas of the working people take hold of you, and help them to fight this rotten society.

I write this in place of the autobiographical notes that are so popular and in such constant demand. It matters more to me to set out the facts and the universally valid demands, which my experience has revealed to me, than to enumerate all the stupid external accidents of my life: date of birth, family background, schooling, first long trousers, the artist's earthly pilgrimage from cradle to grave, urge to create, joy of creation, first success, etc. etc.

Constant tooting on one's own trumpet is utterly futile.

Zu meinen neuen Bildern
On My New Paintings

> Written in November 1920 and first published in January 1921 in the art journal *Das Kunstblatt*, this essay continues the essentially Marxist argument set out in the previous two articles. The 'new paintings' referred to here were those watercolours, some with collaged elements, that Grosz made in 1920, using a ruler, other geometric instruments and unmodulated washes of colour in order to achieve a mechanistic, almost anonymous effect (see cat. 79, 82, 83).

Art today is an utterly secondary matter. Anyone capable of looking beyond the (mostly somewhat individualistic) confines of his own studio will see this. All the same, art is an activity that calls for some clear decisions on the practitioner's part. It is not immaterial where you stand in this business, or what attitude you adopt to the issue of the masses, which to the clearsighted is an issue no longer. *Are you on the side of the exploiters, or on the side of the masses, who are out to destroy those exploiters?*

This is not a question to be brushed aside with all the old impostures about sublimity and sacredness and the transcendental nature of the artist's activity. Today's artist is for sale to the highest-paying jobber or patron. In the bourgeois state, this particular way of playing the market is known as patronage of the arts. Painters and writers today care nothing for the people. How else are we to explain the almost total absence of any reflection of the ideals, the aspirations or the will of the insurgent masses?

Painters and poets, of course, have their own, no doubt interesting and aesthetically valuable artistic revolutions. But, ultimately, these are workshop matters. Many artists sincerely torment themselves, only to subside into nihilistic bourgeois scepticism just because they are unable to escape from their own individualistic isolation. They fail to get a grip on revolutionary issues because they do not think about them enough. To this day, some artistic revolutionaries are still depicting Christ and the Apostles, at a time when it is our duty to redouble our propaganda to purge the world of supernatural powers – God, angels and all – and to improve man's insight into his realistic relationship with the world around him. The antiquated symbols and mystical ecstasies of the religious humbug that still fills painting today –

what are these to us? Life demands too much nowadays for us to tolerate this kind of nonsense.

So what should you do? What should your paintings be about?

Go along to a proletarian meeting, and watch and listen while people like you discuss some minute improvement in their lives.

Understand that it is they, the masses, who are working to change the way this world is organised! Not you! But you can take a hand in the work of organisation. You can help, if only you are willing! And in the process you can learn to base your artistic work on the revolutionary ideals of working people.

As for those works of mine that appear in this publication, I have this to say. I am trying once more to give an absolutely realistic image of the world. I strive to be comprehensible to *every* human being, without any of the deep waters now expected, into which you can never descend without a diving suit crammed full of spiritual, cabalistic humbug and metaphysics. The effort to create a clear, simple style brings one involuntarily close to Carrà. Nevertheless, I remain worlds apart from him. He meant to be appreciated on a metaphysical level, and his whole approach is bourgeois; my works are to be understood as training exercises – *systematic work* on the ball – with no prospect of eternity! In my so-called artistic works, I set out to build an entirely real platform. Man is no longer shown as an individual, with psychological subtleties, but as a collectivistic, almost mechanistic concept. The fate of the individual no longer counts. I would also like to show quite simple sporting symbols – as in ancient Greece – which everyone might understand and enjoy without added explanation.

I keep colour in check. Line is drawn not individualistically but photographically. Construction is used to give sculptural roundness. Back to stability, structure, functionality – sport, the engineer, the machine – but without dynamic, futuristic romanticism.

Control over line and form is reintroduced. The aim is no longer to conjure up colourfully expressionistic psychic wallpaper. – The sobriety and clarity of the engineering drawing is a better model than a disorderly mess of cabalism, metaphysics and the mystic ecstasies of the saints.

It is not possible to write down all there is to say about one's own work with total precision, especially when one is in constant training. Very often, each new day brings a new slant and new revelations. I have one more thing to say. I see the future evolution of painting as lying in the workshop, the purely craft aspect, and not in the artistic Holy of Holies. Painting is a manual craft like any other, which can be done well or badly. At present we have a star system, just as we have in other branches of the arts. This will disappear.

Photography will play a major role. It is now much better and cheaper to have your photograph taken than it is to have your portrait painted. What is more, today's artists habitually distort everything – and seem curiously loath to create a resemblance. Expressionistic anarchism must cease. Painters today revel in it – as they must, since they are politically unenlightened and have no relationship with working people. A time will come when the artist will no longer be a soggy bohemian anarchist but a bright, healthy worker within the collective community. Until the working masses achieve this, the brain worker will swing to and fro in a state of cynical unbelief. Only then will art burst from the narrow channel in which it now trickles anaemically through the lives of the 'upper ten thousand' and once more spread in a copious stream to reach the whole of working humanity. Then the things of the mind and spirit will cease to be the monopoly of Capital.

Here, as elsewhere, Communism will lead to the enrichment and forward evolution of humankind, and to the true classless culture.

ABWICKLUNG
Winding Up

Written as an introduction to Grosz's one-man exhibition at the Flechtheim Gallery, Berlin, in 1923, this autobiographical sketch marks a shift from the impersonal position outlined in the previous essay.

When I first became conscious of the world, I soon discovered that its colour and glitter did not add up to much; for that matter, neither did my fellow human beings. In those days I was an idealist and still very much of a Romantic; I felt isolated, and shut myself away.

Ignorant as I was in those days, I had altogether too high an opinion of art, and so I ended up with some very warped ideas. I had a blinkered hatred of the human race. I saw everything from the viewpoint of my little attic studio. Downstairs and all around me were members of the petty bourgeoisie, landlords and small business people, whose talk and ideas sickened me. And so I became a misanthrope, a sceptic and an individualist. Foolish and ill-educated as I was, I believed that I had a monopoly on wisdom and knowledge, and I took pride in my supposed ability to see through the fog of stupidity that surrounded me.

I started with drawings that expressed the mood of hatred I was in. For example, I drew a regulars' table in a bar, surrounded by incurables, like fat, red masses of flesh crammed into ugly, grey sacks. In search of a style to reproduce the bleak lovelessness of my subjects as starkly and uncompromisingly as possible, I studied the most direct utterances of the artistic instinct. I copied the folk drawings in urinals, because they seemed to me to convey strong feelings with the greatest economy and immediacy. And so I gradually developed this blade-sharp drawing style as a means of imparting observations that were dictated by my utter misanthropy.

On the street, in cafés, in music halls, etc., I carefully stored my observations in little notebooks, also often subsequently analysing my impressions in writing. At that time, before the War, I projected a major three-volume study entitled 'The Ugliness of the Germans'. However, this never progressed beyond Chapter 1, because there was as yet no Malik Verlag to publish it.

I was in Paris for a while. Not that Paris made any particular impression on me; I have never shared in the excessive adulation of that city of idlers. My knowledge, in that prewar period, may be summed up as follows. Human beings are swine; all talk of ethics is a fraud, designed for fools. There is no meaning to life beyond satisfying your hunger for food and for women . . .

The outbreak of war clearly showed me that the majority of the masses were devoid of will. As they thronged enthusiastically through the streets, every man subjugated by the will of the military, I felt the effects of the same will in myself – but without the enthusiasm, because I was aware of the threat to the individual freedom in which I had previously lived. Having lived in anarchic isolation from mankind, I now ran the risk of enforced association with the human beings I so loathed. My hatred concentrated itself on those who wanted to force me. I regarded the War as a monstrously hypertrophied form of the normal struggle for possessions . . .

I began to see that there was a better purpose in life than working just for myself and for my dealer. I decided to become an illustrator. To the extent that high art stood for the beauty of the world, it did not interest me. What interested me was the work of the committed outsiders and moralists of painting: Hogarth, Goya, Daumier and their like. I drew and painted out of a spirit of contradiction, and through my work I sought to convince the world that it, the world, was ugly, diseased and perfidious . . .

The German Dada movement had its roots in the realisation, which came to my fellow soldiers at the same time as it came to me, that it was utter madness to believe that the world is ruled by mind or spirit or spirits. Goethe in the barrage, Nietzsche in the kitbag, Jesus in the trenches . . .

What did the Dadaists do? They said this: huff and puff as much as you like – recite a sonnet by Petrarch, or by Rilke, or gild the heels of your boots, or carve Madonnas – the shooting goes on, the usury goes on, the starving goes on, the lying goes on. What earthly good is art? . . .

I no longer hate human beings indiscriminately. Now I hate their bad institutions, and those in power who defend those institutions. If I have a hope, it is that those institutions, and the class of individuals who protect them, may disappear. My work serves that hope. Millions of

25. Signet for the Malik Press.

Grosz as an Art Theorist

26. Jacket of *Die Kunst ist in Gefahr*, Berlin, 1925.

people share that hope with me; and those are not the art experts, not the patrons, not those with money to spend. So, whether you call my work art or not depends on whether you believe that the future belongs to the working class.

DIE KUNST IST IN GEFAHR: EIN ORIENTIERUNGSVERSUCH
Art Is in Danger: An Attempt at Orientation

> Written with Wieland Herzfelde, this is one of three essays published as a book by the Malik Press in 1925. The other two are *Paris als Kunststadt* (Paris as City of the Arts) and *Statt einer Biographie* (Instead of an Autobiography). In part *Die Kunst ist in Gefahr* is an attack on contemporary avant-garde styles and attitudes. More importantly, it also seeks to demonstrate that all art wittingly or unwittingly embodies a political point of view.

Let us step into the art arena. From melodramatic actor to eccentric clown, a strange assortment of people disport themselves there – much jollity and sunshine, but also brawls, fought tooth and nail, down to the last broken paintbrush and buckled pair of compasses. Activity – publicity – noise; but also dignified withdrawal, abnegation, remoteness. Individualism runs riot, even in the academy drawing schools. Art magazines of all shapes and sizes – triangular, square, oblong – battling against each other, crammed with problems and theories. Pick them up and you start wondering: Who is right about art? . . .

One group rejects all tradition; they swing their implements in a fine frenzy and paint more wildly than any Aborigine. Others are strictly Gothic and off-the-peg Catholic. An aberrant minority declares itself Zionist or Buddhist. Yet others come across as Tuscan; inspired by the Old Masters, they provide high-society beauties, or headstands and knock-about – all with a slight Parisian flavour. Even the Cubists, guitar and all, refuse to become extinct – though classicism has rallied of late, and Ingres, Flaxman, Poussin and Genelli show signs of rising from the grave. Then there are the Futurists, the worshippers of simultaneity, the votaries of noise. Others again cook up a metropolitan *ragoût fin* of Old Russian icon and sweetened-up Cubism. Many (honesty being the best policy) dispense with innovation and experimentation altogether and stick to sound, traditional home cooking. To them, the optical laws and colouristic researches of the Impressionists (such as the bold cropping used by the Japanese, *Fujiyama Seen Through a Fishing Net*), and the experiments of the Pointillists and Neo-Pointillists, are all still total novelties . . .

Who judges rightly? Which standpoint is to be endorsed? How do artists, those 'most sensitive nerves of society', express themselves today? How and where is their influence detected? . . .

Kandinsky made music – and projected his inner music on to the canvas rectangle. Paul Klee sat at his Biedermeier sewing table and crocheted his delicate, maidenly handiwork. The so-called new art had nothing left to represent but the painter's own feelings; consequently, the true painter had to paint his inner life. – Result: disaster. Seventy-seven art movements. And all of them claim to paint the *true* soul . . .

People went further and designed constructions. Speaking of dynamism, people soon realized that the most straightforward expression of dynamism was in the spartan drawings of the engineer. Compass and straight-edge supplanted the soul and its metaphysical speculations. Enter the Constructivists. They take a clearer view of this age. They take no refuge in metaphysics. Their aspirations are free of antiquated, bankrupt prejudices. They want sobriety; they want to work to fill real needs. They want artistic production to have a verifiable objective once again . . .

In the art world today – perhaps even more than in the past – any demand for commitment to a cause meets with indignant and contemptuous rejection. It is of course conceded that every age has produced committed works of great merit; but these works are valued not for their commitment but for their formal, 'purely artistic' qualities. In such quarters, there is no realisation that all art, in every age, has been committed to a cause: the only change has been in the nature of the cause and the clarity of the commitment . . .

The *Gothic* artists stood entirely in the service of Christian propaganda. In the Middle Ages, artists made whatever appealed to the kings, patricians and merchant princes . . . *Menzel* is the artist of Prussianism and of the early industrial age in Germany . . . *Delacroix* is the painter of the cosmopolitan bourgeoisie, supported by history and tradition, devoted to the cause of heroism, progress and a powerful France. *Toulouse-Lautrec* sees through the celebrated French tourist and pleasure industry; he unmasks bourgeois eroticism . . .

These examples may suffice to show that commitment is not just something that exists in art but something that is typical of it. True, the artist's commitment to a cause is not always a fully conscious one; but the effect is the same . . .

The artist's work always expresses the relationship between him and the world; and that, inevitably, is the commitment expressed in the art . . .

Any artist today who does not mean to be a dud, an antiquated wet squib, has only two choices: either technology or class-war propaganda. In either case, he has to abandon 'pure art'. Either he enrols as an architect, engineer or commercial artist in the – unfortunately still very feudal – army that develops industrial power and exploits the world; or, as a portraitist and critic who shows the age its own features, as a propagandist and champion of the revolutionary idea and of its adherents, he serves in the army of the oppressed, who fight for their rightful share of the world's valuables and for a rational, social organisation of life.

UNTER ANDEREM EIN WORT FÜR DEUTSCHE TRADITION
Among Other Things, a Word in Favour of German Tradition

> First published by the art journal *Das Kunstblatt* in 1931, this essay betrays a thoroughgoing disillusionment with dogma and a retreat into the past. Aware that he might be thought to be harbouring Nazi sympathies, Grosz specifically states that he does not intend this to be 'an art manifesto *à la* Schulze-Naumburg' – Paul Schulze-Naumburg was a rabid nationalist architect and the author of the notorious *Kunst und Rasse* (Art and Race, 1928).

I consider Germany now to be the most interesting and also the most mysterious country in Europe. I have the feeling that our country is destined to play a great role. It often seems to me that we are living in an age like the end of the Middle Ages. Then, too, everyone was under heavy pressure – and yet that horrific age made its artists fruitful, and Bosch and Bruegel painted cosmogonies unique in the history of art.

Perhaps we have before us another such age, a new Middle Ages. Who knows? At all events, it seems to me that humanistic ideas are dying out. People set no great store by the Rights of Man that were so ecstatically proclaimed a century ago . . .

Of course, you cannot live as an 'Old Dutch Master' today. But in prints, drawings and paintings, in this faithless and materialistic age, you must show people their own hidden, diabolical face. Let us tear down the stacks of ready-made goods and all the mass-produced trash, and show the grisly void beneath. Political upheavals will powerfully influence us. Take a long, cool look at your ancestors. Look at them: Multscher, Bosch, Bruegel, Mälesskircher, Huber, Altdorfer. So why keep on making pilgrimages to the philistine French Mecca? Why not hark back to our own forebears and continue a 'German' tradition?

Between ourselves, let them call us second-class, so long as we have expressed a little of our national identity. In any case, the French are the last people likely to take an interest in the stragglers of their own three schools.

Of course, no Matisse can flourish in Nether Pomerania, or in Berlin. What of it! The air and everything else is hard here – a bit inhospitable, linear. You tend to catch cold and get chilly feet – this is not the sun-baked, tranquil soil of the South.

To avoid misunderstandings, I do not intend this as an art manifesto *à la* Schulze-Naumburg . . .

What I do say, in all due modesty, is this. We ought to pay more attention to our own good, and not at all minor, tradition in painting and in drawing. It seems to me only right and proper to establish continuity with our great medieval masters and with their powers of design – just as the French do, and just as they cultivate their own people and tradition by drawing inspiration from old Neapolitan frescoes, Oriental carpets, Ingres, Negro sculpture or Bushman paintings.

Ugh! I have spoken.

Translated from the German by David Britt

The Catalogue

1
CAFÉ 'VERLORENES GLÜCK'
The Lost Happiness Café
1912
pen and coloured crayon, 23 × 21.5 cm
Private collection

In January 1912 Grosz moved from Dresden, having received a diploma with distinction at the Academy of Art, to Berlin, where he enrolled as an advanced student at the School of Arts and Crafts. By May he had filled five sketchbooks, four of them with drawings of streets, railway stations and cafés. He explored every part of the expanding city, especially its fringes, other underprivileged areas, pubs and cabarets. The subject of this marvellously atmospheric drawing is imaginary but probably derived from memories of things seen during his nocturnal wanderings.

2
BLAUER MORGEN
Blue Morning
1912
pen, indian ink, watercolour and coloured pencil, 53.5 × 45 cm
Private collection

Executed while Grosz was an art student in Berlin, this drawing reveals two of his major interests at that time. The first, evident in the style of the building (above all that of the relief decoration on the wall, upper left), was in the mannered ornamentation of Jugendstil, the German version of Art Nouveau. Grosz, already moderately successful as an illustrator, had published several Jugendstil-inspired drawings in humorous magazines. The other interest was thematic. Grosz then lived at Südende, an outer suburb of Berlin where the expansion of the city was at its most obvious and dramatic. It was populated by the relatively poor and unemployed whom Grosz often drew aimlessly standing on street corners with building sites in the background.

The scene shown here is clearly imaginary; it does not appear to be like Südende, and is more similar to the affluent and more central district of Charlottenburg which from the turn of the century contained many Jugendstil apartment blocks.

Sometimes entitled *Auf dem Weg zur Arbeit* (On the Way to Work), the drawing is here given the title preferred by the artist's son, Peter M. Grosz.

Catalogue

4

AM TEMPELHOFER FELD
Tempelhof Field
c. 1912
pencil, 28 × 41.5 cm
Private collection

This drawing is representative of a large number in which Grosz depicted the furthest limits of the city, the depressing areas inhabited by the poor in which rows of apartment blocks are confronted by fields and scrubland. Berlin was expanding rapidly at this time, incorporating villages and rural communities as it did so. When this drawing was made Tempelhof Field, now the site of one of Berlin's airports, was used for army manoeuvres.

3

ZIRKUS
Circus
1912–13
transfer lithograph with watercolour additions, 40.5 × 49 cm
Private collection

Only two examples are known of this print, and the other lacks the watercolour additions.

Grosz loved popular entertainment of every kind. In a memoir of his childhood he described his excitement when Barnum and Bailey's circus arrived at the small town on the Baltic where he was brought up: 'It was like a visit from fairyland as the white Pullman coaches painted with gold decorations and foreign script pulled into our little station. I wandered around the site of the circus for an entire day... In the town, too, everything was more lively than usual... The exotically strange circus types who appeared in various parts of town contributed to the transformation' (Grosz, 1929, p. 17).

44   *Catalogue*

5

HELIGOLAND
1913
pencil, 36.5 × 31.5 cm
Private collection

In 1913 Grosz spent several months in Paris, studying at the Colarossi art school, where he practised drawing briefly held poses in the life room, to facilitate a more spontaneous style. He returned to Germany after taking a holiday on the small German island of Heligoland in the North Sea, where this lively drawing was made.

6
ARBEITER
Workers
1912–13
transfer lithograph, 31.5 × 46 cm
Private collection

Grosz reproduced some of his student drawings of workers, unemployed men and vagrants in Berlin as transfer lithographs. His drawings of this period are unlike his later treatment of similar subjects in their lack of a political or social message. Grosz was chiefly interested in their picturesque, narrative or, as here, dramatic potential. The dark, moody style is realted to that of the popular Berlin artist Heinrich Zille (see fig. 3).

7
SECHSTAGERENNEN
Six-Day Bicycle Race
1913
pencil and charcoal, 20 × 25.7 cm
Lent by the Syndics of the Fitzwilliam Museum, Cambridge

The Six-Day Bicycle Race was one of Berlin's most popular spectacles. Held in the Sportpalast, the enormous arena in the Potsdamerstrasse, it demanded phenomenal feats of endurance from the international riders who took turns with a partner to race around the cambered circular track for six days and nights without interruption. Meanwhile the public (which always included actors, singers and many other celebrities – even the Crown Prince) became hysterical as signs of despair and exhaustion multiplied on the track, and loudspeakers announced the award of a prize every fifteen minutes. The prizes were not only monetary: suits, motorcycles and bottles of spirits could also be won. Grosz was one of the many artists and intellectuals who found the event irresistible. One reputable literary journal even organised a competition after the war, judged by Bert Brecht, for the best poem about the race.

A sketchbook of 1912 (Stiftung Akademie der Künste, Berlin) includes two rapid ink sketches made at that year's Six-Day Race. One (on the verso of page 22) is related to this pencil drawing.

8

KEILEREI II
Brawl II
c. 1913
Pen, 39 × 53 cm
Private collection

As an advanced student in Berlin, Grosz became fascinated by the atmospheric tales of the supernatural by Edgar Allan Poe, Gustav Meyrink and Hanns Heinz Ewers while at the same time maintaining his long-standing interest in lurid pulp fiction. Enthused by his reading, he made numerous drawings of street fights, brawls in bars, murders and other violent deaths (cf. cat. 9, 10, 11). These were clearly imaginary, although no doubt partly based on scenes observed in the low dives he frequented. For all his liking for the fantastic and grotesque, he never lost a strong sense of the real world.

9

DIE AFFÄRE MIELZYNSKI
The Mielzynski Case
*c.*1912–13
pen and ink on paper, 22.8 × 27.94 cm
Richard L. Feigen & Co.

The unusual title suggests that this violent scene was inspired by an actual murder. Grosz certainly followed reports of criminal cases in the press but whether the 'Mielzynski Case' was one of them or a figment of his imagination has not been confirmed. Beyond doubt is the debt owed by the style of this drawing, especially its almost spidery line, to the work of the Expressionist Alfred Kubin (1877–1959) who specialised in violent, grotesque and fantastic subject-matter.

10
SCHLÄGEREI
Brawl
1913
pen and ink, 26.5 × 23 cm
Galerie Pels-Leusden, Berlin

The almost manic style of these drawings was new. In 1912 Grosz gradually abandoned the use of a soft pencil in favour of a fine-nibbed pen whose dense networks of nervous lines helps establish a sinister, emotionally charged atmosphere. The effect is not unlike that achieved by drypoint and Grosz did indeed produce a few prints in that technique at just this time.

Grosz may have depicted violence in order to sublimate his boiling resentment at the claustrophobic atmosphere of militaristic, authoritarian Germany. However, it is more likely that he was simply indulging an appetite for excesses of every kind. The pleasure he took in making drawings like this also helped him abandon his 'boyhood ambition for gigantic oil paintings, ladder-backed easels and brushes the size of brooms' (*Autobiography*, p. 87).

11

DER ÜBERFALL
The Attack
1915
pencil, 28.5 × 22.2 cm
The Hirshhorn Museum and Sculpture Garden, Smithsonian Institution
Gift of Joseph H. Hirshhorn Foundation, 1966

One of many scenes of violence and murder dating from this period, this drawing is one of the few in which Grosz used a very soft pencil whose marks were then rubbed and softened with his fingers and a stump, achieving atmospheric effects that are almost painterly. Both the emotive subject and style are related to Expressionism.

The rendering of light which draws attention to the solitary figure on the balcony is especially effective.

Catalogue

12

LUFTANGRIFF
Aerial Attack
1915
pen and ink, 19.9 × 26.8 cm
The Museum of Modern Art, New York
John S. Newberry Fund

This explosive scene, drawn during the first full year of World War I, shows the destructive bombing of cities that had not yet become reality. Both the subject and the markedly Expressionist style are related to the work of Grosz's friend, the painter and writer Ludwig Meidner (1884–1966) who, from the unbearably hot summer of 1912, was obsessed by visions of catastrophe.

Meidner was important for Grosz. His idiosyncratic use of Futurist fragmentation influenced Grosz's drawing and painting for several years. So did his passionate political ideas. Associated with the Berlin Expressionist (and pacifist) journal *Die Aktion*, Meidner was a leftwing republican and, after the war, a member of several revolutionary artists' organisations. He also kept open house once a week where Grosz met several of those with whom he was to work especially closely. One of them was Wieland Herzfelde.

The inscription in the bottom left-hand margin reads *Fliegebombe* (Flying Bomb). The title given here is that preferred by the owner.

14
GEFANGENEN
Prisoners
1915
lithograph, 40 × 38.5 cm
Private collection

These prisoners look like Russians. During his military service in 1914–15 Grosz once guarded men like these. In a letter of 6 February 1945 to his friend Ulrich Becker, he remembered that 'They arrived like begging dogs with dirty tin mugs and old plates; they even fished things out of dustbins with their caps...' (Knust, 1979, p. 343).

13
SCHLACHTFELD
Battlefield
1914
pen and ink, 23 × 28 cm
Collection of Roy and Jenny Wright, London

Grosz volunteered for army service on 11 November 1914. He served in the Royal Prussian Emperor Franz Grenadier Guard Regiment, and, while being sent to the western front, became seriously ill with a sinus infection from which he partially recovered in a military hospital before being given an honourable discharge in May 1915. Military records confirm that he never experienced battle. However, this image, together with several others of similar battle subjects (cf. cat. 14), is vivid enough to suggest at least a memory of something directly seen.

Catalogue 53

15

DER TOTE MANN
The Dead Man
1915–16
pen and ink, 28.4 × 22.1 cm
Henry Boxer Gallery, London

Almost identical to *Mord (*Murder), an image included in the print portfolios *Kleine Grosz Mappe* (Little Grosz Portfolio, 1917) and *Ecce Homo* (1923), this drawing is more elaborately worked. It includes tonal cross-hatching; there is a street lamp; the corpse is more detailed; and a hat and broken cane are lying on the ground. Above all, this is a nocturnal scene: in the prints the murder has taken place beneath a blazing sun. However, the knowing naïvety of the style, producing the appearance of an elaborate graffito, is common to both drawing and prints. So is the evil-looking mongrel bitch, a familiar member of Grosz's cast of characters at this time.

16
KRAWALL DER IRREN
Lunatics Riot
1915–16
pen and indian ink, 31.8 × 22.6 cm
Staatliche Museen zu Berlin,
Kupferstichkabinett

Soon after Grosz was released from the army for the first time his graphic style changed. His line became bold, razor-sharp and deceptively simple. He abandoned the use of tone in favour of clear, supple contours. He also imitated the artlessness of naïve drawings, especially graffiti on lavatory walls which he admired and copied.

The primitive mannerisms evoke the atmosphere of a world gone mad, in which all civilised behaviour has been abandoned. The lunatics have taken over the asylum, fighting, murdering and setting buildings ablaze. What we see here was, of course, taking place throughout war-torn Europe, with the difference that the real lunacy – on the battlefield – was being encouraged in the name of civilisation and reason.

In 1920 the critic Leopold Zahn referred to Grosz in an essay entitled *Über Infantilismus in der neuen Kunst* (Concerning Infantilism in Modern Art). Grosz, he wrote, 'attempts to see the big city from the perspective of a precocious, depraved street urchin, and draws that miserable quarter on the fringe where, from childhood on, people are surrounded by images of deprivation, vice and crime. Heartlessly and mockingly grimacing, he points to the baseness which he discovers beneath every façade' (*Das Kunstblatt*, Vol. 4, 1920, p. 86).

17

DAS ENDE DES WEGES
The End of the Road
1913
watercolour, charcoal and pencil,
29.1 × 22.8 cm
The Museum of Modern Art, New York

Even the colours in this gruesome scene suggest the stink of corruption and decay. An ordinary family, their circumstances made plain by the room's simple furniture and furnishings, has committed suicide. Perhaps the woman hanged herself with her husband's assistance before he drank the poison still running from the overturned bottle. Their bloated baby lies beside him.

Grosz produced many similarly horrific and brutal images at this time, indulging his taste for the morbid and desire to shock. However, there is already a hint of a more serious intention: a determination to reveal the uncomfortable truths lurking behind the respectable façades erected by seemingly average people.

18

KABARETTSZENE
Cabaret Scene
1913–14
wood engraving with pencil corrections,
19.9 × 13.7 cm
Berlinische Galerie, Berlin,
Landesmuseum für Moderne Kunst,
Photographie und Architektur

Although he made prints at every stage of his career, Grosz was not really a printmaker. That is to say that the overwhelming majority of his prints were not created with a specific reproductive process in mind. They were made first as drawings which were then reproduced as lithographs with the aid of transfer paper or the camera. While studying at the School of Arts and Crafts in Berlin, however, Grosz did produce a small number of drypoints and this wood engraving. It is the only one known, and once belonged to his fellow student (and later Dadaist) Hannah Hoech, who noted on the verso that Grosz had made it while 'still a student of Orlik'. She may also have added the signature which is not in Grosz's handwriting.

The influence on Grosz of his teacher Emil Orlik (1870–1932) has been insufficiently emphasised. Orlik's etchings and drawings are closely observed and spontaneously realised. They left an abiding impression on Grosz.

Catalogue 57

19
TRAPEZKÜNSTLERIN
Trapeze Artist
c. 1915
Pen, ink and wash, 28 × 22.1 cm
Henry Boxer Gallery, London

58 *Catalogue*

20
VERA TRUPPE
The Vera Troupe
1917
pen and ink, 33 × 21 cm
Private collection

Grosz was fascinated by the circus, variety, music hall and cabaret acts. He drew them often and made a series of studies of the Vera Troupe. On 18 November 1917 Grosz's patron Count Harry Kessler noted in his diary that 'he has a passion for artistes, for music hall. He says that the Americans and English invest all their artistic sense in the music hall. He himself wanted to become an artiste' (quoted after Kessler, exhib. cat., 1988, pp. 311–12). Indeed, Dada was about to give him the chance. Several of his performances at Dada soirées were grotesquely exaggerated cabaret numbers. In one he pretended to urinate against a painting by Lovis Corinth while intoning the words 'pee makes the best varnish'.

Catalogue 59

21

VARIETÉ TÄNZER
Variety Dancers
c. 1915
coloured crayon and ink, 22.5 × 17.1 cm
Richard L. Feigen & Co.

'The firm-hipped and corsetted artistes . . . exerted a secret sweet charm. Here one could admire through opera glasses the entire fleshly glory in contrast to the current fashion for covering everything up. The plump thighs and calves in silk tricots played a big role in my fantasies' (*Autobiography*, p. 27).

Stylistically, this drawing may owe something to Kokoschka's example, especially in its colour range and use of the crayon to emphasise the contours. Although Kokoschka lived in Berlin in 1910 he was back in Vienna before Grosz arrived in the German capital. However, his work was well known there and Grosz probably saw it at *Der Sturm* (The Storm) Gallery.

22
AKROBATEN
Acrobats
c. 1916
Coloured ink on paper, 22.8 × 29.2 cm
Richard L. Feigen and Co.

Grosz's humour was frequently savage, macabre and exploitative. Here he mixes the grotesque with the more straightforwardly humorous: the dog imitating the female acrobat, for example.

Catalogue

23

BEI SIMSEN
At Simsen's
1915
pencil, 22.5 × 29.1 cm
Hirshhorn Museum and Sculpture Garden, Smithsonian Institution. Gift of Joseph H. Hirshhorn Foundation, 1966

This is a traditional pub, frequented by the traditionally minded. The cheap cigar and sign on the table in the foreground say as much. The *Stammtisch* is the table reserved in such places for the landlord and his favoured regulars.

24

LIEGENDES AKT
Reclining Nude
1915
pen and ink, 27 × 32.5 cm
Private collection

62   Catalogue

25
STEHENDER AKT
Standing Nude
1915
ink and wash, 27 × 19 cm
Private collection, London

As a student in both Dresden and Berlin, Grosz was obliged to spend hours drawing from the live model. He knew the benefit of such regular exercise and continued to draw from life throughout his career. The many nude studies made in 1914 and 1915 (cf. cat. 24, 26, 27) differ markedly from those that precede them, however, and in their lack of idealisation and interest in expressive ugliness betray a change in attitude to people in general that was caused by the experience of war. In his diary for 18 November 1917, Grosz's patron Count Harry Kessler described such drawings as this as 'brutally truthful, a continuation of the North German, Berlin tradition of von Schadow, Menzel, Liebermann; completely non-French in their heedless ugliness; although Grosz himself says that he admires Ingres especially' (quoted after exhib. cat. Harry, Graf Kessler, *Tagebuch eines Weltmannes*, Deutsches Literaturarchiv im Schiller Nationalmuseum, Marbach am Neckar, 1988, p. 311).

The model here was almost certainly Fanny Klink, a prostitute who often posed for Grosz at this time. The nature of his interest in whores was once amusingly described by his friend Fritz Harig: 'An old whore who for 20 years had displayed her tattoos at fairgrounds regularly stood on the Grossbeeren Bridge... She often accosted me and I brought her to Grosz's attention. "How was it?", I asked him later. Grosz was wildly enthusiastic: "Fabulous things were there", he said, "I filled an entire sketchbook with drawings"' (Fischer, 1976, pp. 22–3).

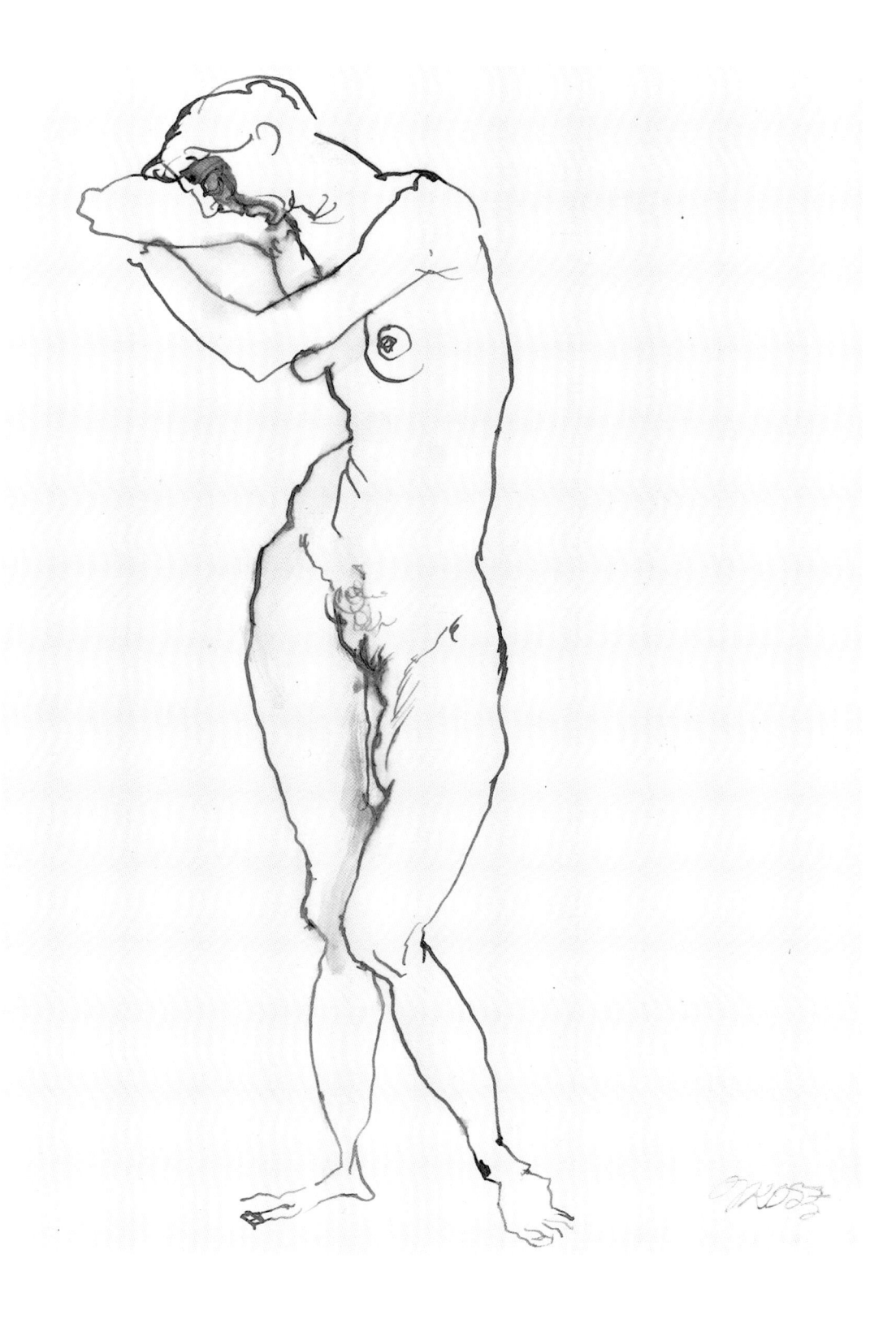

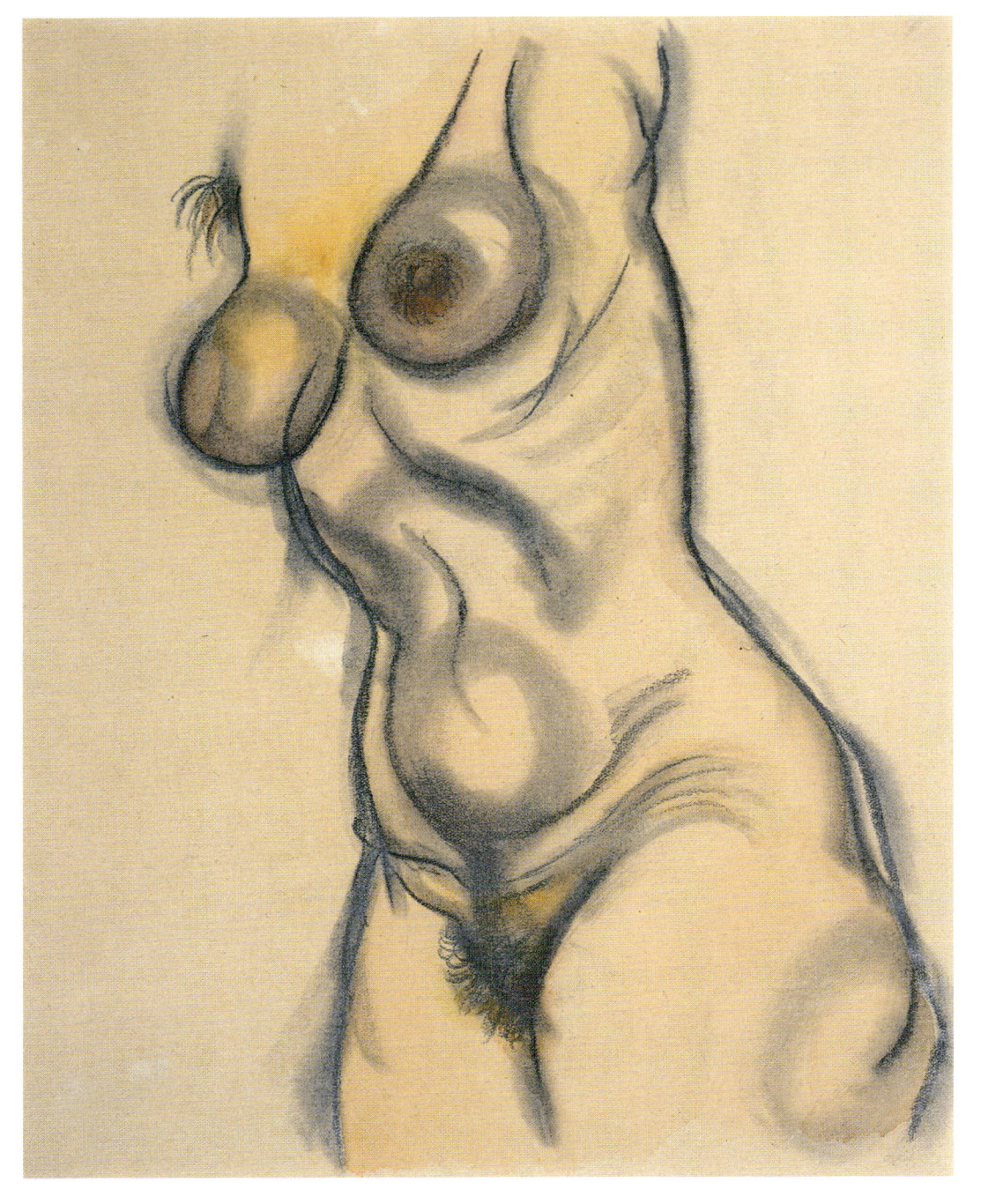

27
DER LIEBESTURM
The Tower of Love
*c.*1915
coloured crayon, pen and ink,
29.2 × 22.2 cm
Richard L. Feigen & Co.

The caption reads 'for Rachilde / The Tower of Love'. Rachilde was the pseudonym of the writer Marguerite Eymery who during the 1880s became known for her erotic horror stories. To judge from this unpublished illustration, 'The Tower of Love' must have been a highly sensational example of the genre and, as such, very much to Grosz's taste for the macabre and grotesque. His drawing shows a sailor or lighthouse-keeper who has rescued a woman from a shipwreck in a storm and now eagerly eyes her dead and bloated body. A related image (reproduced in cat. Sabarsky, no.17) shows the sailor ascending the spiral staircase of the lighthouse with an oil lamp in one hand and the woman's severed head in the other.

The sharp, angular style and impetuous use of crayon both to colour in the forms and emphasise their contours are characteristics of several works of this period (cf. cat. 20, 21).

26
HALBAKT
Nude Torso
1916
watercolour and wax crayon,
32.3 × 26.6 cm
Private collection

This extraordinarily vigorous life drawing testifies to Grosz's refusal to idealise or prettify the naked female form. He sought out models whose bodies were old or ill-used (see cat. 25), emphasising in his studies of them the folds of the flesh and the skeleton beneath the skin. Grosz's debt to Expressionism is also evident here. The bold, spontaneous marks and livid colours are especially reminiscent of both Kokoschka's and Schiele's earlier treatment of young, emaciated girls, which however were probably unfamiliar to Grosz at this time.

Catalogue 65

28

QUERGEBÄUDE VIER TREPPEN
Tenement, Four Flights Up
1916
offset lithograph, 28.5 × 36.5 cm
Private collection

With a title couched in the language of estate agents, this image depicts in deadpan fashion a place in which even suicide seems unexceptional. A man has hanged himself in the wardrobe at the rear while a couple makes love in full view of two card-players and an opium addict lying on a couch. None of them is remotely interested in his mean and depressing surroundings.

In its pronounced linearity and obvious reliance on the radical simplifications of graffiti, this print (which Grosz included in *Ecce Homo*) is related to such drawings as *Lustmord in der Ackerstrasse* (cat. 30) and *Krawall der Irren* (cat. 16).

29

Two Men in a Room
1915–16
Lithograph, 32 × 24 cm
Collection of Roy and Jenny Wright, London

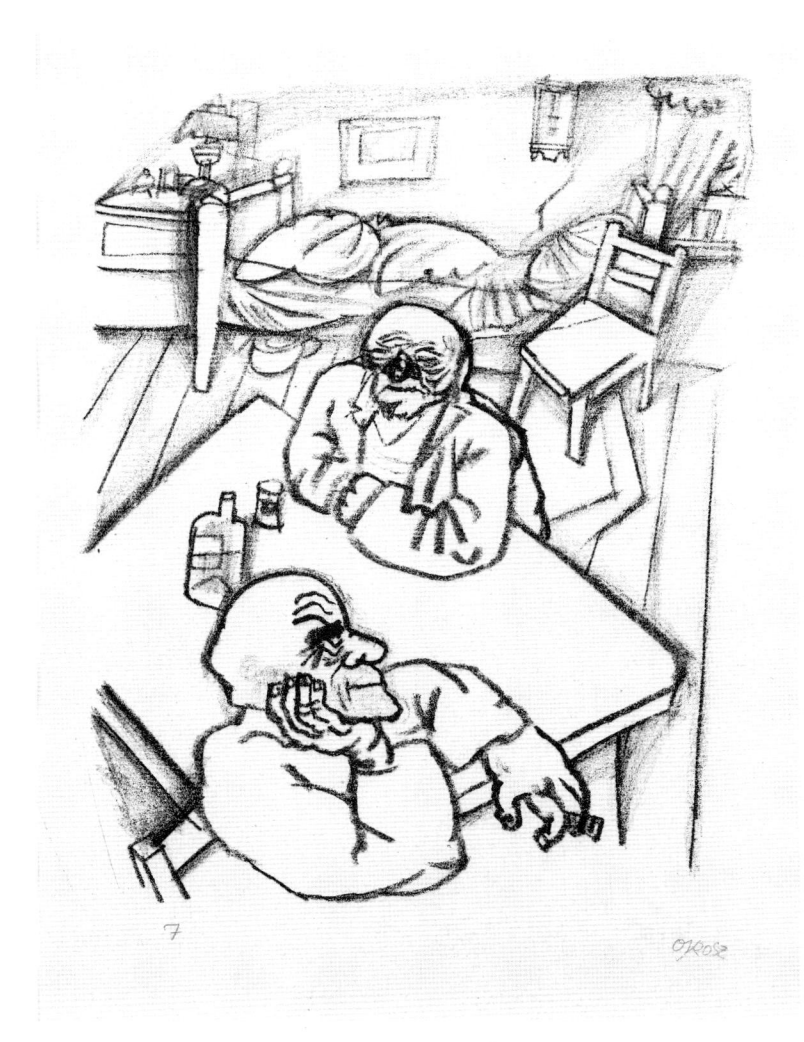

66   Catalogue

30

LUSTMORD IN DER ACKERSTRASSE
Sex Murder in Acker Street
1916–17
pen and indian ink, 35.6 × 28.3 cm
Leopold Museum, Privatstiftung, Vienna

In a seedy room an unspeakable event has taken place and the murderer, guiltily viewing his beheaded victim, washes her blood from his hands. The bundle of twigs on the chair hints at sexual perversion, but most of the details establish an unexceptional, even mundane setting. The jacket and cane hung over the screen, the gramophone and lucky horseshoe, are contrasted with the axe and corpse so as to emphasise the horrific nature of the act. A bourgeois idyll has been destroyed by blind sexual compulsion.

The title echoes the style of sensational newspaper headlines while a caption, written in English, reads 'Jack the Killer – drawing by Dr. William King Thomas'. Jack must refer to Jack the Ripper whose gruesome activities in Whitechapel had fascinated Grosz since his boyhood. Dr Thomas was one of several pseudonyms the artist used on numerous occasions. Most were invented, but Thomas, or rather Thomas William King, actually existed. He was a ship-owner who gained notoriety in the 19th century by blowing up one of his own vessels in the harbour of Bremerhaven, killing hundreds of people in the process, in an attempt to defraud an insurance company.

At this time Grosz executed many drawings and paintings of criminal acts, suicides and murders, most of them sexually motivated. As he wrote in his autobiography, 'The catastrophe had begun . . . I drew drunken, vomiting men who cursed the moon with clenched fists, murderers of women who sit playing cards on a packing case in which the corpse can be seen, and a man who, with fear in his eyes, washes his bloody hands. . . I drew solitary men who flee along empty streets like lunatics' (p. 102).

Catalogue 67

31
GOLDGRÄBER
Gold Diggers
1917
pen and ink, 18.5 × 23 cm
Private collection

Grosz's early, starry-eyed vision of America was largely inspired by pulp fiction and the novels of James Fenimore Cooper and Karl May. May was a German who set numerous adventure stories in a variety of exotic locations, especially the American Wild West, none of which he actually visited. Every German schoolboy avidly read May's accounts of the Indian scout Old Shatterhand and his friend the Indian brave Winnetou (they still do). These stories, together with penny dreadfuls about gangsters and detectives in New York and Chicago, largely shaped Grosz's conception of the United States. Many of his early drawings of cowboys, Indians and gold prospectors look like illustrations for unwritten popular novels, while several of the poems he composed at about the same time deal with similar subjects in a similarly effusive vein. One of them, entitled *Song of the Gold Diggers*, includes the lines: 'Gold! Gold! Gold!!! / Gold Diggers move / to the front! / The Klondyke beckons again!!! The knives and spades hold firm –. / The engineers are already arriving, / Black magician in an American suit. / America!!! Future!!!'

32
TEXASBILD FÜR MEINEN FREUND CHINGACHGOOK
Texas Picture for My Friend Chingachgook
1915–16
transfer lithograph, 26.9 × 21.2 cm
Busch-Reisinger Museum,
Harvard University Art Museums
Museum Purchase

This, the second of the nine prints in the *Erste George Grosz-Mappe*, is also one of two which reflect the artist's fascination for America. (The other is *Erinnerung an New York.*, Memory of New York) The Mohican Chingachgook is a central character in James Fenimore Cooper's series of 'Leather-Stocking' stories which Grosz read as a boy.

Grosz seemingly thought seriously about moving to America at this time. His friend the French artist Jules Pascin was already there, and so was his half-sister Cläre. As he wrote to Robert Bell in 1916, 'It's not necessarily romantic if the thoughts I had as a boy about emigrating to the fabulously wealthy and victorious land now increasingly take hold of my imagination' (Knust, 1979, p. 34).

In a letter to Otto Schmalhausen Grosz referred to 'the longing in my blood for sun, for brown Peruvian towns and the romance of cowboys, but in contrast the love of the most fantastic [of all] civilisations, of the elastic elevator, of the gigantic manifestations of the new, great American world. . .' (22 April 1918, Knust, 1979, p. 60).

Catalogue 69

33
MÄDCHEN UND IHRE LIEBHABER
Girl and Her Lovers
1915–16
lithograph, 24.5 × 15.2 cm
Collection of Roy and Jenny Wright

First published in the *Kleine Grosz Mappe* (1917), this amusing image about blossoming romance in the big city also appeared in a remarkably early American collection of Grosz's graphics (*George Grosz, Twelve Reproductions from his Original Lithographs*, Chicago, 1921) under the more colourful English title 'Anything Doin'?'

34
TRAUM FANTASIA
Dream Fantasy
c. 1916
coloured crayon and ink, 22.2 × 29.2 cm
Richard L. Feigen & Co.

The consciously naive style of this eccentric drawing emphasises the animalistic nature of its subject. The female figure dressed in erotic underwear advertises herself as a sexual object; the genitalia of the men are clearly visible beneath their clothes; the dogs are obviously on heat. But, as though in a dream, the connection between the details is tenuous.

35
TUMULT
Tumult
1916
ink and brush, 44 × 34 cm
Sammlung Karsch/Nierendorf, Berlin

Drawn during World War I, this bold, fragmented image of a city in uproar reflects something of Grosz's feelings about the conflict and its effect on general behaviour. In the light of the street battles which took place in Berlin immediately after the War, it also seems remarkably prophetic.

36
DIE GESUNDBETER
The Faith-Healers or *Fit for Active Service*
1916–17
pen, brush and indian ink, 50.8 × 36.5 cm
The Museum of Modern Art, New York
A. Conger Goodyear Fund

One of Grosz's most savage attacks on the German military mind, this justly famous drawing was often reproduced between the Wars: in the second issue of *Die Pleite* (April 1919), in *Gott mit Uns* (1920), in *Das Gesicht der herrschenden Klasse* (1921), and in *Die Gezeichneten* (1930). In each publication it appeared with a different title.

In the presence of a group of bored or distracted officers, an army doctor uses an ear trumpet to examine a corpse in an advanced state of decay. He pronounces the corpse *Kriegsverwendungsfähig*, here abbreviated to the letters *KV*, literally meaning 'capable of war use', in other words, 'fit for active service'. The drawing is also intended to suggest another word, often heard in the German army: *Kadavergehorsam* – the obedience of a corpse.

'The Faith-Healers' dates from the moment when the tide of World War I had turned. German generals, their forces seriously depleted, were obliged to recall to active service men previously discharged because of illness or injury. They resorted, as the macabre phrase had it, to 'digging up the dead'. Grosz was one of the men recalled – on 4 January 1917 – only to be released again on medical grounds four months later.

Bertolt Brecht's poem *Die Legende des toten Soldaten* (The Legend of the Dead Soldier) concerns a corpse that was disinterred before being pronounced fit, and was probably directly inspired by this unforgettable drawing.

Catalogue 73

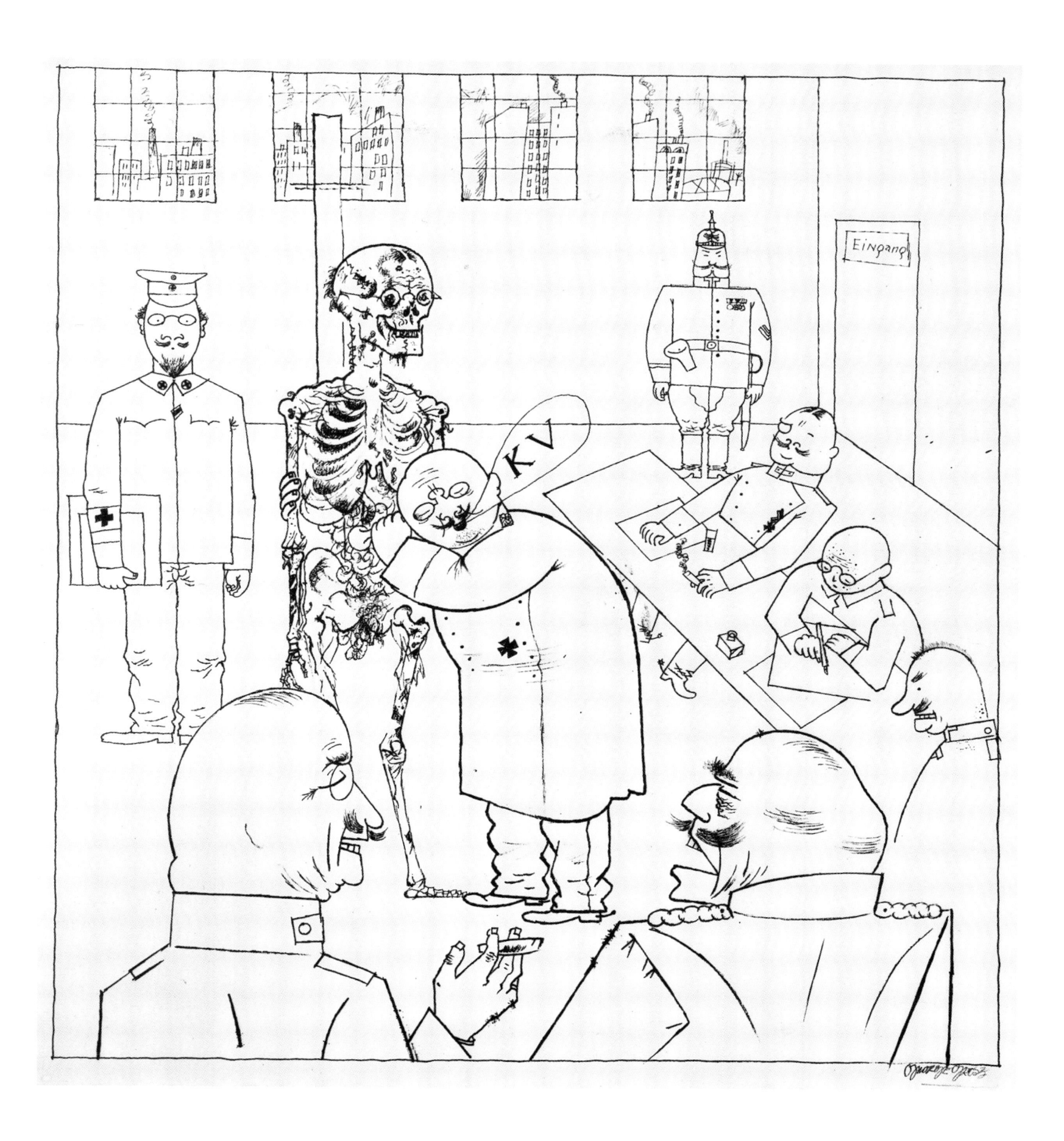

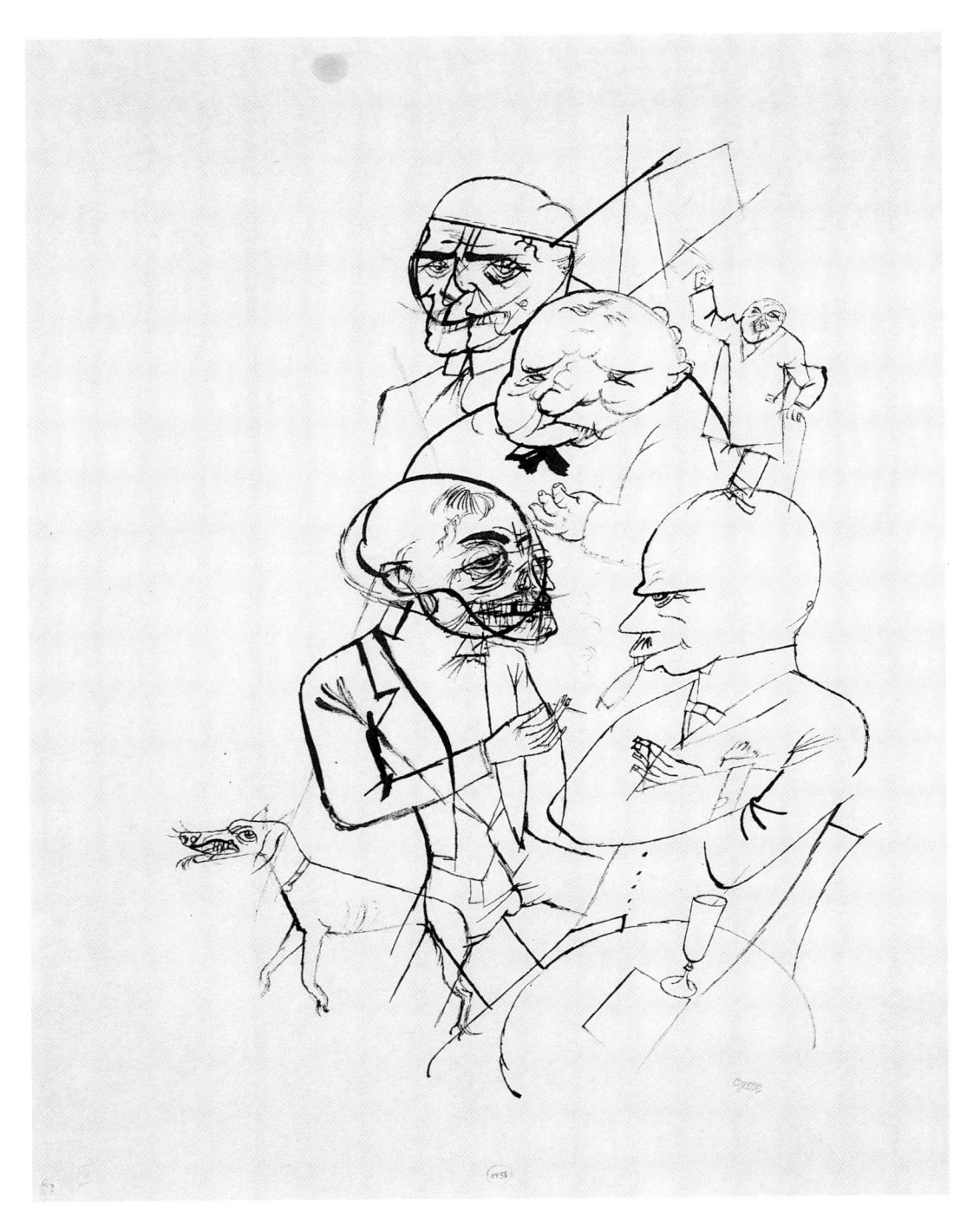

37

GEGENSÄTZE
Contrasts
*c.*1917
brush and ink, 59 × 46.1 cm
Graphische Sammlung der Staatsgalerie Stuttgart

In 1917 Grosz made several drawings in which some of the heads are semi-transparent so as to reveal the skull beneath the skin. The significance of these heads, two of which appear here, is unclear. They seem to point not merely to the transience of all life but to the characters of the individuals portrayed.

38
BETRACHTUNG
Scrutiny
1917
pen and ink, 42.3 × 38 cm
Private collection

The dynamically counterposed rectangles on which this relatively simple composition is based testify to Grosz's debt to Futurism. So do the overlapping, transparent planes. The wide-eyed, leering collector is using a magnifying glass to scrutinise a picture of a female nude.

'I'm looking forward to the porno photos – I . . . foster and cherish my small and discriminating collection . . . just as every good citizen does his goldfish in a bowl or his window boxes. . . I hereby appoint you my commissioner and representative for this genre. . . I request you . . . to collect and buy up all pornographic postcards, photos . . . drawings, inscriptions on pissoir walls . . .' (letter to Otto Schmalhausen, 22 April 1918, Knust, 1979, p. 76).

Although this drawing is clearly not a self-portrait, Grosz was as enthusiastic a collector of pornography as this letter to his future brother-in-law suggests. He also produced sexually explicit images at every stage of his career.

Catalogue 75

39
MONDNACHT
Moonlit Night
1915–16
transfer lithograph, 43.5 × 54.5 cm
Private collection

Published in the *Erste George Grosz-Mappe* (First George Grosz Portfolio), this is a wonderfully atmospheric image of sinister events taking place in a nocturnal city street. The contrast between the romantic title and the scene described is also exploited in a poem of the same title which Grosz published in the September 1916 issue of *Die Neue Jugend* (The New Youth): 'You silvery, kitschy moonlit night, / I am aroused by alcohol, / And the shoe of the eternal Jew incessantly squeaks before me. / The moon roundly decomposes into milky white. / Damn it!'

Although all the images in the portfolio were reproduced lithographically, the appearance of this one, the ninth, is strikingly different from the others. At first sight its texture and tonal range make it look as though it was drawn directly on the stone, but, as Dückers points out, closer inspection reveals it was reproduced from an original made in chalk on paper (Kaiser-Wilhelm Museum, Krefeld).

40
DOPPELBILD
Double Image
1916
pencil drawing, 26 × 16.5 cm
Soufer Gallery, New York

Grosz frequently employed the repetition of angular forms, a pictorial convention derived from Italian Futurism, so as to suggest movement. Here it is also used to comic effect since it evokes the confused mind and uncontrollable body of a man tottering home after a hard night's drinking. The dog, seemingly on heat, puts in frequent appearances in Grosz's work.

41

IM LOKAL
In the Pub
1917
ink drawing, 33 × 21 cm
Soufer Gallery, New York

Clearly a low dive, this is the haunt of rogues and criminals and may well have been based on one of many pubs Grosz regularly visited.

The inscription, made many years later, is to Bernard Reis and his wife. Reis was one of Grosz's post-War patrons in the United States.

42

NACHTKAFFEEHAUS
Café at Night
c.1917
pen and ink, 35.8 × 21 cm
Graphische Sammlung der Staatsgalerie Stuttgart

Like their Viennese equivalents, Berlin cafés played a unique social role and Grosz spent much of his time in them. He also drew and painted them often, presenting them not only as pleasant and lively places where customers played cards, had animated conversations and made assignations with women but also as microcosms of urban society in which every imaginable type of person could be observed (cf. cat. 53, 65, 90, 140). Frequently they provide a backdrop for private dramas in which the lonely and troubled drink themselves into oblivion or contemplate suicide.

Catalogue 79

43

STRASSENSZENE MIT ZEICHNER
Street Scene with Draftsman
c.1917
pen and ink, 33.4 × 21.5 cm
Graphische Sammlung der Staatsgalerie Stuttgart

> In order to achieve a style . . . that captured the extreme, plain hardness and charmlessness of my subjects, I studied the extreme products of the compulsion to make art. In pissoirs I copied folkloristic drawings which seemed to me to be the most direct expressions and shortest translations of powerful feelings. I was stimulated, too, by children's drawings because of their lack of ambiguity. I thus gradually arrived at this razor-sharp drawing style which I used to depict what I saw, dictated as it then was by an absolute hatred of humanity.
> (*Abwicklung*, pp. 83–4)

44

NIEDERKUNFT
Childbirth
1917
pen, ink and watercolour, 50.8 × 35.3 cm
Graphische Sammlung der Staatsgalerie Stuttgart

Dedicated and presented to Theodor Däubler, the art critic who wrote the first essay about Grosz's work, this watercolour was reproduced in *Ecce Homo* (1923) and was one of the five images in that collection that offended the authorities. They demanded the removal and destruction of the five offending prints, and took Grosz and his publisher to court for peddling pornographic pictures. The objections were understandable. The details here range from the repulsive to the sexually explicit, and the tawdry colours complement the licentious and depraved imagery. The scene is entirely in keeping with Grosz's savage view of humanity, expressed in most of his drawings and writings at the time. 'I tried to convince the world by means of my work that this world is ugly, sick and mendacious' (*Abwicklung*, p. 36).

Catalogue 81

45

SELBSTBILDNIS
Self-Portrait
1916
pencil, 48.5 × 41 cm
Private collection

Grosz smoked a pipe partly because it contributed to the American image he wished to cultivate – most Germans of his age preferred cigars. The lengths to which he was prepared to go in order to acquire good pipes and tobacco are revealed in his lengthy correspondence with the journalist Mark Neven DuMont, who moved to England in 1925. Much of it is devoted to pleas for supplies from a country where pipe smoking was regarded as manly and sophisticated. But the pipe here also adds to the impression of maturity which Grosz obviously wanted to give: he looks considerably older than twenty-three, his age in 1916.

46

SELBSTBILDNIS
Self-Portrait
1917
pen and ink, 32 × 21 cm
Sammlung Karsch/Nierendorf, Berlin

On 4 January 1917 Grosz was recalled to the army. A day later he was hospitalised and returned home on sick leave in April. The precise nature of his illness remains unclear. He claimed in his autobiography that he had tried to desert, had hit an officer, and was saved from execution by the intervention of his patron Count Harry Kessler who persuaded the authorities to send him to a military lunatic asylum instead. Letters written at the time to his future brother-in-law Otto Schmalhausen reveal his deep emotional turmoil. In one he refers to his 'disgust, loathing, total . . . breakdown. . .' (15 March 1917, Knust, p. 48). This self-portrait, obviously made after his demobilisation, hints at the mental problems he was experiencing.

Selbstporträt 1917

47

DADA-ZEICHNUNG 'MANN MIT MESSER, FLASCHE UND MOND'
Dada drawing 'Man with Knife, Bottle and Moon'
1918
brush and ink, 48 × 31.5 cm
Richard A. Cohn, Ltd, New York

48

DER BESESSENE FORSTADJUNKT
The Possessed Forestry Assistant
1918
lithograph, 50 × 65 cm
Private collection

The intended meaning of this intriguing print – reproduced in *Ecce Homo* – is unclear, and the details compound rather than explain the mystery. There seems to be no connection between the love-struck forester's assistant, the man with a collecting box around his neck and the face, clearly that of an individual, and not, like the others, a generalised type, at the bottom right. At least the reason for the obsession is explicit; but the naked woman is not depicted whole, simply in a way which emphasises her behind. Not only Grosz's drawings testify to his predilection for the female buttocks: he also photographed his wife naked from the rear on numerous occasions.

84   *Catalogue*

49
VORSTADT
Suburb
1918
pen and ink, 25.7 × 20 cm
Sammlung Karsch/Nierendorf, Berlin

A splendid example of Grosz's faux-naïf style derived from his close study of graffiti. It includes several details familiar from numerous other drawings: the balloon in the sky, gasometer, gallows, figure observing the scene from an upper window, and woman in transparent clothes walking her dog. His features may be rudimentary, but the man in the bowler hat is obviously Grosz himself.

50
AUFRUHR
Uproar
1918
ink and brush, 47 × 30.8 cm
Sammlung Karsch/Nierendorf, Berlin

A vision of tumult and destruction created during and reflecting the events of the final year of World War I. In the background a building has been set ablaze and a cross erected beside a tree, while in the centre a man is raping a terrified woman. The marks, seemingly made in a frenzy, the fragmented composition and unconnected faces and figures powerfully evoke rapidly occurring events and an atmosphere of mindless violence.

51
Whisky
1918
pen and ink and watercolour,
58.4 × 33.6 cm
Wilhelm-Hack-Museum, Ludwigshafen

Composed of interlocking geometric planes, pulsating with jarring colour suggestive of nocturnal shadows penetrated by bright moonlight and the beams of electric lamps, this dramatic watercolour combines imagery derived from the music hall and circus and hints of the violent and sinister. A man plainly up to no good tugs at a shirt cuff while glancing back at a headless corpse lying prone. In the foreground a female conjurer or juggler stands beside a table covered with what appear to be magic tricks.

The signature ('Grosz Sept. 1918 Südende') is in old German script. So too is the dedication: *Herrn Kunstkritiker Däubler zur Erbauung und Anregung* (To the art critic Däubler, for his edification and stimulation). Däubler was the first to publish an article about Grosz's work.

This watercolour was reproduced in full colour in *Ecce Homo*.

Catalogue 87

52

BERLIN – FRIEDRICHSTRASSE
1918
pen, brush and indian ink, 48.9 × 32.4 cm
Stiftung Archiv der Akademie der Künste,
Berlin, Kunstsammlung

Grosz thought this drawing significant enough to publish as a single print and later as the first image in his most important portfolio, *Ecce Homo* (1923).

Within the restless composition whose dynamic, counterposed lines are related to Futurism, Grosz's already established repertory of representative types pack the street beneath the railway arch, or are glimpsed through apartment windows. Familiar from many other works of this period, they include a beggar, a blinded war veteran selling matches, a student with duelling scars, a bowler-hatted black marketeer, whores, an officer and a common soldier.

In contrast to Unter den Linden, known to Berliners as the *Laufstrasse* ('promenading street'), and the Leipziger or *Kaufstrasse* ('shopping street'), the Friedrichstrasse was, thanks to its innumerable pubs and bars, the *Saufstrasse* or 'boozing street'. With its large railway station it was not just one of the busiest and most central areas of Berlin: it was also one of the most dissolute and dangerous, infested with criminals, spivs and prostitutes. Here, in the final year of the War, Grosz reveals in cross-section a collapsing social order against a chaotic background in which even the buildings are unstable. Death lurks close to the centre of the spectacle.

53

MENSCHEN IM CAFÉ
People in a Café
1917
pen, brush and ink, 65.2 × 85.5 cm
Trustees of the British Museum, London

One of the finest and most vivid drawings Grosz ever produced, this dynamic composition combines an interior and exterior view. It also includes many elements used in other drawings and paintings of the same period – the corner building, hearse and hot air balloon, for example, as well as the man with a naked female corpse, shown here on the left. The face at the bottom left together with the profile to its right are self-portraits. Grosz often included himself in such scenes of chaos and turbulence, as though condemning what he observes. The composition, energised by rhythmically arranged curves and angles, owes much to Futurism. So, too, do the repeated superimpositions of transparent objects and figures.

54

FAHRENDES VOLK
Tavelling People
c. 1918
pen, brush and ink, 50 × 29.2 cm
Henry Boxer Gallery, London

In 1929 Grosz wrote about his childhood for the art journal *Das Kunstblatt*. Some of his article's most vivid passages concern visits from circuses to the small town where he lived. Once even Barnum and Bailey, the world's biggest circus, put in an appearance, and Grosz watched astonished as the 'freaks', who included General Tom Thumb, drove through the town in coaches. 'What I would not have given to travel the world with tightrope walkers and jugglers and to live in a white caravan ornamented in gold. Naturally not as the person I was but as a world-famous barrel jumper or a much admired trapeze artiste' (quoted after *Eintrittsbillett*, pp.17–18).

This drawing, with its overlaid images of elephants, palm trees, a big wheel, the Eiffel Tower (from which a suicide seems to be leaping), and in the foreground, a drummer advertising the show, reflects not only Grosz's abiding enthusiasm for spectacular popular entertainment of every kind, but also the exotic thrills that the circus and fun fair promised.

55

OLYMPIAKINO, BERLIN
Olympia Cinema, Berlin
1917
pen and ink, 29 × 22.3 cm
Private collection

There was an Olympia Cinema in Berlin, and since Grosz was an enthusiastic moviegoer we can assume that he went there. Here, however, the cinema itself has been relegated to the background, and the major interest is provided by vivid depictions of people and buildings. These are similar to those that appear in many of the drawings and paintings Grosz made both at this time and later. Some of the details – the horse-drawn carriage, the tram, the dog – also come from the standard Grosz repertory. So do the central characters, the superannuated whores

Catalogue 91

56

BELEBTE STRASSENSZENE
Lively Street Scene
c.1918
pen and ink, 55.8 × 38 cm
Sammlung Karsch/Nierendorf, Berlin

Several of the figures here are identifiable as friends of the artist. At the top left, observing the scene through the transparent wall of the house, is the hunchbacked poet Max Herrmann-Neisse of whom Grosz later made two oil portraits (see fig. 13). The bearded man on the left of the group of three figures immediately beneath Herrmann-Neisse is the writer and critic Theodor Däubler. One of Grosz's earliest supporters, he published the first essay about his work. In Däubler's pocket is a copy of his best-known novel *Nordlicht* (Northern Light). Shown in profile on the right of the same group is Else Lasker-Schüler, bohemian poet, habituée of the Café des Westens, wife of the dealer and impresario Herwarth Walden, and author of a poem about Grosz. At the bottom left in profile is Grosz's brother-in-law Otto Schmalhausen whom he nicknamed Oz. Married to Eva Grosz's sister, Charlotte, he was an artist and graphic designer who suffered from hypochondria, a condition satirised by Grosz in several hilarious drawings. Beside Oz, dressed as a hiker, stands Robert Bell, Grosz's friend and failed artist who, in spite of his name, was German.

fastening on to a soldier the worse for drink.

The high viewpoint and strong diagonals of the composition, together with the lack of a single vertical or horizontal anywhere, suggest turbulence and, perhaps, imminent collapse, which are more clearly depicted in other drawings of the same period. The nervous, fragile line and perfunctory squiggles representing smoke in the background testify to Grosz's abiding interest in graffiti.

57
GROSSSTADTSTRASSE MIT KUTSCHE
Big City Street with Coach
*c.*1918
brush and ink, 46 × 59 cm
Graphische Sammlung der Staatsgalerie Stuttgart

Behind the coach and crowd jostling on the street is an urban panorama of smoking factory chimneys, a gas works, seedy hotels and posters. The hotel in the centre is the Pension Thanatos, the Greek word for death, clearly a meaningful invention. The light bulb and letters AEG on the poster advertise the German General Electricity Company. In profile at the bottom left is a smiling caricature of the artist himself.

58
SCHÖNHEITSABEND IN DER
MOTZSTRASSE
Beauty Contest in Motz Street
1918
lithograph, 37.2 × 49.1 cm
Collection of Roy and Jenny Wright, London

Running between the western districts of Wilmersdorf and Schöneberg in Berlin, the Motzstrasse was a desirable place to live. According to Grosz, however, the splendid façades of its houses masked a venal reality. Indeed, at just this time, the street became associated with a number of sexual scandals which were reported in the press. The most notorious concerned a lieutenant of the army reserve and his wife who staged a series of sexually explicit performances (advertised as 'Beauty Contests') in a flat in the Motzstrasse. On the evening of a police raid a newspaper reported that the paying audience included 'a priest, a doctor, several businessmen, a few fitters and turners as well as four married women of good middle class background. . .' (quoted after Hans Ostwald, *Sittengeschichte der Inflation*, Berlin, 1931, p. 131).

59
SELBSTPORTRÄT (FÜR CHARLIE CHAPLIN)
Self-Portrait (for Charlie Chaplin)
1919, transfer or photo lithograph, 49.5 × 33.5 cm
Öffentliche Kunstsammlung Basel, Kupferstichkabinett

Charlie Chaplin's films appealed by no means just to the mass movie-going public. They were also widely admired by artists and intellectuals, especially in Europe. In Berlin, Chaplin's 'little man' became a hero to the Dadaists who identified with his unequal but always victorious struggle against authority and the chaos he caused. Their admiration multiplied when Chaplin's films were banned by the authorities during and immediately after World War I.

Grosz loved the cinema. In 1922, asked by the art journal *Kunstblatt* for an opinion about the 'new naturalism' which then seemed to be in the air, he replied that 'Film is the most modern pictorial form of all, possessing as it does every dynamic, simultaneous and futuristic possibility. Is it surprising that Chaplin and Fatty [Arbuckle] seem more alive than the best art exhibition?' (*Abwicklung*, p.79)

This dynamically composed image, in which figures, details and collaged texts are juxtaposed and overlaid in the Futurist manner, locates the dandified, self-assured and intensely masculine artist at the centre of a chaotic urban scene, holding himself like a boxer and wielding his pen as though it were a scalpel. Grosz loved to attend boxing matches; he counted several champions among his friends; and did some boxing himself. For a time he trained with a punchbag in his studio.

The whereabouts of the original drawing are unknown.

60
CAFÉ
Café
1918
ink drawing, 40 × 29 cm
Soufer Gallery, New York

61
AN EVA, MEINE FREUNDIN
To Eva, My Girlfriend
1918
lithograph, 65.5 × 50 cm
Private collection

Grosz met his future wife Eva Peter when both were students of Emil Orlik at the School of Arts and Crafts in Berlin. Said to have been a talented painter, she also worked as a fashion designer, and, between 1917 and her marriage in 1920, ran a shop on the Kurfürstendamm selling clothes and crafts. At the First International Dada Fair she exhibited 'the world's first Dadaist cushion': appropriately, there were two of them.

Eva's relationship with Grosz (who called her 'Maud' or 'Daum' as fancy took him) was never easy. She disliked several of his closest friends (especially Wieland Herzfelde), was repeatedly worried by his bouts of heavy drinking, and during their years together in the United States, never quite managed to settle. She also found Grosz's keen sexual appetite a mixed blessing, as this confession to her future brother-in-law Otto Schmalhausen reveals. 'George loves me *purely sensually* – only my thighs, mouth or suchlike; because of that I feel degraded, demeaned... Whenever I give myself to him ... he is the most tender, lovable man; otherwise he is terribly cruel, finds fault, insults me, although often unintentionally... I remember things said in Herzfelde's presence which tormented me so much that I rushed out crying... Our love knows only extreme highs or lows; the harmony I dream about occurs only on the rarest occasions. And yet in spite of, or precisely because of this I love him and am justifiably proud of having been his girlfriend for two years' (letter dated Whitsunday 1918, quoted after Bergius, p. 181).

According to the writer Walter Mehring, a friend of both Eva and Grosz, she was 'the ideal model for his ceaselessly raging artistic, alcoholic and erotic excesses. Whenever he wanted to include the female figure in all its voluptuous perfection – in his nude studies ... his sadistic anti-militarist caricatures ... his garishly coloured, obscene watercolours of petit-bourgeois orgies – everywhere ... Eva incarnate appeared before him. Almost no other artist has drawn and painted his beloved, his own wife with such monomania ... in every conceivable position...' (Mehring, 1983, p. 249).

In this lithograph she sits at the single still point of a turbulent composition in which her lover's sexual fantasies are described. Grosz, wearing a bowler hat, stands in profile beneath her.

Catalogue 97

62

AUS DEM ZYKLUS PARASITEN
From the Cycle Parasites
1919
lithograph, 69 × 53 cm
Private collection

The title raises expectations of a series of images dealing with individuals who live from the labours of others. Perhaps Grosz planned such a series, but, if so, this is the only print or drawing known. The man is obviously a pimp, nonchalantly standing aside while his whores perform for the benefit of some unseen spectators.

63

SCHÖNHEIT, DICH WILL ICH PREISEN!
Beauty, I wish to praise thee!
1919
pen, brush, ink and watercolour, 42 × 30.2 cm
Sammlung Karsch/Nierendorf, Berlin

A prostitute sits at a table in a low dive while three potential costumers undress her with their eyes. In the background a second prostitute signifies that she too is available for hire. The irony in the title is made clear by the ugly and rapacious appearance of the central figure. Even the combination of glowing, poisonous and clashing colours hints at lasciviousness and vice. Grosz's technique – clearly defined contours filled in with thin, pure and luminous washes – looks forward to the great watercolours of the following year in which the use of a ruler and collaged elements contribute to an almost anonymous effect (see cat. no. 83). This watercolour, one of the finest Grosz ever created, was reproduced in colour in the portfolio *Ecce Homo*.

Catalogue 99

64
DIE FEIER
Celebration
1919
ink on tracing paper, 28.5 × 22.7 cm
Soufer Gallery, New York

100   *Catalogue*

65
CAFÉ AM RHEIN
Café on the Rhine
1919?
Brush and ink, 46.7 × 59.5 cm
Graphische Sammlung der Staatsgalerie Stuttgard

The café may be situated on the banks of Germany's most romantic river – the fairytale castle on the hilltop in the background locates it – but its drunk, promiscuous and violent customers are indistinguishable from those in one of Berlin's lowest dives. At the bottom, wearing a bowler hat, is Grosz himself, somewhat apart, sober and watchful. The inscription at bottom right identifies the setting as [Bad] Godesberg, but it is not in Grosz's handwriting.

66
AUF DER PIRSCH
On the Hunt
1919–20
pen and ink, 32 × 24.3 cm
Sammlung Karsch/Nierendorf, Berlin

The kind of hunting alluded to in the German title is usually of game, thus reducing the activity depicted to its essentials. The woman pursued by the ardent gentleman tipping his Bavarian hat seems less interested in yielding to his overtures than the comely females in the background, who are obviously prostitutes.

67
ORGIE
Orgy
1919
pen, ink, pencil and watercolour, 36.8 × 28.4 cm
Galerie Pels-Leusden, Berlin

The male figure is clearly a self-portrait – even though the amputated right hand implies a war injury that Grosz himself never sustained. The bottle and glass on the table and size and position of the female figures suggest that Grosz is not present at a real orgy but seeing two depersonalised but voluptuous female bodies in a drunken vision.

    The watercolour washes, especially those covering angular geometric areas and details not enclosed by an ink-drawn contour, may have been influenced by the work of August Macke, the Rheinland painter who exhibited with the Blaue Reiter (Blue Rider) group in Munich before World War I. The old German script at the bottom left is a dedication which reads: *s. lieben Theo zum Andenken von George Grosz 1920* ('to his dear friend Theo, a souvenir from George Grosz 1920'). Theo was probably the writer and critic Theodor Däubler whose first essay about Grosz's work appeared in 1916.

Catalogue 103

68

KNÖDELESSEN
Eating Dumplings
c.1920
pen and ink, 44 × 38.5 cm
Kunstmuseum, Düsseldorf, Graphische Sammlung

The political affiliations of these two gluttons are made clear by the bust of the Kaiser on the wall beside the window behind them. Wilhelm II abdicated in 1918 and went into exile in Holland, but German nationalists continued to long for the restoration of the monarchy and the stability it supposedly represented.

69

DER ZUCHTHÄUSLER
The Convict
1919
lithograph, 68 × 53 cm
Private collection

The German title identifies the convict as someone sentenced to penal servitude, and he presents himself to the viewer together with the dissolute life of which he dreams and from which he is now excluded. Nevertheless, Grosz has portrayed him with sympathy. Like the crippled war veteran and the prostitute, the convict often appears in Grosz's work as the victim of a cruelly authoritarian society.

Catalogue 105

70
BALTIKUMER
1919
pen, brush and ink, 45.9 × 59.5 cm
Stiftung Archiv der Akademie der Künste, Berlin, Kunstsammlung

The German word *Baltikum* describes the former Russian provinces of Courland, Livonia and Estonia which border the Baltic Sea. The name *Baltikumer* was given to volunteers assembled from the German Eighth army who, in contravention of the armistice of 1918, captured Riga from occupying Bolshevik forces on 22 May 1919. In October 1919 the German government yielded to Allied demands for the irregulars' removal but some remained behind, joining the counter-revolutionary White Russian army under General Avalov-Bermondt. Grosz's drawing shows these militaristic types fighting among themselves.

71
DIE KOMMUNISTEN FALLEN UND DIE
DEVISEN STEIGEN
*The Communists Fall and the Foreign
Exchange Rises*
1919
pen, brush and ink, 38.2 × 55.9 cm
Stiftung Archiv der Akademie der Künste,
Berlin, Kunstsammlung

The title borrows a phrase from a pamphlet written by the leading Communist activist Rosa Luxemburg under the pseudonym 'Junius' and entitled *Die Krise der Sozialdemokratie* (The Crisis of Social Democracy). Pubished in Zurich in 1916, it argues that, since the workers from all the combatant nations were killing each other in World War I, the proletariat was, in effect, committing suicide. 'Dividends rise', she wrote, 'and the workers fall.' What Grosz shows, however, is a scene not from the war but from the German revolution. A businessman and an officer satisfy their appetites while workers are clubbed and bayoneted to death in the background.

Catalogue 107

72

ZUR ERINNERUNG AN ROSA LUXEMBURG
UND KARL LIEBKNECHT
In Memory of Rosa Luxemburg and Karl Liebknecht
c.1919
brush and indian ink, 59 × 40.5 cm
Leicestershire Museums, Arts and Records Service

Luxemburg and Liebknecht led the extreme Spartacist wing of the Independent Social Democratic Party which had opposed German participation in World War I and agitated for a republic. Named after Spartacus, the slave who led a revolution in ancient Rome, the Spartacists formed the core of the German Communist Party when it was founded on 31 December 1918. According to an unsubstantiated story, Grosz immediately became a member, receiving his party card from Rosa Luxemburg herself.

In the first week of January 1919 the Communists demanded the removal of the recently installed Social Democratic government and called a general strike. It was bloodily ended by volunteer militia. A price was put on the heads of Luxemburg and Liebknecht who were captured and brutally murdered on 15 January 1919. Their bodies were then dumped in the Landwehr Canal in Berlin. Grosz shows their shrouded corpses beneath the ghostly figure of a judge whose robe leaves a bloody trail behind it. Justice was as guilty of the murders as the military.

Catalogue 109

73

SIND WIR NICHT VÖLKERBUNDFÄHIG?
Are we not eligible for the League of Nations?
1919
pen and ink, 56 × 38.4 cm
Graphische Sammlung der Staatsgalerie Stuttgart

A comment on Germany's frustrated efforts to join the League of Nations, founded at the Paris Peace Conference in January 1919. (She was eventually admitted in 1926.) Grosz obviously considered Germany ineligible. The troops marching beneath the old imperial flag signify the continuing popularity of militarism while the other characters, stock types from Grosz's repertory, point to Germany's moral collapse: the inadequate professional figure with his comic shoes, hat, cigar and umbrella; the well-heeled couple out riding; the crippled soldier; the cross-eyed officer with a face scarred not in battle but in a student duel; and finally the profiteer vulgarly displaying his wealth in the form of a diamond tiepin, heavy gold watchchain and ten-mark cigar. The juxtaposition of such contrasts to make a point is a device familiar in Grosz's work. Interestingly, it was also somewhat later exploited by Grosz's friend John Heartfield in his photomontages. The small 'wanted' poster on the wall at the right probably refers to one (misspelled) Eugen Leviné, a German Communist who took part in the Munich revolution, which briefly resulted in the Bavarian Soviet Republic, and was executed by firing squad in June 1919. The sign around the neck of the veteran selling matches reads 'blind'. The signature – Böff (variant of Georges le Boeuf) – was one of Grosz's favourite pseudonyms. The drawing appeared in the portfolio *Das Gesicht der herrschenden Klasse* (The Face of the Ruling Class) under the title 'Post-war Idyll'.

"Sind wir nicht völkerbundfähig"

74

DREI MÄNNER
Three Men
1919
pen and ink, 17.5 × 15.2 cm
Private collection

A characteristic confrontation of three social types, already permanent members of Grosz's satirical repertory company. A more elaborate version of this drawing was reproduced as No. 35 in the collection of drawings *Das Gesicht der herrschenden Klasse*. There it has the title 'Oh Marburg, Oh Marburg, you wonderful city in which many murderers have such good friends!'. Marburg is the location of one of Germany's oldest universities, and the title plays on a familiar student drinking song. The figure in the cap with the prominent scar on his face is a patron, or *alter Herr*, of one of the student duelling fraternities. Those associations were, as the swastika on the man's tie emphasises, hotbeds of reaction and nationalism.

Grosz used the same faces again and again. Compare the right-hand figure here with that on the right of cat. 84, drawn about three years later.

112   Catalogue

75

ECCE HOMO
1919–20
pen and ink, 52.5 × 38.5 cm
Sammlung Karsch/Nierendorf, Berlin

Within a composition determined by a configuration of sharply angular lines Grosz has disposed two standing figures and four faces, all of them types representative of Berlin during the turbulent years following World War I. Both the pictorial structure and the partial transparency of the details were obviously derived from Futurism but Grosz's formal language is here used to suggest disintegration and decay. The explosion demolishing the house in the background was probably suggested by the revolutionary rioting and street fighting with which Berlin was plagued during the winter of 1918 and 1919. This drawing was reproduced in the portfolio *Im Schatten* (In the Shadows, 1921) under the title *Dämmerung* (Dusk). A closely related but later watercolour of the same title was reproduced in full colour in the portfolio *Ecce Homo*.

76

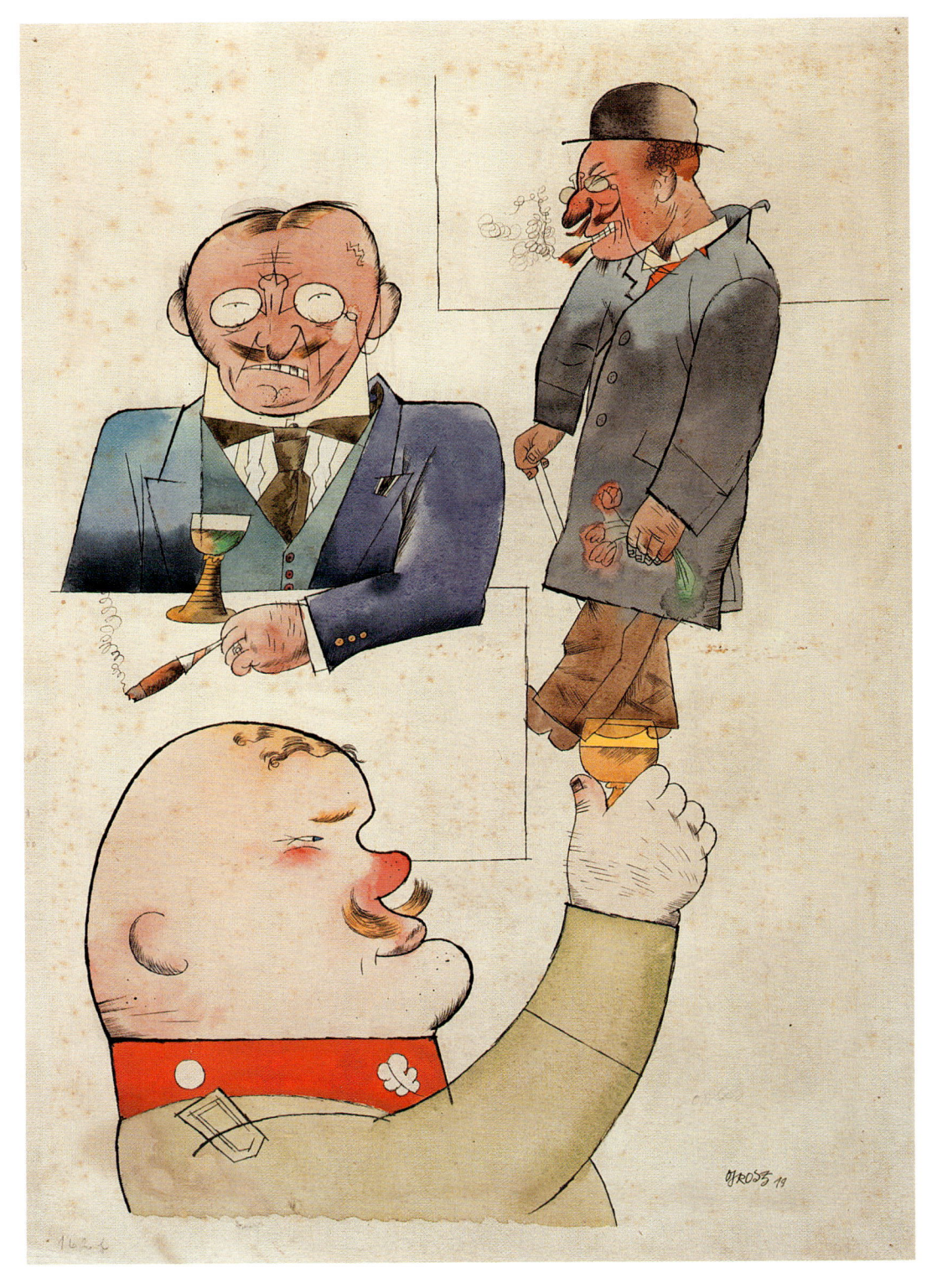

DEUTSCHES LIED UND DEUTSCHER WEIN
German Song and German Wine
1919

watercolour and indian ink, 43.7 × 30.4 cm
Collection E.W.K., Bern

These respresentative types, two somewhat motheaten, contrast with the romanticised title taken from a popular drinking song. The character in the centre wears the ribbon of the Iron Cross in his lapel while the walking man holding a bunch of flowers looks improbably as though on his way to an assignation with a female.

77

MEIN DEUTSCHLAND
My Germany
1919–20

proof sheet for *Dadaco*, 58 × 46 cm
Berlinische Galerie, Berlin,
Landesmuseum für Moderne Kunst,
Photographie und Architektur

Dadaco was an anthology which aimed to provide information 'about all present day Dadaists'. Disagreements between its editor, Richard Huelsenbeck, and publisher, Kurt Wolff, prevented its appearance at an advanced stage and all that remains is a number of printer's proofs of texts and illustrations. This is one of them. It consists of 'pulls' of three blocks made after two drawings and the beginnings of a collage by Grosz. The face at the top left is taken from the foreground figure in *Deutsches Lied und deutscher Wein* (1919, cat. 78).

Catalogue 115

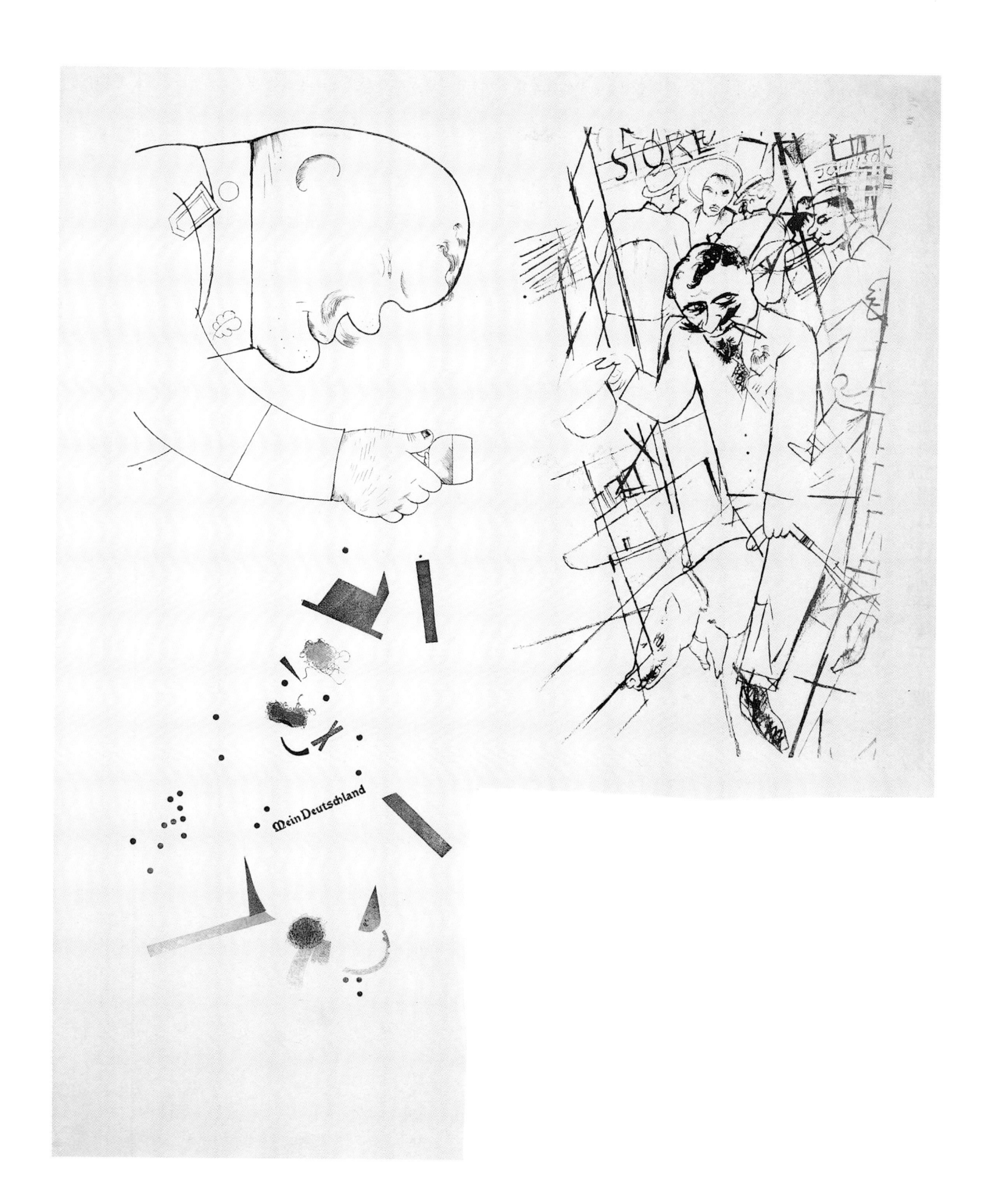

78

DR BILLIG
1920–21
pen, brush and ink, 30 × 22 cm
Collection of Roy and Jenny Wright, London

This was conceived as an illustration for Richard Huelsenbeck's novel *Dr Billig am Ende* (Dr Billig at the End) of 1921, but never published. Those drawings that were published depict scenes of drunkenness, sexual activity and violent death against the background of a big city. They are among the best book illustrations Grosz ever made, probably because the world Huelsenbeck describes is so similar to that which Grosz habitually depicted. Here, for example, is Friedrichstrasse at midnight:

> The war has turned all these harmless, middle-class people into beasts. They shriek like lunatics; squabbles and fights break out; they whistle and howl as though they were animals in a circus. Meanwhile the red and violet light shines out of the first floor windows of the cafés on to the aroused street – the cities are drunk on booze, and the clouds wander above the rooves like green devils. Billig feels all this, and he hears the threatening noise of the underground railway beneath his feet which seems to announce the coming of a storm; the yells and screams and rattles of the trains drive him onward; he is surrounded by the chatter of the horses' trotting legs. A hundred different faces are a hundred different types which embody and portray a hundred different life-stories.
> quoted after Huelsenbeck, p. 165

One of the founders of Dada in Zurich, Huelsenbeck returned to Berlin in 1917 bringing Dadaist ideas with him. He emigrated to New York not long after Grosz, who helped Huelsenbeck find his feet by lending him money, and spent his last years working as a psychiatrist.

79
BÜHNENBILDENTWURF ZU G.B. SHAW, 'CAESAR UND CLEOPATRA'
Stage set design for G.B. Shaw's 'Caesar and Cleopatra'
1920
watercolour, pen and ink, 42.5 × 48 cm
Private collection

In the course of his career Grosz designed the sets and costumes for twelve plays (cf. cat. 110), one of which was Shaw's comedy at the Deutsches Theater in 1920. What makes this lucid watercolour (for a backdrop) especially interesting is its relationship to the anonymous style Grosz was developing at the same time (cf. cat. 82, 83). In contrast to Grosz's humorous ideas for the costumes (Caesar wears a kilt, for example), his set designs were exceedingly sober, even reminiscent of technical drawings in their use of flat washes and precise ink outlines drawn with geometric instruments.

80

KU KLUX KLAN
1920
pen and ink, 65 × 52.5 cm
Private collection

Grosz's attitude to the USA was ambivalent. He anglicised his name during the First World War both to irritate German nationalists and to signal his admiration for a country which he knew only from popular literature and movies. He adored boxing, jazz and Charlie Chaplin, and, like his friend Bert Brecht, had a sneaking admiration for gangsters. However, thanks not least to the novels of Upton Sinclair, published by the Malik Press in Berlin, Grosz was also aware of the social injustice and racial hatred that were widespread in America.

This drawing was made as an illustration for Sinclair's *100%*, a novel about the workers' struggle against capitalism, strikes and their suppression. Ten of Grosz's illustrations accompanied the text and they included another, less detailed version of this drawing. An unfinished variant of the same composition is on the reverse. Malik published the complete works of Upton Sinclair, each of them with a dustjacket design based on a photomontage by John Heartfield. Sinclair, who believed that 'the history of the industrial world is written in blood', was the perfect author for the publishing house founded by Wieland Herzfelde.

81

BERLINER STRASSENSZENE
Berlin Street Scene
1920

pen and ink on paper, 52.7 × 35.6 cm
The Metropolitan Museum of Art,
New York,
Gift of Priscilla A. B. Henderson, in memory of her grandfather, Russell Sturgis, a founder of the Metropolitan Museum of Art, 1950

A mixture of contrasting social types, this impressive drawing is dominated by the monocled army officer in the foreground who wears the medal for outstanding bravery, the *Pour le Mérite*. Lurking in the centre between the respectable middle-aged men and young woman is a common criminal.

This drawing was reproduced in *Ecce Homo*.

82

BRILLANTENSCHIEBER IM CAFÉ KAISERHOF
Diamond Profiteers in the Café Kaiserhof
1920
pen, ink, watercolour and collage, 42 × 30cm
Sammlung Karsch/Nierendorf, Berlin

First exhibited together with several other similar works (cf. cat. 83) at the *First International Dada Fair* in 1920 (where it was given the subtitle 'Tatlinian Sketch Plan'), this deceptively simple image was also reproduced in a book, *Mit Pinsel und Schere* (With Brush and Scissors), published in 1922. The book consisted of illustrations of watercolours and collages made in an anonymous, mechanistic style. None was signed. All were rubber-stamped with the artist's name and address, and all represented an attempt to create a new, 'constructive' (or 'Tatlinian'), impersonal kind of art embodying revolutionary ideals. In an essay written in 1920, *Zu meinen neuen Bildern* (Concerning My New Pictures; see pp. 35–6), Grosz envisaged the 'future development of painting taking place in workshops, in pure craftsmanship, not in any holy temple of the arts. Painting is manual labour.' He also acknowledged the influence of Italian Metaphysical painting, especially that of Carlo Carrà. The whereabouts of most of the originals of these 'new pictures' are unknown; but reproductions show that the majority had little or no satirical dimension. They were visions of a utopian yet chillingly faceless world. A few were humorous or critical: this is one of them, attacking a type familiar in the Berlin of the 1920s: the hard-faced profiteer and spiv.

There are more collaged elements in this watercolour than are immediately obvious. The eyes, nose and trousers of the figure on the left and the hair and shoe of the balding man to his right are fragments of photographs. The eyes and moustache of the central figure were also cut from photographs. The newspaper clipping on the table is part of a report about the trial of a profiteer, while the banknote in the foreground is real. In the background is the old imperial German flag, replaced in 1919. This emblem, frequently employed by Grosz, proclaims that nothing had changed in the new German republic.

Catalogue 121

83
Daum marries her pedantic automaton 'George' in May 1920. John Heartfield is very glad of it
1920
pencil, pen, brush, ink, watercolour and collage, 42 × 30.2 cm
Berlinische Galerie, Berlin, Landesmuseum für Moderne Kunst, Photographie und Architektur

The original title is in English, and Wieland Herzfelde explained why in a commentary in the pamphlet cum catalogue for the *First International Dada Fair* where this watercolour was first exhibited: the foreign language was necessary 'because the subject concerns intimate matters to which not everyone should be privy.'

Herzfelde then embarked on a jokey description of the imagery as an attack on the bourgeois institution of marriage which is 'a concession to society. Resembling a machine, it unfailingly transforms the man into a constituent part of itself, into a small cog within a larger system of wheels and gears, so that marriage actually means a renunciation of the bride in favour of the world in general. At the same time eroticism and sexuality are renounced. It is different for the woman. For her, marriage turns everything upside down. If the symbol of the young girl is a naked figure who covers her private parts with her hand . . . in marriage, sexual desire is no longer denied but even emphasised . . . from the first moment of marriage . . . the woman is able to give vent to all her secret longings and set her body free while the man addresses other sober, pedantic and calculating tasks' (quoted after cat. Berlin 1994, p. 418).

Grosz did indeed get married in May 1920 – to Eva Peter who had been his girlfriend since 1916. (They were students together at the School of Arts and Crafts in Berlin.) He called her Maud, or Daum (Maud almost backwards). Her photograph appears in the top left-hand corner of this complex montage which is dominated by her partly clothed image in the centre. Several other collaged elements are included: other photographic details, fragments of typography and a piece of real lace attached to the border of Eva's drawers. Her eyes and hair and the hand touching her breast are also cut from photographs and the top of her boots appears to have come from a trade catalogue.

The robot, here representing Grosz, is an image central to Berlin Dadaism which proposed among other things that the artist should suppress every sign of subjectivity or individualism in his work and become like a machine. The background here is therefore rendered in a mechanistic, almost anonymous style which Grosz partly derived from Italian metaphysical painting (cf. cat. 82).

Daum marries. . . may have been conceived as an elaborate invitation to the wedding, 'an authentic George Grosz celebration, [that] took place in [Eva's] mother's house on Savignyplatz in whose lobby he would die 39 years later.' Those present included 'the Berlin Dadaists . . . and the three most prominent avant-garde doctors: Dr Heinrich Klapper, Dr Döhmann (author of *Wanton as a Beaver*, bacteriologist and orientalist), and the psychoanalyst Dr Richard Huelsenbeck (co-founder of the *mouvement dada*)' (Mehring, 1983, pp. 248-9).

In spite of Herzfelde's interpretation, the precise significance of the imagery is anything but clear. As in another Dadaist work on a similar theme, Marcel Duchamp's *The Bride Stripped Bare by her Bachelors Even*, its meaning, if it was even intended to have one, remains a mystery.

Catalogue 123

84

DEUTSCHE TYPEN
German Types
*c.*1922
pen and ink, 48.2 × 43.2 cm
Achim Moeller Fine Art, New York

Several of these representative types put in frequent appearances in Grosz's satirical drawings. Compare the face of the man on the right with that of the right-hand figure in *Drei Männer* (cat. 74), for example.

In his essay in this catalogue Christopher Clark refers to the '"negative solidarity" between the extreme left and the extreme right, in propaganda as in politics' during the Weimar Republic (see pp. 26–7). Grosz's caricature of the wealthy Jew in this drawing is as crude as anything that later appeared in the Nazi propagandistic paper *Der Stürmer*.

This drawing was published in *Ecce Homo*.

85

SONNIGES LAND
Sunny Country
c. 1920
pen, ink and watercolour, 41.8 × 29.5 cm
Theodore B. Donson Ltd, New York

This memorable and unusual watercolour contrasts the idyllic with the gross. The castle, landscape and windmill in the background might come from an illustration for a fairy-tale. But they are insignificant by comparison with the enormous pigs and the two butchers. Given the presence of the man with a pig's head at table in the foreground, the suggestion seems to be that pigs are victims but also predators, or rather, as Grosz frequently asserted, that human beings are swine.

Catalogue

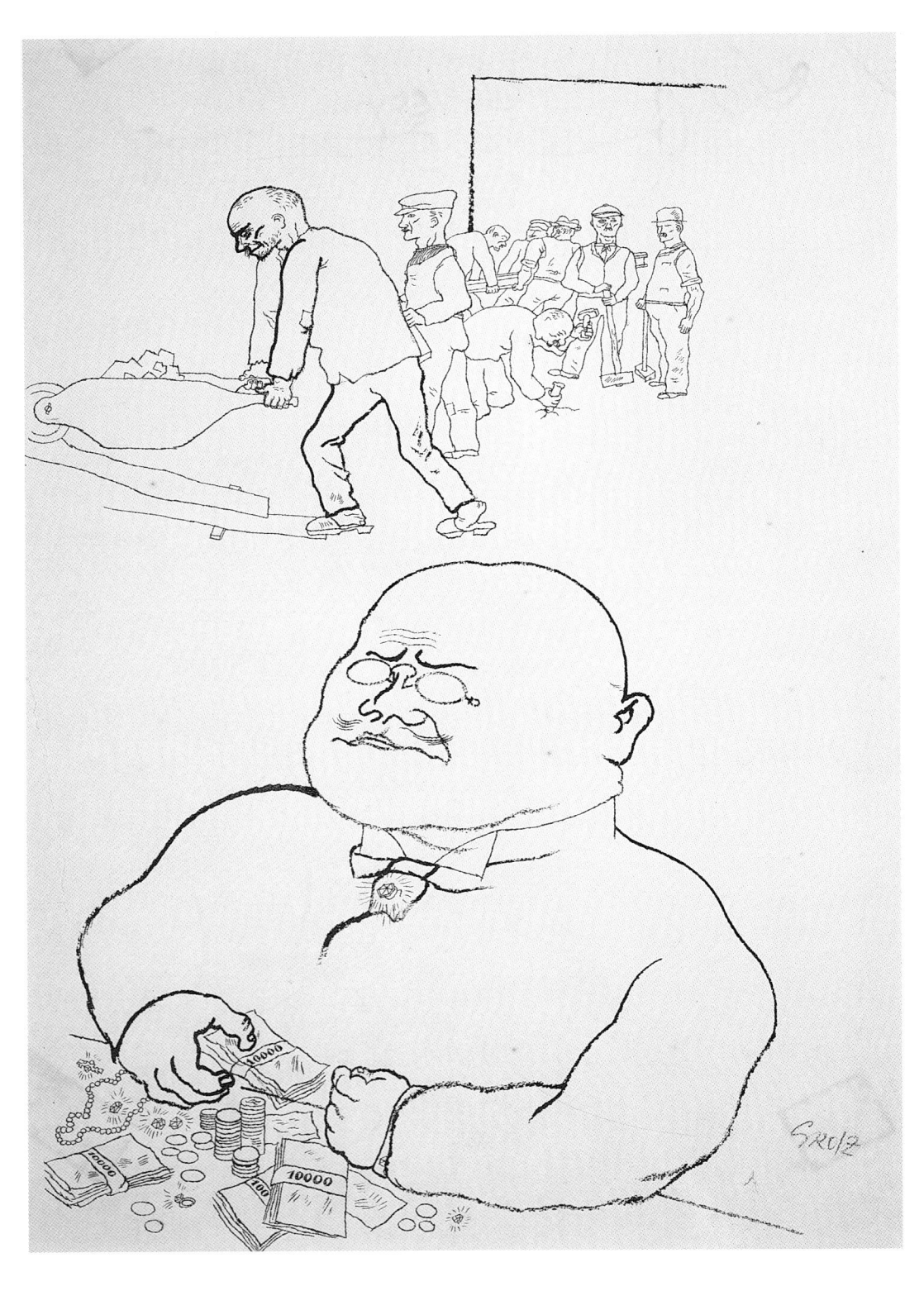

86
INFLATION
c.1923
pen, ink and charcoal, 50 × 32.5 cm
Private collection

Between the end of World War I and 1924 when the German currency was stabilised, inflation assumed devastating dimensions (see Chronology). But it did not damage everyone. Industrialists borrowed to pay off debts, build cartels and acquire tangible assets before repaying the loans in near-worthless currency. On the other hand, workers, civil servants, war veterans and pensioners had their savings wiped out. They saw the value of their wages, salaries and pensions plummet within minutes of receiving them. As Grosz wrote in 1922: 'Humanity has created an evil system – a top and a bottom. A few make millions while countless thousands have barely enough to survive. . . But what does that have to do with art? Precisely the fact that many painters and writers, in a word almost all so-called "intellectuals", still tolerate these things, without making a clear decision to oppose them. Today, when all the muck has to be cleared away, they cynically stand aside – today, when all these demeaning factors, this cultural hypocrisy, and all this damned indifference must be fought against. The belief that private initiative alone makes you happy dominates everything. The purpose of my work is to help undermine this belief and reveal to the oppressed the true faces of their rulers' (exhib. cat. *George Grosz*, Hanover, 1922).

87
AM TISCH
At Table
1920–21
watercolour, pen and ink, 46.3 30.2 cm
The National Museum in Warsaw

Grosz's watercolours from this period are, strictly speaking, coloured drawings. However, this does not mean that they fail to exploit the unique potential of the medium, its characteristic luminosity and transparency. The washes which have added colour to the pot plant and jackets testify to Grosz's technical skill. The contrast between the repulsive male faces and the moods and characters they reflect is sharpened by the inclusion in the background of the bare-buttocked young female who leaves us in no doubt about the kind of establishment depicted.

Catalogue 127

88
HAIFISCHE
Sharks
1920–21
lithograph, 50 × 65 cm
Private collection

In innumerable prints and drawings Grosz depicts females naked, or rather he reveals their naked bodies beneath seemingly transparent clothes. The title is characteristically ambiguous. Who are the sharks? The men who wish to possess the woman, or the woman anxious to exploit the men? Of course, all three are predators: each feeds off the others. This image is related to the watercolour *Schönheit, dich will ich preisen!* (cat. 63). The necklace and fur stole worn by the woman are the same, and so is her pose. The man in the centre also appears in the watercolour.

89
DIE BESITZKRÖTEN
The Toads of Possession
1920–21
pen and ink, 52.7 × 41 cm
Scottish National Gallery of Modern Art, Edinburgh

Some of Grosz's left-wing critics, Brecht among them, suspected that the artist was less in sympathy with his working-class subjects than he claimed (see p. 11). Indeed, in those many drawings where the poor and downtrodden are juxtaposed with their wealthy exploiters, the former are treated in a considerably more clichéd and less vivid way than the latter. This celebrated image is a case in point, although it must be said that the grasping industrialists with their diamond tiepins, pince-nez and cigars were so prominent and familiar as members of Grosz's repertory company that they became almost as clichéd as the labourers behind them (cf. cat. 86, 87).

Grosz defended himself against such criticism in an article in *Prozektor* (Moscow, 1928, no.14): 'I do not think it necessary to meet the demands of a "chauvinistic Bolshevism" which imagines the proletariat neatly combed and dressed in the old heroic costume . . . I see it as still oppressed, still at the bottom of the social ladder, poorly clothed, badly paid, living in dark, stinking accommodation, and often governed by the bourgeois ambition to "better itself". . . One cannot represent the worker in the style of agitprop posters alone, with rolled-up shirtsleeves and bulging biceps. . . One must remember that the mass of the German proletariat has not yet become aware of its strength, as the workers in the Soviet Union have. To force . . . the worker openly to acknowledge his misery and enslavement . . . is the purpose of art, and I serve that purpose' (quoted after *George Grosz, Eintrittsbillett zu meinem Gehirnzirkus*, Leipzig and Weimar, 1988, pp. 111–12).

This drawing was reproduced on several occasions under various titles. In *Die Pleite, Beilage des Gegners* (Bankruptcy, Supplement to The Opponent) Vol. 2, No. 6, it was accompanied by a quotation from Heinrich Heine: 'Today the verminous rich man has powerful friends. / He sits with a money bag beneath his arse / and victoriously drums the Dessau March.' In *Das Gesicht der herrschenden Klasse* (The Face of the Ruling Class, 1921) it appears as *Die Besitzkröten*, the title now generally used. In the portfolio *Die Räuber* (The Robbers, 1922), the title, like those of the eight other images, is taken from Schiller's drama *Die Räuber* (1781): 'Under my rule it shall be brought to pass that potatoes and small beer shall be considered a holiday treat; and woe to him who meets my eye with red rosy cheeks! Haggard want and crouching fear are my insignia, and in this livery will I clothe thee' (Act 2, Scene 2).

In the portfolio *Die Gezeichneten* (1930), the drawing again appears as *Die Besitzkröten*.

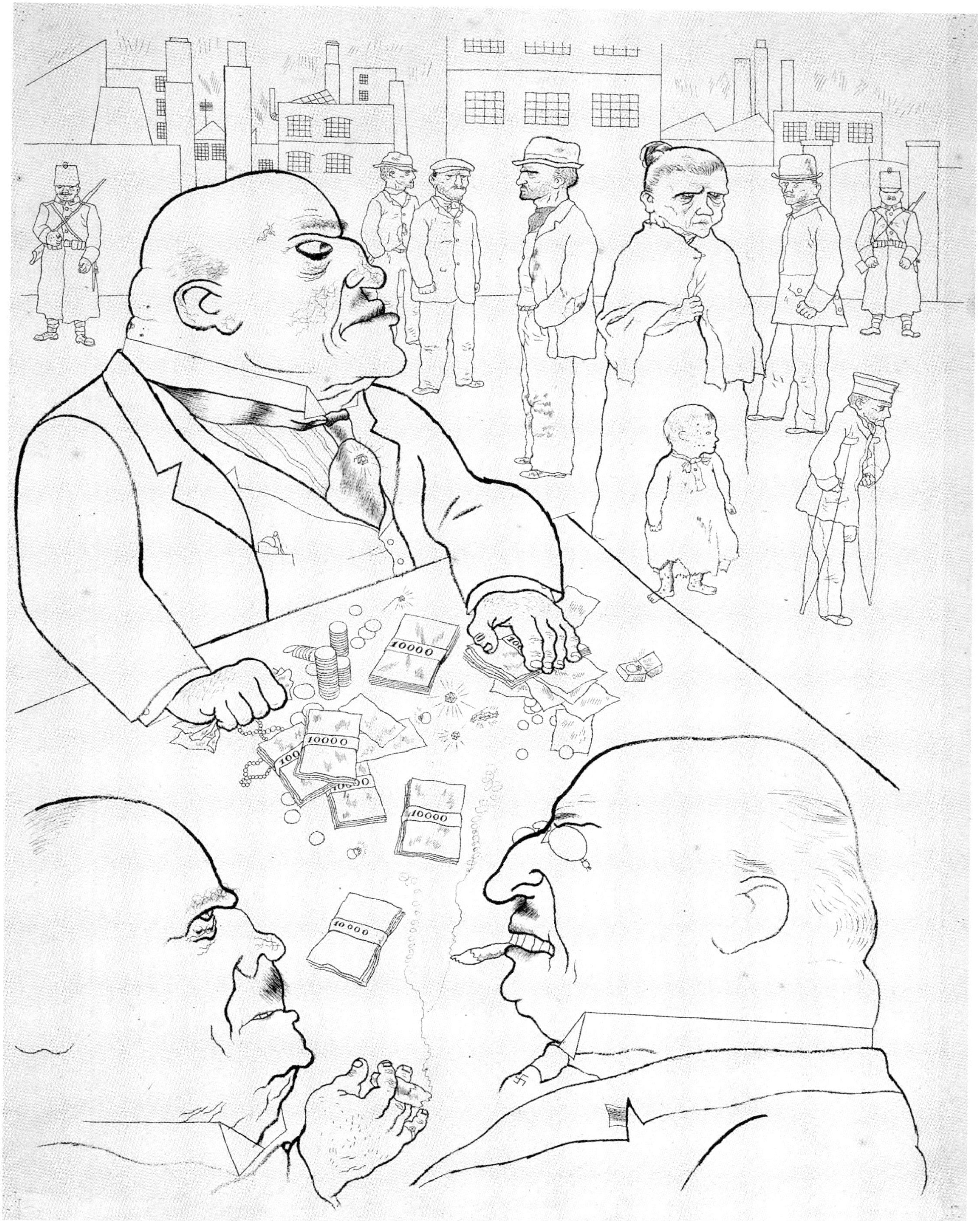
10000
10000
10000
10000
10000
10 000

90

KLEINES CAFÉ
Small Café
c.1921–4
pen and watercolour, 60.9 × 47.9 cm
Museum Ludwig, Cologne (Haubrich Donation)

The curious nun-like costume of the waitress is impossible to explain: it is unlikely that she and here colleagues were dressed like medieval serving wenches. The trade of the two seated women is obvious enough, however, thanks to Grosz's use of the naked body revealed in whole or in part beneath the clothes. The man smoking a cigar in a holder is the prostitutes' pimp, or more likely a potential customer.

91

AN DER GRENZE
On the Verge
1920–21
lithograph, 65.5 × 50 cm
Private collection

A depiction of alcohol-aided seduction at home or more likely in a *Séparée*, a private area in a restaurant reserved for such a purpose. The meal has been finished, the coffee and liqueurs have been served. The woman, already half undressed, offers no resistance. This print was reproduced in *Ecce Homo*. Several related drawings showing various stages of the seduction are known.

92
WERBUNG
Courtship
1921
pen and ink, 39 × 30 cm
Private collection

The ambiguous title means both 'courtship' and 'plying for trade' – a characteristic confrontation of the seemingly irreconcilable but intimately related behaviour that this drawing illustrates. The man in the foreground is insinuating himself into the affections of two unattractive bourgeois women, one a devout Christian, while glancing over his shoulder at a group of parading whores.

The common man so spiritually and sexually suffocated in his domestic life that he longs for the illicit pleasures promised by the world outside is a familiar theme in contemporary German literature and film.

93
DIE GUTEN JAHRE
The Good Years
*c.*1920
pen, ink and watercolour, 45 × 36 cm
Galerie Pels-Leusden, Berlin

The woman may still – just – be interested in her man, but she is beginning to be as bored by their relationship as he. Brutal, aggressive and moody, he can no longer be aroused by her provocative *déshabillé* and eyes the unseen door, planning his escape from an idyll gone sour.

Although certainly not earlier than 1920, the drawing should probably be dated somewhat later on stylistic grounds.

Catalogue 133

94
LAPPE UND VORRATSHAUS
Laplander and Storage Shed
1922
pen and ink, 23 × 18 cm
Private collection

This drawing was presumably made on the way to the Soviet Union. Grosz travelled there in the company of the Danish writer Martin Andersen-Nexø in 1922. They went by way of North Norway and Finland.

95
HAUSSUCHUNG
House Search
1921
chalk, pen and ink, 54.5 × 49 cm
Stiftung Archiv der Akademie der Künste, Berlin, Kunstsammlung

The full title reads: 'House Search – These people, who were also only working to live, had sold themselves for the purpose of attacking their fellow creatures like sharp-toothed dogs'. During the political upheavals of 1919 and 1920 house searches by the police and military looking for Communist agitators were common in Berlin and elsewhere.

This drawing appeared as an illustration in Franz Jung's novel *Die rote Woche* (The Red Week, Malik Verlag, 1922) and before that in *Der Gegner* (Nos 8/9, 1920–21) where it formed part of a sequence of three. The sequence begins with two armed soldiers battering down a door, continues with this scene, and ends with an emaciated worker slumped over a table. The text to the illustrations in *Der Gegner* reads: 'For the sake of "internal peace" . . . the "Greens" [police] are sent as friends to the people . . . and the unemployed man is granted his daily death allowance.'

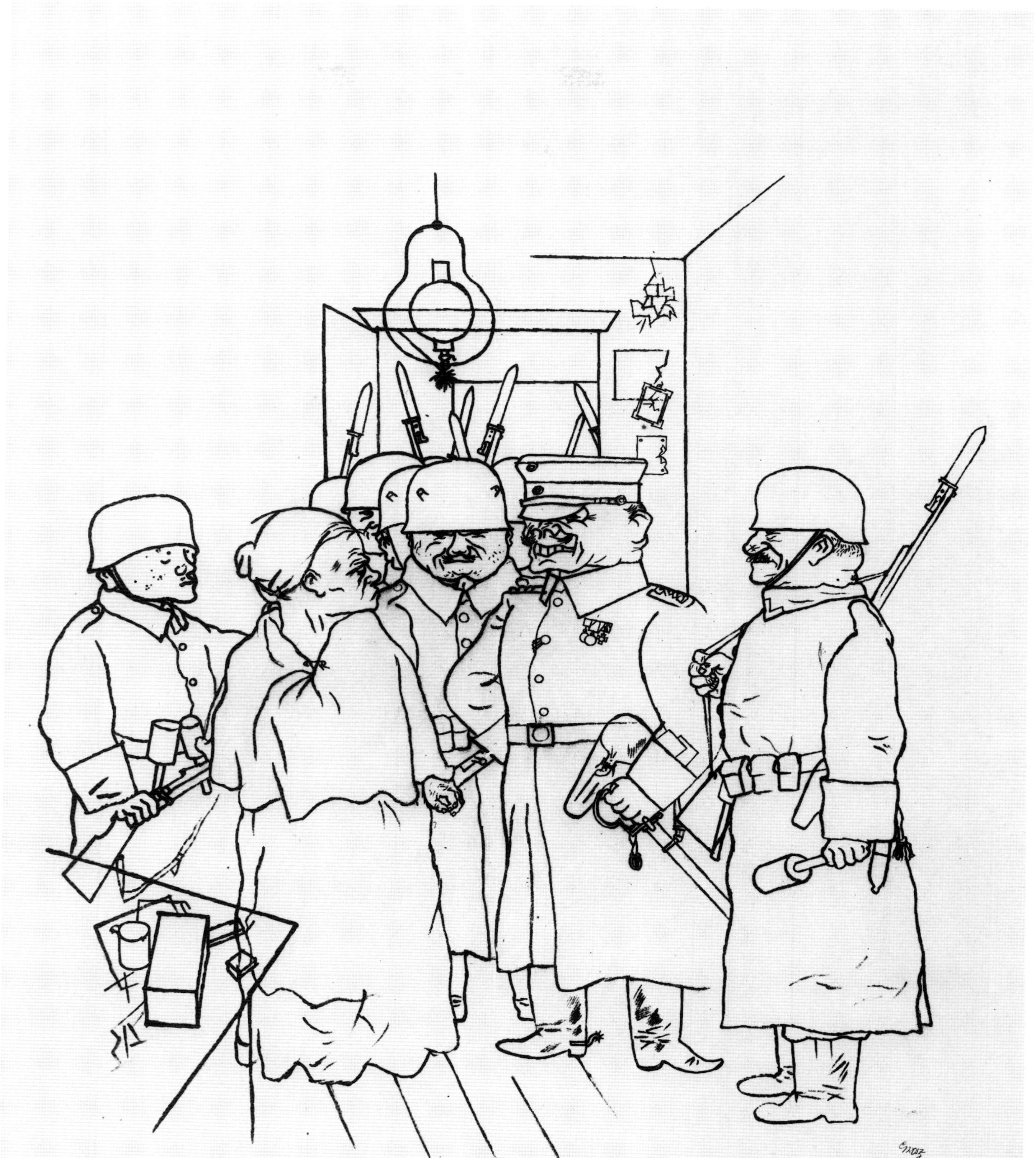

96

VIER MENSCHEN VOR DER KIRCHE
Four People in Front of a Church
1921–2, brush and ink, 65.1 × 50.2 cm
Private collection

Grosz delighted in mocking average middle-class families whom he depicted at home or, as here, in their Sunday best and at their most respectable. What above all intrigued him was the contrast between the façade such people so assiduously cultivated and the turbulent passions and violent thoughts kept out of sight behind it. Early in his career he had depicted scenes in which their emotions found expression in unspeakable acts. Now he is content to allow facial expressions and poses alone to hint at the disturbing nature of their true personalities.

97
NACHWUCHS
Next Generation
*c.*1921
pen and ink, 75 × 59 cm
Private collection

This drawing, reproduced in *Ecce Homo* and *Die Gezeichneten* (The Marked Men) has the title 'Albert, Wholesaler in Screws' (*Albert, Schraubengrosshändler*) written on the verso. This, as Dückers has pointed out in his catalogue raisonné of the prints (p. 161), refers to a passage in Grosz's autobiography about a spectacularly unlikely career made by one of his friends in post-war Berlin called Albert. He

> was conscripted with me for a second time [and] was a great dreamer who dreamed and mused about fairies and golden vessels. 'Tell me', I asked him, 'how did you get rich so fast?' At that moment we were smoking ten-mark cigars and drinking Albert's breakfast drink, Pommery & Greno Extra Brut with porter. 'Ah well', he replied . . . pointing to a heap of old, rusted rails and screws, 'that's how I got rich!' There were so many careers then. Just like a fairytale.

The characters depicted, then, were among the innumerable fixers and entrepreneurs who made fortunes by exploiting the unlikely opportunities presented by the aftermath of the War. The face in the foreground is presumably that of the resourceful Albert himself.

98

DER INDIANERHÄUPTLING
The Indian Chief
1921–2
pen and brush, 65 × 52 cm
Private collection

A portrait of the nationalist and revanchist politician Konstantin Fehrenbach, German Chancellor between June 1920 and May 1921. A strident critic of the Treaty of Versailles, he demanded an end to reparations and German disarmament. Whose scalp he has just bloodily removed is not known.

99

DOLCHSTOSS VON RECHTS
Stab in the Back from the Right
1922
brush and ink, 64.8 × 50.3 cm
Stiftung Archiv der Akademie der Künste, Berlin, Kunstsammlung

A coalminer is metaphorically stabbed in the back by the hand of a profiteering industrialist. First published in Grosz's collection of drawings *Abrechnung Folgt!* (The Reckoning Is Coming, 1923) under the title 'United Front', this powerful image alludes to conditions in the Ruhr, the industrial and coalmining heartland of Germany. When this area was occupied by the Allies after World War I, much of its production was diverted to meet demands for reparations, which caused repeated demonstrations and uprisings. At the time of the Kapp Putsch in 1920 much of the area was in the hands of the Communist-armed militia known as the 'Red Army of the Ruhr' and plagued by daily street battles. For the left, the fate of the Ruhr was an object-lesson in the unequal suffering of workers and industrialists since the profits of the latter seemed unaffected by the Allies' demands.

Catalogue 139

Grosz claimed not to enjoy illustrating books but, grateful for the money such work brought in, he accepted numerous commissions of that kind. Most of them, however, were for books written or published by friends or political allies. This drawing is one of 31 'charming decorations' made for a book of humorous stories, many of them in the Saxon dialect, by Hans Reimann who specialised in satires and grotesques. The book, *Hedwig Courths-Mahler, Schlichte Geschichten fürs traute Heim* (Hedwig Courths-Mahler, Plain Stories for the Beloved Home, 1922), poked fun at the clichéd style of Hedwig Courths-Mahler, an enormously popular author of romantic fiction.

This illustration is for a very short story titled *Schniedeking* which gave Grosz the opportunity to rework one of his favourite themes: a man thinking erotic thoughts about a much younger woman. The man is called Schniedeking. While out walking one day, he follows a 'musical girl' to her home. Having noted her address and ascertained what he believes to be her name, he sends her a telegram consisting of 'three heavyweight words: "I love you"', and then waits two weeks for an answer which never comes. The story ends as laconically as it began: 'Fräulein Krölund was probably not the girl of his desires, or she was already in love with another, or God knows what. The episode has never been explained.'

101

GANOVEN AN DER THEKE
Rogues at the Bar
c.1922
ink and watercolour, 58 × 46.7 cm
Private collection, courtesy of Galerie Kornfeld, Bern

A wonderful evocation of character and atmosphere, this watercolour seems to record the moment, as though in a snapshot, at which a stranger enters a den of thieves. The characters responding to the intrusion might be actors in a contemporary film about low-life Berlin by Pabst.

100

GRUSS AUS SACHSEN
Greetings from Saxony
1920
pen and ink, 59 × 42 cm
Sammlung Karsch/Nierendorf, Berlin

Catalogue 141

102

AUS DER JUGENDZEIT
Youth Remembered
1922
pen, brush and ink, 63.6 × 43 cm
Hirshhorn Museum and Sculpture Garden, Smithsonian Institution
Gift of Joseph H. Hirshhorn Foundation, 1966

An old man sits, a mug of beer beside him, dreaming about the conquests of his halcyon days.

Such drawings have made Grosz an easy target for feminist critics. His women, whether shown as the victims of violent assault, whores or nudes, are treated as sexual objects. A letter written to his brother-in-law (3 March 1918) seems revealing in this respect: 'Between ourselves: I can't stand "depth" in women where it's mostly combined with an ugly preponderance of masculine characteristics – angularity and skinny thighs; my view is the same as [the critic Alfred] Kerr's: "I alone have a mind"' (Knust, 1979, p. 58). On the other hand Grosz's capacity for irony should never be underestimated.

103

KRAFT UND ANMUT
Strength and Grace
1922, watercolour and indian ink, 53.3 × 44 cm
Museum Ludwig, Cologne
Haubrich Donation

A familiar confrontation between a self-assured man and a musing, half-dressed woman. Their relationship is not entirely clear, however. Who is tired of whom? And who is the dominant, exploitative partner? The petulant puff of cigar smoke is an especially vivid detail.

Catalogue 143

104

VERSTIMMTE FLÖTE
Dissonant Flute
1922
lithograph, 65.5 × 50 cm
Private collection

Grosz often juxtaposed a crippled soldier, an ugly war profiteer and an erotically suggestive female to telling effect. Here a further dimension is provided by the title. Not only the flute is out of tune: the times themselves are *verstimmt* – depressed and bad-tempered. The flute and truncated limbs of the veteran probably also allude to his impotence, of which sight of the woman makes him painfully aware.

105
DIE SCHANDE
Infamy
1922
brush and ink, 63 × 50 cm
Private collection

A rejected version of a drawing for the cover of an anthology of poems by Oskar Kanehl which was published by Franz Pfemfert, the editor of the Expressionist and pacifist journal *Die Aktion*. The book was subtitled 'Poems of a Soldier Liable for Conscription'.

The drawing that was used for the cover shows a soldier with an artificial hand and foot slumped against a bloodstained cross. It was reprinted in *Abrechnung Folgt!* (The Reckoning is Coming, 1923).

The original has scarlet additions within the outline lettering. Grosz often combined black, white and red in his dramatic cover illustrations.

face registers both contentment and greed as he surveys his mine and employees. As so often, Grosz identifies desire for wealth and power with sexual drive. This is made clear by the position of the expensive cigar: all that counts is the gratification of appetites. Here the use of pen and brush to produce a variety of expressive lines, marks and textures is especially effective. The contours of the face of the main figure alone suceed in implying, by varying the weight of the line from nose to chin, a great deal about the man's character and habits.

107

SIEGFRIED HITLER
1922–3
brush, pen and indian ink, 63.2 × 46.7 cm
Busch-Reisinger Museum, Harvard
University Art Museums
Gift of Mr Erich Cohn

The title alludes to the manipulation of Germanic mythology by the Nazi Party. So does Hitler's costume which, with its necklace of bear's teeth and sword, makes him seem both menacing and ridiculous. The drawing was reproduced on the front page of the satirical journal *Die Pleite* (Bankruptcy) in November 1923, the same issue in which *Der weisse General* (cat.109) appeared. Beneath the illustration two quotations from speeches by Hitler were printed: 'I propose that *I* take over the political leadership of the German government' and 'Tomorrow will see either a national government in Germany or us dead'. The same text appeared on a poster based on a photolithograph of the image.

In November 1923 Hitler, together with General Ludendorff, led an unsuccessful putsch in Munich. He was arrested and imprisoned in the fortress at Landsberg zu Lech where he wrote *Mein Kampf*. In the same year he became the undisputed leader of the National Socialist Workers' Party, which, however, remained an insignificant force for some years. Grosz's portrait testifies to the artist's prescience.

106

ICH WILL ALLES UM MICH HER
AUSROTTEN, WAS MICH EINSCHRÄNKT..
I Will Root Up from my Path...
1922
lithograph, 70.6 × 53.8 cm
Fogg Art Museum,
Harvard University Art Museums,
Louis E. Bettens Fund

Like the drawing *Toads of Possession* (cat. 89), this image was reproduced in the portfolio *Die Räuber* (The Robbers). The title was taken from Schiller's celebrated play, and each print was accompanied by a quotation from the drama, in this case the text, 'I will root up from my path whatever obstructs my progress toward becoming the master'. It is one of the most memorable images of an exploitative industrialist Grosz ever created. The coarse and bloated

Catalogue 147

108

EBERT DER PRÄSIDENT
President Ebert
1923
pen and ink drawing, 64.6 × 51.4
Busch-Reisinger Museum,
Harvard University Art Museums
Gift of Mr Erich Cohn

One of the many criticisms levelled at the Weimar Republic by the extreme left was that its government and judiciary were nothing more than a continuation of the old imperial order in a thinly disguised form. That is the point of this scathing portrait of the Republic's first President, Friedrich Ebert, a saddlemaker's son and leader of the Social Democratic Party. He may not wear a crown or the court or military costume favoured by the deposed Kaiser, but nevertheless he is an absolute monarch in petit-bourgeois clothing. This is made clear by the curtain and column, details familiar from many formal royal portraits, in the background. Everything else, however, points to Ebert's pretensions, vulgar tastes, and lack of charisma: the lucky horseshoe, cigar, three-piece suit and watch-chain across the comfortable belly. Even the glass of beer (a Berlin speciality known as *Weisse*) betrays his decidedly average taste. The portrait in the background is of Karl Kautsky, the chief ideologue of the 'Marxist Centre' of the Independent Social Democratic Party. Unlike Ebert's SPD, it voted against the war budget in 1916 and was absorbed by the Communist Party after the War. Kautsky's image on the wall points to the difference between Ebert's version of socialism and what Grosz saw as the authentic variety.

Catalogue 149

109

DER WEISSE GENERAL
The White General
1922–3
pen and indian ink, 51.8 × 46.5 cm
Collection E.W.K., Bern

This drawing was made for reproduction in the eighth issue of the satirical paper *Die Pleite* (Bankruptcy) where it appeared in November 1923, and was also published as an illustration to a book of Oskar Kanehl's poems on the German revolution, *Strasse Frei* (Clear the Street, 1928), and in Grosz's collection of drawings *Das neue Gesicht der herrschenden Klasse* (The New Face of the Ruling Class, 1930). It was also printed as a transfer lithograph.

Frequently dated 1919, the year when the German revolution was at its height, but certainly made later, the drawing looks back to the bloody period when strikes and uprisings against the government in almost every major city were savagely suppressed by volunteer militia or Freikorps under the command of the Social Democratic Minister for Internal Affairs, Gustav Noske. Those on the left like Grosz never forgave Noske, his militia or the government.

This is not a portrait of a specific person but a generalised image of one of the militia officers who, with the classic features and monocle of the Prussian aristocrat, is shown surrounded by the bleeding corpses of his victims. The white swastika was used by the Freikorps as early as March 1919 and adopted by the Nazis later.

The title also alludes to the White Russian forces who fought against the Bolsheviks and thus prefigured the activities of the Freikorps.

Catalogue 151

110
CAFÉ
1926
brush and ink, 31.5 × 64.8 cm
The Museum of Modern Art, New York
Acquired through the Lillie P. Bliss Bequest

The pronounced horizontal, an unusual format in Grosz's work, is easily explained. The drawing was made as one of the designs for Paul Zech's play *Das trunkene Schiff* (The Drunken Ship), produced by Erwin Piscator at the Berlin Volksbühne in 1926. Described as a 'scenic ballad', the drama is based on the adventurous life of the French poet Rimbaud. Employing characteristically unconventional techniques (which he further developed in his production of *Schwejk* – see cat. 128), Piscator back-projected Grosz's drawings on to a triptych-like screen at the rear of the set. The two side-wings were opened and closed at intervals. The compositions of the drawings take account of this in their description of both the various locations of the action and Rimbaud's fevered fantasies. Many of Grosz's designs for the play are of tropical landscapes but some occupy more familiar territory. The café here is obviously in France, but the guests are similar and in some cases identical to those in Grosz's Berlin scenes. The central couple – the man with a pig's head about to be kissed by a woman – who also appears in other drawings and watercolours, for example *Circe* (cat. 134).

111

DER WEG ALLEN FLEISCHES, VI
The Way of All Flesh, VI
1923
pen and ink, 46 × 60 cm
Robin Garton Ltd, Devizes, Wiltshire

This is the last and most elaborate of six related drawings about gluttony, physical cruelty and the transience of life. Since each has the same title, all were probably conceived as a print portfolio which, however, was never published. They were included in the collection entitled *Das neue Gesicht der herrschenden Klasse*.

Here, in a savage but humorous image of butchery and indifference, the amputated corpse of a woman lies on an operating or dissecting table while her spirit, holding a palm branch, floats free. Some of the amputated limbs have been stuffed into a bucket, and the mongrel dog seems to be feasting on other remains. Licking his lips, the surgeon sharpens his knife in readiness for his next victim. Meanwhile his assistant sweeps up litter and cigarette butts from the floor. His – and the surgeon's – dispassionate attitude to the grim work is suggested by the objects that surround them, especially the cigarettes, newspaper and mug of beer on the operating table. The ghoulish proceedings, emphasised by the insanitary clutter of the room in which they take place, are in stark contrast to the idyllic scene glimpsed through the window.

Catalogue 153

112

BILDNIS ANNA PETER
Portrait of Anna Peter
1926–7
pencil, 67.6 × 53.2 cm
The Museum of Modern Art, New York
Gift of Paul J. Sachs

From about 1924 Grosz made an increasing number of drawings exclusively in pencil, fully exploiting the medium in his depiction of tone, texture and subtle detail. He used it in a series of soberly realistic portraits of menial and unemployed workers (see cat. 113), members of his family and friends. Anna Peter, the subject of this characteristic drawing, was his mother-in-law.

A renewed interest in oils which Grosz also used to paint naturalistic portraits occurred at the same time. The sobriety of these drawings and paintings betrays a shift in attitude to which Grosz himself drew attention in *Abwicklung* (Winding Up), an autobiographical essay of 1924: 'Today I no longer hate people indiscriminately; today I hate their bad institutions and the men of power who defend them. And if I have any hope, it is that these institutions and the class of people that protects them shall disappear.'

Neither overtly political nor satirical, the work of this period is factually descriptive and exhibits a deep sympathy with its subjects. Grosz's new but obviously traditional approach was also the product of a developing impatience with stylistic experiment.

A relatively dry, realistic and matter-of-fact manner was adopted by several other German artists more or less concurrently. Moving with the conservative – if not reactionary – current that gathered strength throughout Europe during the mid-1920s, they jettisoned the challenging and subjective in order to take on board a more generally accessible pictorial language. This increasingly evident trend was the subject of a famous exhibition staged at the Mannheim Kunsthalle in 1925. It included a group of Grosz's drawings and paintings, and its title, *Die Neue Sachlichkeit* – 'The New Objectivity' – entered the language as a term descriptive not only of this kind of art but also of related styles in architecture, literature, music and the cinema.

113
REINMACHEFRAU
Charwoman
1924
graphite, 65 × 52.3 cm
The Brooklyn Museum, Dick S. Ramsay Fund

Shifts in Grosz's style were never absolute. He frequently employed two or more approaches concurrently. While he was making drawings like this – closely observed, relatively objective, and consciously academic – he was also producing caricatures and satirical scenes in a more characteristic manner. For him, a style was not an end in itself but a means to an end, selected because of its appropriateness to the subject. Pencil, used again now after an interval of several years, gave him the opportunity to make sympathetic studies of the real people he encountered, many of whom were underprivileged, unemployed or menial labourers. The cutting edge of his pen-drawn contours had prevented him from depicting such people in anything more than a schematic and clichéd fashion. Now he could treat them as clearly distinguished individuals whose faces betray their feelings and something of their lives (see also cat. 112).

Several other German artists, among them Grosz's friend Rudolf Schlichter, changed their style in a similar way at the same time, and some German photographers also produced direct, sober and factual images of individuals who are nevertheless representative types. The best known of them was August Sander who travelled the country making cunningly artless camera portraits which together became a kind of picture gallery of society in all its aspects. Published in his book *Antlitz der Zeit* (Face of the Time, 1929), his subjects were anonymous, identified only by their profession or status – 'The Grammar School Boy', 'The Middle-Class MP', 'The Policeman', and so on.

114

SELBSTBILDNIS MIT HUND VOR DER STAFFELEI
Self-Portrait with Dog in Front of an Easel
1926
transfer lithograph, 57 × 45 cm
Private collection

By 1926 much of Grosz's anger had gone, and his savage drawings of representative social types had become more mellow, wryly observed satires. He was also producing soberly naturalistic portraits whose control of detail and tonal values betray a growing respect for tradition (cf. cat. 112, 113). The stylistic change reflected a shift in attitude that was in part conditioned by Grosz's domestic circumstances. Disillusioned by Communism, he was now a family man, obliged to make a living. Some of this can be sensed in this lithograph in which Grosz shows himself in an affectionate light, contented, and even slightly self-indulgent. Instead of grimly observing the surrounding chaos, he is relaxed and contemplative. And the Scotch terrier on his lap is strikingly different from the thin, snarling mongrels that patrol the streets in earlier drawings. The dog, whose name was Dubb, was one of several owned by the artist over the years.

115

STRASSE IN BERLIN
Street in Berlin
c.1922–3
ink, watercolour and gouache, 59.8 × 46 cm
The National Museum in Warsaw

Catalogue 157

116
ZWEI MÄNNER
Two men
1925
pen and ink, 31.75 × 24 cm
Private collection, New York

A study in contrasting ages, physical and racial types, this bold and fluid drawing was presumably made on the spot. How else was such spontaneity achieved? Grosz always drew with the unerring certainty of a sleepwalker, committing himself to a definitive linear statement without need of pencil underdrawing or any other kind of crutch. The economy of his line also verged on the miraculous. Here nothing whatsoever is redundant.

117
PARIS
1925
pen, brush and watercolour, 72 × 54 cm
Stiftung Stadtmuseum, Berlin

When Grosz first went to Paris in 1913 he claimed to dislike the city and its cultural pretensions. But his attitude changed: although he never revised his opinion of most French contemporary art, he later came to love Paris and France in general. He stayed in Paris with his wife for over a month in 1924 and went there again in 1925 in the course of a three-month journey which included visits to Boulogne and Brittany. In the autumn of the same year he again spent several weeks in the French capital.

This accomplished watercolour was among the first to reflect Grosz's wry affection for the French. The three main figures are seen not through the eyes of a bitter satirist but through those of someone wishing gently to poke fun at fashionable clothes and attitudes. The restrained, gentle colours serve the same purpose.

Catalogue 159

118
SCHAUFENSTER IN BERLIN
Shop Windows in Berlin
1926
pen, brush and indian ink, 64.5 × 45 cm
Private collection

Grosz was perennially fascinated by street furniture, advertisements, window displays and the activities of pedestrians. Here his interest was engaged more by the shops than the perfunctorily indicated figures. The hairdressing salon is advertising 'The popular haircutting chair for children', the '*Bubikopf* [pageboy] cut' that was fashionable at the time, as well as 'hairdressing of every desired kind'. Next door is a gentlemen's tailor.

119
STRASSE IN BERLIN
Street in Berlin
c.1925
watercolour and ink, 72.3 × 54 cm
The National Museum in Warsaw

Most of Grosz's street scenes employ contrast and telling detail in order to expose social inequality and hypocrisy: beggars or unskilled workers confront industrialists or bureaucrats, prostitutes, policemen or prospective clients. But many of the street scenes of this period are more frankly illustrative and lack any moralising purpose possibly because they were created with a view to selling them through Alfred Flechtheim's gallery where this watercolour was exhibited at a one-man show in 1926. The artist is simply amused and fascinated by the uniform and pose of the traffic policeman, the ruddy face and ample belly of the male, pigeontoed pedestrian, and the aggressively alert expression on the face of the muzzled dog.

Catalogue 161

120

LETZTE FLASCHE
Last Bottle
*c.*1924
watercolour, 68.5 × 49 cm
Dr and Mrs George Dean

Executed in the soft and fluid style characteristic of the watercolours of this period, this image of erotic anticipation employs a device that Grosz had used on several previous occasions: not merely a bottle as a phallic symbol but a bottle of champagne being opened so as to suggest imminent ejaculation. The watercolour was reproduced in black and white and under the same title in Grosz's collection of drawings *Über alles die Liebe* (Love Above All, 1930).

121

IN DEN BESTEN JAHREN
In the Best Years
*c.*1923
watercolour, 62.6 × 49.5 cm
Sprengel Museum Hannover

Representative of the shift, occurring in Grosz's work during the mid-1920s, from corrosive satire to less acid social observation, this watercolour is nevertheless full of implication. The woman arranging her pearls seems unaware of the shiftily rapacious and possessive glance of her older male companion. His repulsive face and its evil expression are enough to betray his attitude to the opposite sex in general. As so often, the cigarette or cigarillo clutched in his gloved hand functions as an emblem of his possibly inadequate sexual drive.

Catalogue 163

122
PASSANTEN
Pedestrians
c.1926
pencil, 46 × 59 cm
Private collection

Together with the watercolour *Auf der Strasse* (cat. 124) this drawing gives an insight into Grosz's working methods and his ability to preserve the freshness of directly observed sketches in more elaborate compositions based on them. The figures here are almost identical to the three pedestrians on the right of the watercolour, and so are the details of the display in the tobacconist's window. The watercolour was clearly derived from the drawing, therefore, and Grosz somehow managed to retain an impression of spontaneity throughout. Yet the drawing itself was obviously not made on the spot but worked up from rapid notations in a sketchbook.

123
CHEZ EMILE HASENBOHLER
1927
brush and ink, 56.5 × 73 cm
Private collection

In 1927 Grosz spent seven months on the French Riviera, hoping that the change of place and climate, and above all the distance from Berlin, would enable him to address different and more saleable subject-matter. This drawing must have been made on a visit to Paris and in (to judge from its name) an Alsatian restaurant.

164 *Catalogue*

124
KURFÜRSTENDAMM
c. 1926
pen, ink and watercolour, 66 × 88 cm
Private collection

125
DIE VON DER LIEBE LEBEN
Those Who Live from Love
c. 1929
brush and ink, 88 × 62 cm
Private collection

This lively and seemingly unfinished drawing was first published in *Über alles die Liebe* (Love Above All, 1930). In a preface Grosz warned his readers not to expect 'any common or garden idyllic love scenes... Realist that I am, I use my pen and brush primarily to portray what I see and observe, and for the most part that is unromantic, sober and hardly dreamlike.'

Nevertheless, this and most of the other 72 images in the collection are considerably milder than Grosz's earlier work: they show him with his sting drawn, the venom neutralised. Contentment, acceptance and even delight in whatever was directly observed shine forth from this drawing. The once razor-sharp line is now blunt, even caressing. Grosz had already used the contrast between a blind, deaf and dumb beggar and well-heeled pedestrians on a busy shopping street so often that it had by now become a cliché. It is here designed not to provoke anger at social inequalities, rather to raise a wry smile of recognition. What Grosz now observes is, as he says in his preface, 'the happy immutability of life'. The revolutionary who believed that art could change the world had become a chronicler for whom humans would never change. He was content with their constancy.

Appropriately enough, *Über alles die Liebe* was published not by the Communist Malik Press but the up-market house of Bruno Cassirer. It was thus intended for a public quite different from that which such books as *Das Gesicht der herrschenden Klasse* (The Face of the Ruling Class) set out politically to educate.

126
PASSANTEN
Pedestrians
c.1926
pen, brush and ink, 46.2 × 60 cm
Hessisches Landesmuseum, Darmstadt

The monogram stamp in the bottom left-hand corner of this vivid street scene was the collector's mark of the industrialist and mine-owner Hugo Stinnes who exploited the inflation and economic collapse in order to establish a monopolising conglomerate. From 1920 he was also an influential member of the German government. Grosz frequently attacked him in his drawings but he responded only with praise and admiration. Indeed, Stinnes, who assembled a distinguished collection of prints and drawings, bought several works by Grosz. Perhaps the artist's failure to wound Stinnes was one of the factors that contributed to his despair about the lack of effect he imagined his drawings had. Later he even came to believe that his attacks on the Nazis unintentionally contributed to the party's popularity.

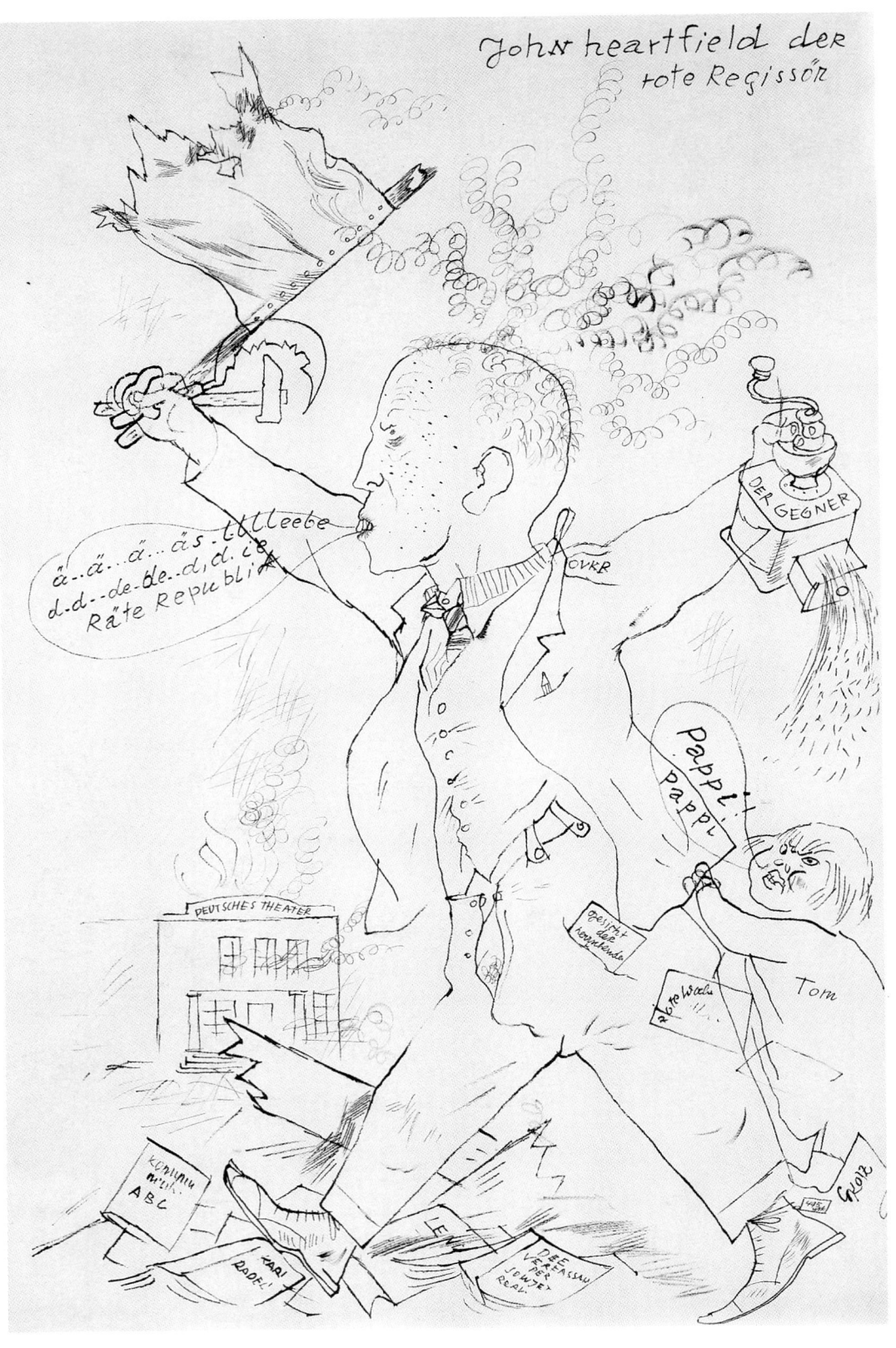

127
JOHN HEARTFIELD DER ROTE REGISSÖR,
John Heartfield the Red Director
c. 1927
brush and ink, 58 × 37.5 cm
Private collection

John Heartfield was the anglicised name adopted during World War I by Grosz's close friend and collaborator Helmut Herzfeld. The brother of the writer and publisher Wieland Herzfelde, he was one of the inventors of photomontage and used the technique to create brilliant propagandistic images. Short, irascible and with a pronounced stutter, especially when roused, Heartfield was an uncompromising Communist. Comparing John with Wieland, the Dadaist Hans Richter remembered the former as 'incomparably weaker . . . but for all that much wilder. He had nothing of [Wieland's] iron will but was consequently much more explosive. An irritable mimosa, a trembling eel, a glass of water slithering hither and thither on a wet table, an artist' (Hans Richter, p. 63).

Grosz shows Heartfield in a combative mood, holding a tattered red flag and a hammer and sickle aloft while stammering the words 'Long live the Soviet Republic!' In his left hand is a coffee mill bearing the title of one of the left-wing journals for which he and Grosz worked. In his trouser pocket is a copy of Grosz's *Das Gesicht der herrschenden Klasse*, while Communist texs lie beneath his feet. Behind him, screaming for attention, is Heartfield's only son, Tom.

Heartfield and Grosz remained lifelong friends even though their political views began to diverge during the 1920s. (Something of Grosz's sceptical attitude to the Communist Party is reflected in it.) Heartfield fled Germany in 1933, first for Prague and then for Britain where, after internment on the Isle of Man, he produced photomontages for various publications, including *Picture Post*, *Lilliput* and *Reynolds' News*. He also worked as a typographer. In 1955 he returned to Germany, living in the German Democratic Republic until his death in 1968. Tom, his son by his first wife, emigrated to the USA where he worked as a typesetter.

A related, less detailed drawing of the same date is illustrated in Sabarsky, No. 75 where Heartfield is not identified. Heartfield is also the man in Grosz's drawing *Beim Frühstück* (At Breakfast) illustrated as No. 92 in the same catalogue.

168   *Catalogue*

128
BERTOLT BRECHT
1927
pen and indian ink, 60 × 46 cm
Schiller-Nationalmuseum, Deutsches
Literaturarchiv, Marbach am Neckar

This casual caricature is chiefly of interest because of its celebrated subject, the Communist playwright, poet and theorist Bert Brecht. Brecht (1898–1956) moved in 1924 from his native Bavaria to Berlin to take up an appointment as *Dramaturg* (literary director) of the Deutsches Theater under Max Reinhardt. He met Grosz soon after and they became friends and collaborators, most successfully when Grosz designed Erwin Piscator's production of *The Good Soldier Schwejk* (1928) based on Jaroslav Hasek's novel which Brecht had dramatised. Their friendship endured after Grosz's disenchantment with radical politics and Brecht's publicly aired suspicions that Grosz identified too closely with the social types he attacked in his drawings.

In 1932 Brecht planned to base a play on the trial for blasphemy brought against Grosz in connection with his print portfolio *Hintergrund* (see cat. 131). The same year Grosz also set out to illustrate a complete edition of Brecht's plays. Both projects came to nothing, however, but in 1932 Grosz did provide drawings for Brecht's poem *Die Drei Soldaten* (The Three Soldiers).

Like Grosz, Brecht anglicised his name (Bertolt became Bert) and briefly developed a romantic admiration for the USA where he eventually went into exile before returning to the Soviet Sector of Berlin in 1949.

This caricature is affectionate but has a sting in its tail. It shows Brecht as a manipulative propagandist, as a Communist counterpart to the Ullstein publishing house, shown in the background as a huge mouth shouting into an enormous megaphone. Brecht has the cheap cigar and leather cap that were his trademarks and is equipped with eight insect-like arms. In one of them he holds a fishing-rod baited with the hammer and sickle. On roller-skates, his winged feet trample everyone in his path while leaving a trail of flames. A tiny adoring woman addresses the genius with the words 'naked I come before you'. He has several people in his pocket – among them 'Piss' (Piscator), Sternberg and Rudolf Schlichter (see cat. 129) – and instead of a heart a 'deadly writing weapon', a typewriter whose keyboard is worked by 'lightning bolts of destruction'.

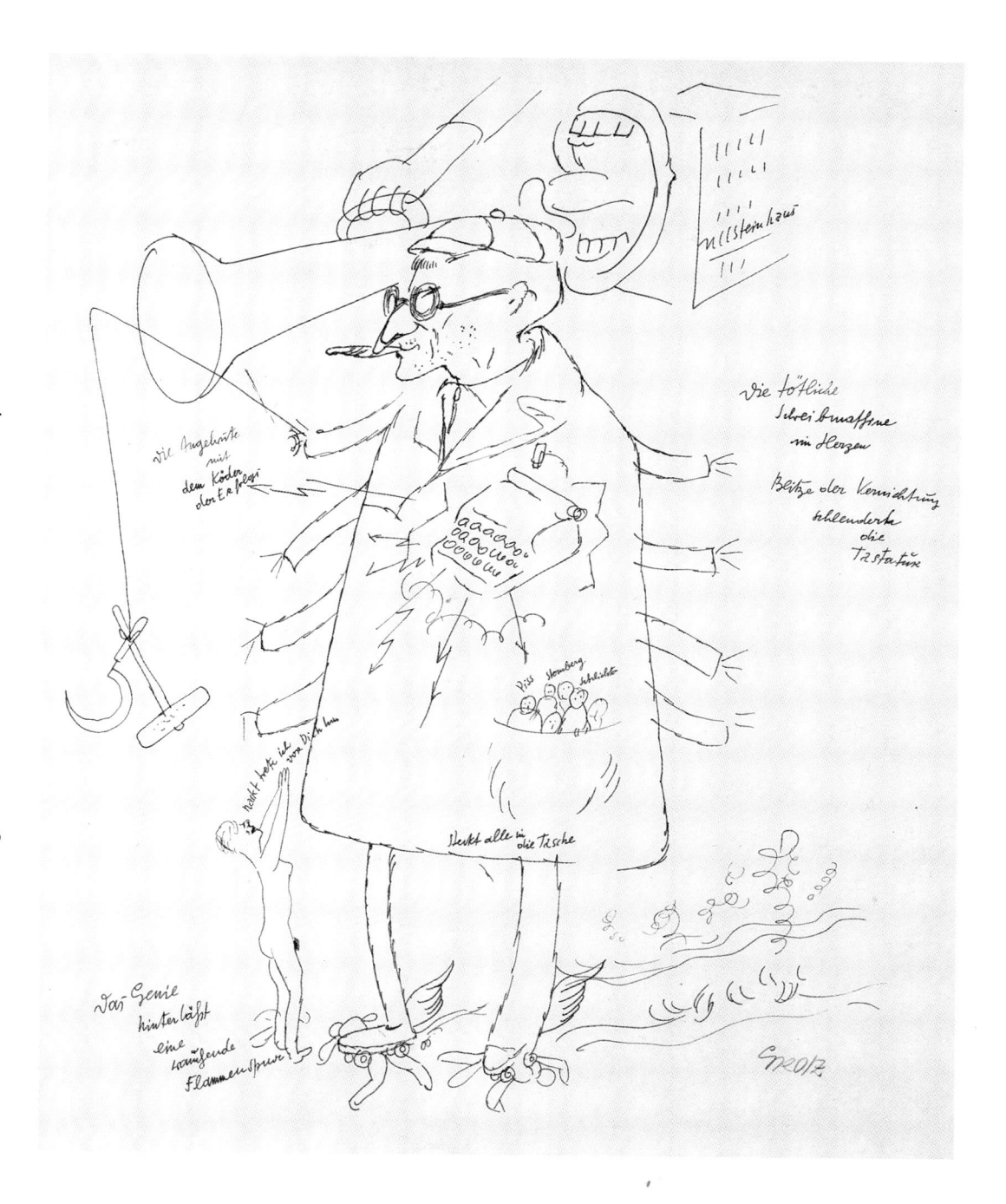

129

RUDI SCHLICHTER
1928
ink, 60 × 46.1 cm
Private collection

Rudolf Schlichter (1890–1955), a close friend of Grosz, was a painter and draftsman of enormous gifts. He was also a Communist, the secretary of the artists' association Rote Gruppe, of which Grosz became chairman in 1924. He often went drinking with Grosz to the Schwanecke pub or his brother Max's restaurant where Brecht was also a regular. Schlichter was a masochist and shoe fetishist, which explains the point of this cruel caricature. Schlichter kept a leather harness in his studio with which he would hoist a prostitute up to the ceiling, prostrating himself before her while slowly lowering the contraption down. Here she is strewing him with flames while he kneels before her. Ignored meanwhile is Schlichter's work in progress: a simple-minded still-life of Communist emblems. The tubes of paint are outnumbered by opened tins of food: once slim and handsome, Schlichter had quickly gone to fat.

A frequenter of some of Berlin's most bizarre brothels, Schlichter fell in love with a beautiful prostitute nicknamed Speedy, whom he eventually married (Grosz was best man.) His two-volume autobiography, *Das widerspenstige Fleisch* (The Rebellious Flesh, 1932) and *Tönerne Füsse* (Feet of Clay, 1933) is a strange but fascinating record of his sexual proclivities. Like Grosz, Schlichter distanced himself from the Communists during the 1920s but, unlike his friend, flirted with nationalism until becoming disillusioned.

In 1929 Grosz made a painting related to this drawing (Grosz Estate) and, curiously, based one of his own still-lifes on that shown here (whereabouts unknown, reproduced exhib. cat. Berlin 1994, p.360). Two other drawings of Schlichter by Grosz are known.

130

MANN, DIE HAARE KÄMMEND, MIT FRAU
Man Combing Hair with Woman
1926
brush and ink, 60 × 46 cm
Richard A. Cohn, Ltd, New York

Grosz was capable of wringing every last drop of narrative out of the most ordinary scene. Here, the expression on the man's face speaks volumes as he attempts to order his thinning hair with both a comb and brush. Is the couple married? Probably not. The location of this moment of intimacy on the morning after seems to be a hotel room. The open suitcase and position of the chamber pot suggest as much.

Maul halten und weiter dienen

131
CHRISTUS MIT DER GASMASKE; MAUL HALTEN UND WEITER DIENEN
Christ with a Gasmask; Shut up and do your duty
1927
Manueltiefdruck, 15.2 × 18.1 cm
Schiller-Nationalmuseum, Deutsches Literaturarchiv, Marbach am Neckar

One of the simplest and most effective political images of the 20th century, this print has an interesting history. Grosz conceived the subject while working on set and costume designs for Erwin Piscator's production of Jaroslav Hasek's novel *The Adventures of the Good Soldier Schwejk*, a huge and savagely funny epic set in World War I. Dramatised by Brecht, it was staged to great acclaim in 1928 at the Theater am Nollendorfplatz in Berlin. Piscator was a Communist and an enormously inventive director who pioneered the use of slide and film projection to complement and comment on the live action on stage. For *Schwejk* Grosz not only designed life-sized two-dimensional figures which at various moments were moved around between the actors but also made drawings for an animated cartoon shown.

Grosz reproduced seventeen of the preparatory images, which totalled some 300 for *Schwejk*, in a portfolio called *Hintergrund* (Background), because they related to what was shown at the back of the set. The portfolio, in which this print is the tenth sheet, was published by Malik on the day of the production's première.

The reproductive process was unusual. Called *Manueltiefdruck* in German, and invented to reprint monochrome books at low cost, it involves making a copy of the original by means of a glass plate covered with a light-sensitive chemical. When the plate is placed over the text or drawing and exposed, the light penetrates the white, transparent areas and hardens the chemical, thus producing a negative which is used to print lithographic copies in the usual way.

This print, together with two other

images from *Hintergrund*, caused the authorities to proceed against Grosz and Herzfelde, the portfolio's publisher, for blasphemy. (One of the others includes a priest balancing a cross on his nose like a performing seal; the second shows a priest preaching in a pulpit while spewing weapons and artillery shells from his mouth.) The trial, the most elaborate of its kind in German history, became a *cause célèbre*. Grosz and Herzfelde were found guilty, but were acquitted on appeal. Further appeals and counterappeals ensured that the legal action continued for several years.

132

CHRISTUS MIT DER GASMASKE
Christ with a Gasmask
1927
pencil and ink, 46.5 × 30.5 cm
Private collection

Grosz later produced several modified versions of the image, one of which is exhibited here. Another appeared in his collection of drawings *Interregnum*, published in the USA in 1936. Grosz gave the original chalk drawing to Wieland Herzfelde. It now belongs to the Akademie der Künste, Berlin.

133

THE LATEST HIT
1929
brush and ink, 64 × 50.5 cm
Soufer Gallery, New York

Grosz wrote and illustrated a number of articles for *Der Querschnitt* (The Cross-Section), the magazine published by his dealer Alfred Flechtheim. This drawing accompanied an article about the Paul Whiteman band, then on a European tour. Grosz loved jazz from his earliest days in Berlin and taught himself to play the banjo.

134

CIRCE
1927
pencil, pen, ink and watercolour, 66 × 48.6 cm
The Museum of Modern Art, New York
Gift of Mr and Mrs Walter Bareiss and an anonymous donor

'Nail a motto over your sty of a bed, definitively, from getting confirmed until pegging out in the paradise beyond . . . "Men are Swine"' (letter to Otto Schmalhausen, 3 March 1918, Knust, 1979, p. 58). The pig as the embodiment of not only venal masculinity but also brutal humanity in general appears more than once in Grosz's drawings and writings (see cat. 85, 110). Here he also alludes to the familiar episode in the *Odyssey* in which the enchantress Circe turns Ulysses' shipmates into animals. An earlier letter to Otto Schmalhausen enthusiastically describes 'the labyrinth of mirrors, the enchanted gardens of the streets! where Circe turns men into swine . . . and the port wine red, kidney-corroding nights. . . Oh, the emotion of big cities!' (letter of 30 June 1917, Knust, 1979, pp. 53-4).

A much less detailed line version of the same subject is reproduced in Grosz's collection of drawings *Das neue Gesicht der herrschenden Klasse* (1930) and the couple also appears in *Café* (cat. 110).

174   *Catalogue*

Catalogue 175

135

SPAZIERGANG
The Stroll
*c.*1926
watercolour
61.8 × 45.1 cm
Private collection, Princeton, New Jersey

This watercolour shows how much Grosz's work changed during the second half of the 1920s. The interest here is not in individual facial characteristics, and no attempt has been made to contrast social types to satirical effect. We are simply invited to compare the different clothes worn by the nanny and the woman (probably the child's mother) as they take a stroll in one of Berlin's shopping districts. Even the technique is looser and more gentle than that of earlier work.

136

DER BLUMENVERKÄUFER
The Flower Seller
*c.*1926
watercolour, 60 × 52 cm
Private collection, Princeton, New Jersey

At the end of the 1920s the economic depression brought a return to the kind of conditions familiar after World War I. The enormous gulf between rich and poor, between the employed and jobless became obvious once again. We are persuaded to think that the dachshund (who puts in an appearance in countless drawings) leads a better life than the flower seller. The juxtaposition depicted here is familiar from Grosz's earlier work, although the style and colour range are quite different. They are also characteristic of watercolours made at the end of the decade, so a date of *c.* 1928 is more persuasive.

Catalogue   177

138
FRÜHLINGSANFANG
The Beginning of Spring
1928
watercolour, pen and ink, 75.6 × 48.6 cm
Private collection

Like all journalists, Grosz took every opportunity to recycle ideas. The encounter here between the old but still frisky man and the seemingly innocent, acne-inflicted girl makes the same point about the persistence of sexual desire as *In den besten Jahren* (*c*.1923, cat. 93) and numerous other drawings and watercolours. As so often, the title adds immeasurably to the effect of the image. The girl is on the threshold of sexual maturity while the man knows only too well that the sap can rise as irresistibly in the autumn as the spring of his years.

137
RESTAURANT
Restaurant
1928
watercolour, 43.5 × 66 cm
Soufer Gallery, New York

Towards the end of the 1920s Grosz exploited a wide range of watercolour techniques, virtually abandoning the graphic effects which had been his speciality for so long in favour of modulated washes laid down on paper made wet beforehand. In style, this painting looks forward to the watercolours of Manhattan which Grosz made after his arrival in the USA in 1932.

178   Catalogue

Catalogue 179

139
SONNTAGNACHMITTAG
Sunday Afternoon
1930
pencil, brush and indian ink, 59.5 × 46 cm
Claudius Ochsner, Zurich

Reproduced in Grosz's collection of drawings *Das neue Gesicht der herrschenden Klasse* (1930) where it is entitled *An Heiliger Stätte* (In a Holy Place), this group portrait was also used as a full-page illustration in the first, American edition of Grosz's autobiography. It was omitted from the later German edition, presumably because it was thought prudent to spare the feelings of those in the drawing who were still alive. They might no longer have wished to be seen in such dubious company.

All the gamblers but one are easy to recognise. They are, clockwise from the top centre: Rosa Valetti; Otto Meissner; Hjalmar Schacht; Franz von Papen; Celly de Rheidt; Kurt von Schleicher; unknown; and Gustav Krupp von Bohlen und Hallbach. All were familiar figures throughout Germany, and the men – politicians and industrialists – were instrumental in bringing the Nazis to power. Rosa Valetti was a cabaret artiste turned actress who created the role of Mrs Peachum in Brecht's *Threepenny Opera* and appeared in the film *The Blue Angel*. Celly de Rheidt was one of the many free, expressive dancers who enjoyed both success and notoriety at the time, not least because they frequently appeared in the nude.

140
QUEEN BAR
Queen Bar
1927
pen and ink drawing, 58.5 × 45.7 cm
Soufer Gallery, New York

Several sketches and a watercolour closely related to this drawing exist. One was reproduced under the title *Eiscreme* in the collection *Das Neue Gesicht der herrschenden Klasse* (The New Face of the Ruling Class, 1930), and it, together with the others, show that Queen Bar was composed from a large number of detailed studies made on the spot. The scene, full of telling details (like the cigarette almost guiltily held behind the chair and the supercilious expressions on the female faces), is obviously an expensive restaurant which boasts a violinist as well as a jazz band – highly fashionable then throughout Berlin – and the clientèle is clearly wealthy and upper class. It is curious, then, that this drawing was illustrated in a guide to 'lascivious' Berlin, *Führer durch das lasterhafte Berlin* (see introduction, p. 1) which concentrated on the city's more notorious and sexually permissive watering-holes. But Grosz had no part in the publisher's choice of illustrations and may not have had advance warning of the use to which his work was being put.

180 *Catalogue*

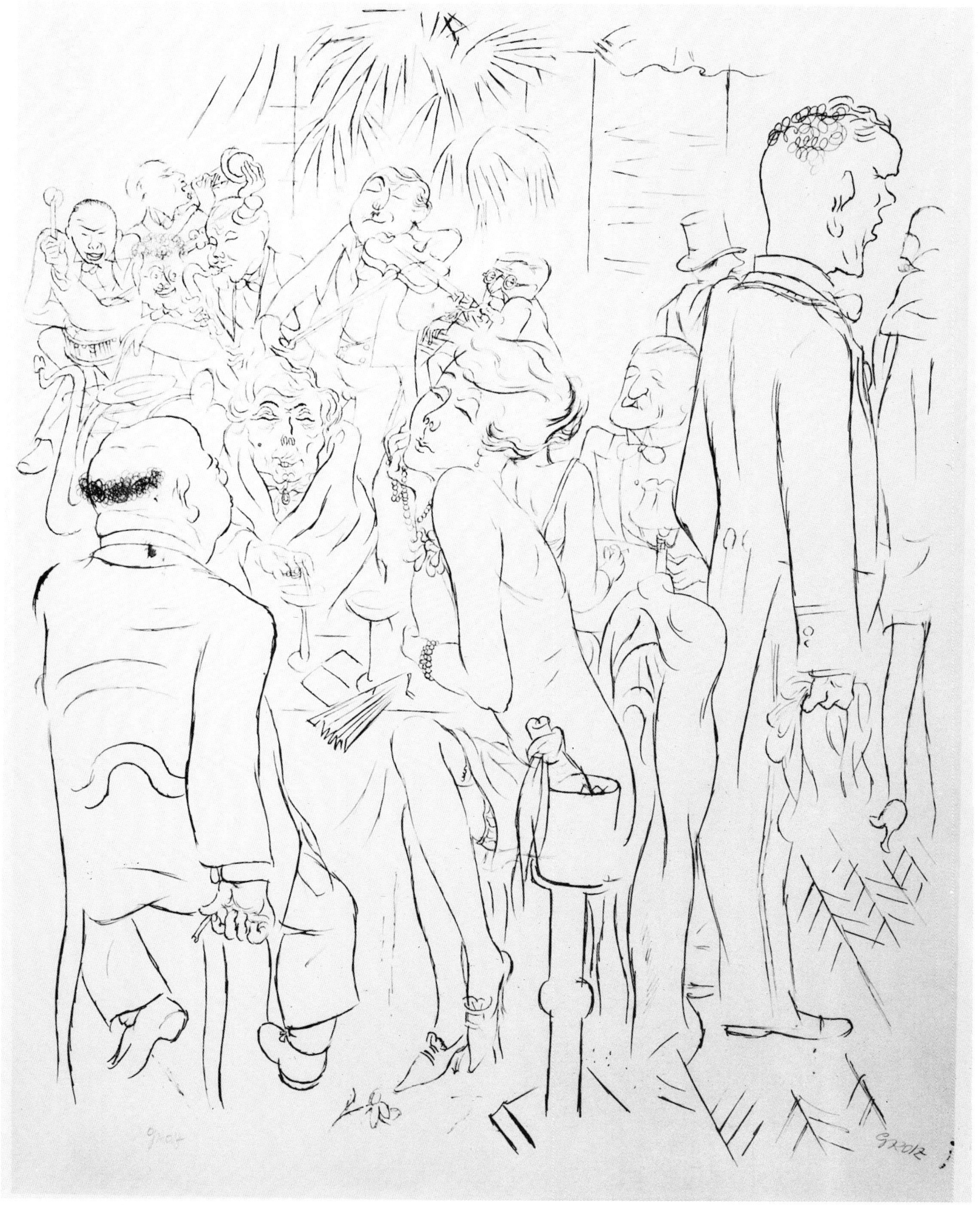

141

Postcard to Erwin Blumenfeld
1931
photomontage, 14.5 × 8 cm
Yorick Blumenfeld

One of innumerable postcards decorated by Grosz and sent to his friends at every stage of his career, this graffiti-decorated portrait of one Dr Otto Briesemeister was received by Erwin Blumenfeld who was briefly associated with Berlin Dada before leaving for Amsterdam where he ran a shop selling leather goods. Blumenfeld (1897–1969) subsequently moved to Paris where he made his name as a fashion photographer, and then to New York. Grosz remained in touch with him for the rest of his life.

The inscription beside the lavatory chain reads: 'Pull slowly then release handle.'

142

EINE ORDONNANZ
An Orderly
1930
watercolour and pen and ink,
66.7 × 48.3 cm
The Museum of Modern Art, New York
The Joan and Lester Avnet Collection

A caption in ink identifies this as one of the costume designs for a production of Arnold Zweig's *Der Streit um den Sergeanten Grischa* (The Case of Sergeant Grischa) at the Deutsches Theater in Berlin in 1930. Although Zweig wrote his pacifist play in 1921 and adapted it as a best-selling novel in 1927, this was the first time it had been staged. It tells the story of Grischa, a homesick Russian who escapes from a German prison camp, assumes a new identity, is recaptured and illegally sentenced to death after much bureaucratic military wrangling.

By comparison with most of Grosz's theatre designs, his watercolours for this production suggest something of the character of each role. Grischa is sympathetically portrayed while the German officers are caricatured with Grosz's customary venom. The significance of the list of names in pencil on the right, the 'servants at the party' (*Burschen beim Fest*), remains unclear. Perhaps these were the actors playing these minor roles.

Catalogue 183

184 *Catalogue*

ILLUSTRATIONS IN BOOKS AND MAGAZINES

143
EHEPAAR
Married Couple
1930
coloured ink and watercolour, 66 × 47.3 cm
Tate Gallery, London
Presented by the Contemporary Art Society, 1955

Typical of many depictions of representative social types, this watercolour is one of several intended for an anthology to be entitled *Die Naturgeschichte des deutschen Bürgertums* (The Natural History of the German Middle Class), for which Grosz is said also to have written an introduction. Because of his move to the USA, the publication did not appear and the text has never resurfaced. In a letter of 8 September 1955, Grosz compared the technique he used here (red ink outline and watercolour wash) to a Rowlandson print (Ronald Alley, *Catalogue of the Tate Gallery's Collection of Modern Art, other than works by British artists*, London, 1981, p. 342). Grosz was a great admirer of 18th century satirical English art which he collected in both Germany and the USA.

At the beginning of his career Grosz wanted to become an illustrator; and that is what he chiefly became. Although he devoted much thought and energy to painting, exhibited often in private and public galleries, and sold works to leading museums, most of his work consists of drawings. Many of them were intended for reproduction and they are among the finest and most characteristic of his creations.

Inexplicably, 'illustrations' and 'cartoons' are generally supposed to be less worthy of serious consideration than the products of 'fine' artists. Grosz did not agree. He believed that art which reached and spoke to a wide public was potentially as significant as whatever was created exclusively for wealthy collectors or museums and sometimes of greater importance. For him, illustrations and cartoons were valid art forms and occupied an important position in art history. He admired and collected the work of other satirical artists and cartoonists, amassing a large number of prints by Hogarth, Gilray, Rowlandson, other British artists of the 18th and 19th centuries, and Daumier with whom he can be most obviously compared. Grosz also followed the careers of contemporary cartoonists closely. Even the work of H.M. Bateman, the regular contributor to *Punch*, was known to him, as, later, were the drawings of Ronald Searle.

Grosz made no qualitative distinction between 'fine' and commercial art. He produced a wide variety of work, ranging from political cartoons to journalistic reportages, for a large number of publications: humorous magazines, propagandistic broadsheets, literary and other quality journals. His drawings also reached the public in other forms: as portfolios of graphics in several differently-priced editions; as collections of drawings in bound books; and as book illustrations. The portfolios and collections are listed in the bibliography to this catalogue, and two of Grosz's most important books are exhibited here. They are *Das Gesicht der herrschenden Klasse* (1921, cat. 149) and

Abrechnung folgt! (1923, cat. 147).

Also exhibited are some of the political journals to which Grosz contributed drawings. They are *Die Pleite* (cat. 152), *Der Gegner*, *Der blutiger Ernst* (cat. 153), and *Der Knüppel* (cat. 154). These journals were published by Wieland Herzfelde's Malik Press, as were many of the approximately eighty-three books for which Grosz provided covers and text illustrations. The following are represented here, either by the complete volumes or original drawings for them: Wieland Herzfelde's *Sulamith* (1917, cat. 145) and *Tragigrotesken der Nacht* (1920, cat. 150); Richard Huelsenbeck's *Phantastische Gebete* and *Dada Siegt!* (both 1920, cat. 144, 148); Oskar Kanehl's *Die Schande* (1923, cat. 105) and Upton Sinclair's *100%* (1921). Some of the more important books illustrated by Grosz but published by presses other than the Malik are also represented here. They are: Edgar Firn's *Bibergeil. Pedantische Liebeslieder* (1919, cat. 146); Richard Huelsenbeck's *Dr Billig am Ende* (1921, cat. 78); and Hans Reimann's *Hedwig Courths-Mahler. Schlichte Geschichten fürs traute Heim* (1922, cat. 100).

144
Richard Huelsenbeck
PHANTASTISCHE GEBETE
Fantastical Prayers
Berlin, 1920
book, quarto
Stiftung Archiv der Akademie der Künste, Berlin, Kunstsammlung

Interestingly, the cover gives the publisher as the Malik Press, Dada section.

145
Cover design for 'Sulamith' by Wieland Herzfelde
1918
pen, ink and collage, 49.5 × 34.9 cm
Stiftung Archiv der Akademie der Künste, Berlin, Kunstsammlung

Printed on a shimmering silvery blue binding, this design for the cover of a collection of Herzfelde's poems (his first publication in book form) ignored all the usual typographic conventions to create a memorable image infused with the spirit of Dada and children's drawings.

The unconnected words, names and phrases which punctuate the composition refer to Herzfelde himself, John Heartfield ('Muti'), and Tom, Heartfield's recently born son. The opening words of the popular war-time song *It's a long way to Tipperary* are also included.

Sulamith was published in a limited, luxury edition of 200 by 'Heinz Barger, Berlin' (a front used by Herzfelde to avoid censorship restrictions) and printed by Count Harry Kessler's Cranach Press in Weimar. Another collage by Grosz was reproduced on the back cover.

TOM
HERZFELDE
WIELAND
A bas
SULAMITH
Wieland
ILLONKA
GE
DI
CH
GEDICHTE
it is a long way to tipperary

146
Edgar Firn
BIBERGEIL
Wanton As a Beaver
Berlin, 1919
book, octavo
Stiftung Archiv der Akademie der Künste,
Berlin, Kunstsammlung

147
George Grosz
ABRECHNUNG FOLGT!
The Reckoning is Coming!
Berlin, 1923
book, quarto
Stiftung Archiv der Akademie der Künste,
Berlin, Kunstsammlung

148
Richard Huelsenbeck
DADA SIEGT!
Dada Triumphs!
Berlin, 1920
book, quarto
Stiftung Archiv der Akademie der Künste,
Berlin, Kunstsammlung

The cover was based on a collage by Grosz and Heartfield called *Sonniges Land* (Sunny Country). Its present whereabouts are unknown and it has presumably been destroyed, but a photograph of the collage is exhibited here.

149
George Grosz
DAS GESICHT DER HERRSCHENDEN KLASSE
The Face of the Ruling Class
1921
book, quarto
Stiftung Archiv der Akademie der Künste,
Berlin, Kunstsammlung

150
Wieland Herzfelde
Tragigrotesken der Nacht
1920
Book, quarto
Private collection, Cambridge

190   *Catalogue*

151
TITELILLUSTRATION ZU 'SCHALL UND RAUCH'
Cover illustration for Schall und Rauch
1920
Berlinische Galerie, Berlin,
Landesmuseum für Moderne Kunst,
Photographie und Architektur

The journal *Schall und Rauch* (Noise and Smoke) was published by the organisers of a cabaret of the same name which opened its doors in the cellars of the celebrated Berlin theatre, the Grosses Schauspielhaus, in December 1919. Max Reinhardt, the theatre's director, supported the cabaret, regarding its performances as the experimental, avant-garde element in his programme. *Schall und Rauch* provided the Berlin Dadaists with a semi-official forum for their activities, although their cabaret turns were less spectacular and irreverent than their earlier appearances at the so-called Dada Soirées. Grosz, Heartfield, Herzfelde and Raoul Hausmann contributed both to the cabaret performances and the journal, which also served as a programme. Grosz and Heartfield made puppets for a play by Walter Mehring with which the cabaret opened entitled 'Simply Classical! An Oresteia with a Happy Ending'. This issue of *Schall und Rauch* (No. 4, March 1920) included a drawing by Grosz entitled 'Why??? My Friend, the Quaker and Dreamer Oz' (The painter Otto Schmalhausen).

Catalogue 191

192　　Catalogue

152
DIE PLEITE
Bankruptcy
1919 Nos 1, 3, 5; 1920, No. 6; 1923, No. 8,
journal (reprint), 50 × 32 cm
Stiftung Archiv der Akademie der Künste,
Berlin, Kunstsammlung

153
DER BLUTIGE ERNST
Bloody Earnest
1919 Nos 4 and 5,
journal, 50 × 32 cm
Stiftung Archiv der Akademie der Künste,
Berlin, Kunstsammlung

154
DER KNÜPPEL
The Cudgel
1923 No. 3; 1925, No. 6,
journal, 50 × 32 cm
Stiftung Archiv der Akademie der Künste,
Berlin, Kunstsammlung

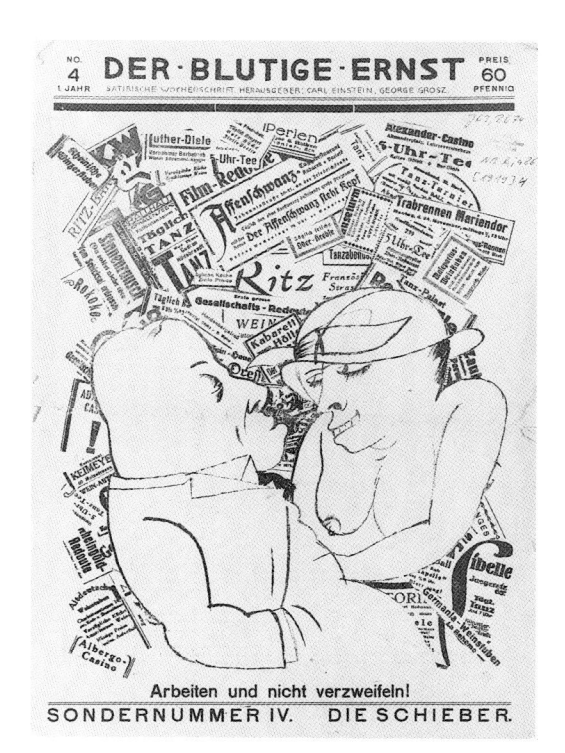

Catalogue 193

ADDENDUM TO THE CATALOGUE

155

GOTTES SICHTBARER SEGEN IST BEI MIR
The Blessing of Heaven is Visibly upon Me
1922
pen, airbrush and ink, 56.5 × 46 cm
Private collection

This hilarious drawing was first reproduced in the portfolio *Die Räuber* (The Robbers), and its title, like that of the images with which it appeared, is a quotation from Schiller's drama of the same name, in this case from Act II, Scene 3. Most of the drawings for *Die Räuber* present dramatic contrasts between industrialists and their exploited workers (see cat. 89, 106). This uniquely depicts a wealthy family at home. It is Christmas Eve when in Germany the candles on the tree are first lit and the presents unwrapped. The mother sings *Silent Night* while one of her sons, his father and grandmother (proudly wearing the diamond necklace she has presumably just been given) pretend to listen. Her second son is already playing with his rocking horse. It is a masterly evocation of bourgeois family life, and, seen in the context of the other drawings for *Die Räuber*, an indictment of a society in which a few are able to relax contentedly while others are cold and starving.

156

GERMANENTAG
Day of the Huns
1921
pen and ink, 45.8 × 37 cm
Private collection

Not illustrated

157

TYPENBLATT
Standardised Types
c. 1921
brush, pen and ink, 43.2 × 55.5 cm
Private collection

Not illustrated

158

PAAR UND TANZENDE
Couple and Dancers
c. 1923
watercolour, brush and ink, 48.5 × 28 cm
Private collection

Not illustrated

159

CAFÉ
1918–19
pen, ink and watercolour, 24 × 31.8 cm
Private collection

overleaf: final page from Wieland Herzfelde, *Tragigrotesken der Nacht*, 1920

Grosz taught himself how to use watercolour, a medium revived in Germany by the Expressionist Emil Nolde (1857–1966) whose work Grosz must have known. Not that there is any evidence of Nolde's influence here – apart from the dramatic use of transparent and translucent colour effects assisted by an always controlled exploitation of the 'bleeding' which occurs when paint is applied wet on wet, or on damp paper. The glowing colours evoke an atmosphere that is both exciting and sinister, and Grosz also employed similar combinations of scarlet, blood red and blue in several oils of this period, for example *Suicide* (1916, Tate Gallery) and *Dedicated to Oskar Panizza* (fig. 4), which he completed in 1918. As he wrote about the paintings he executed then: 'My favourite colours were a deep red and a blackish blue. I felt the ground on which I stood tremble and its tremors were visible in my oils and watercolours' (*Autobiography*, p.104). A self-portrait in profile and looking out of the picture is at bottom right.

Catalogue 195

ENDE

Chronology

1893
26 July, Georg Ehrenfried Gross born in Berlin, only son of Karl Ehrenfried Gross and Marie Wilhelmine Luise, née Schultze. He has a half-sister, Cläre, and a sister, Martha, both considerably older. His parents own a public house in the centre of the city where the family lives.

1899
The business fails; the family moves to Stolp in rural Pomerania where the father, a freemason, is employed as steward and caretaker at the local lodge.

1900
Death of father.

1901
Moves back to Berlin where, in the poor working-class district of Wedding, the mother and sisters make a living sewing blouses and letting rooms. 'Behind the tarred fire wall there was the usual view of the rear courtyard, the grey, big city backdrop of asphalt and stone; and I longed for Stolp, the forests, meadows and the smell of hay on summer days' (*Autobiography*, pp. 11–12).
Enters primary school.

1902
Returns to Stolp where the mother is employed by a Hussar regiment to run the officers' mess. Grosz, now at secondary school, is an avid reader of adventure stories. 'We played trappers and indians. In the spirit of Leather-Stocking and Karl May we shot at each other with airguns and homemade catapults' (*Autobiography*, p. 13).

1905
Begins the earliest known sketchbook, filling it with cowboys and indians, landscapes, and copies of drawings by Menzel, Grützner and Wilhelm Busch.

1907
Joins a Sunday drawing class.

1908
Drawings and watercolours inspired by illustrations in magazines and popular novelettes. 'I remember one book called *The Soho Charnel-House*... Mabel King the lady detective, Texas Jack the daring rough-rider and Captain Stormer were our models and heroes... Many of these wonderful stories were set in ... a romantic, pre-war America. I do not know whether this ... was responsible for my lasting enthusiasm for that country' (*Autobiography*, p. 18).

Expelled from school after returning a slap from a trainee teacher. The school's drawing master encourages him to apply for a place at the Dresden Academy of Art. His mother 'decided with a heavy heart on a profession for me that was as uncertain as a lottery ticket' (*Autobiography*, p. 53).

1909
Passes the entrance examination and moves to Dresden where one of his contemporaries at the Academy is Otto Dix. Seemingly unaware of contemporary avant-garde art in the city, even though the Expressionist group Die Brücke (The Bridge) is based there. Also uninterested in politics: a workers' demonstration demanding the universal franchise fails to engage him. Visits Karl May, author of adventure stories, in the Radebeul suburb of Dresden.

1910
Publication of his first drawing in *Ulk*, the humorous supplement of the *Berliner Tageblatt*. With the fee buys a pair of patent leather boots.

1911
Receives a diploma with distinction from the Dresden Academy. Spends time in Thorn, a town on the Vistula where his mother is now a cook in the military garrison.

1912
In January arrives in Berlin and rents a flat in the south-western suburb of Südende. Supported by a state scholarship and funds from his half-sister Cläre, now married and also living in Berlin, he enrols at the School of Arts and Crafts where he becomes a 'master student' of the graphic artist Emil Orlik. Apart from interruptions in Paris and for war service, Grosz officially continues his

studies until 1917. For the first time draws intensively from whatever he experiences at first hand. 'I then began to make simple sketches from nature in the manner of the old Japanese school of draftsmen... I made quick notations... of people walking, reading newspapers or eating in cafés, and every imaginable thing around me' (Autobiography, p.86). 'The sketchbooks piled up. What one did was nothing special but nevertheless highly instructive. It was especially good for me since I had drawn almost entirely only "out of my head" until then' (Introduction to *Der Spiesser-Spiegel*).

Paints in oils for the first time. A growing taste for violent, macabre and supernatural subjects. 'The strange, mysterious, often consciously deranged held me in thrall... In spite of an innate liking for the fantastic and grotesquely satirical, I had a highly developed sense of reality' (*Autobiography*, p. 84).

1913

In Paris between August and November where he draws intensively from life at the Atelier Colarossi, a private art school. Meets Jules Pascin whose spontaneous style of drawing and erotic subjects he admires. 'Not that Paris made any particular impression on me; I have never shared the excessive adulation of that city of idlers' (*Abwicklung*, p. 83).

In July holidays on Heligoland and in Hamburg and Thorn. Several drawings published in humorous Berlin papers. Back in Berlin, sees Italian Futurist and German Expressionist works in the 'First German Autumn Salon' at the Sturm gallery. Under their influence he discovers a strikingly individual voice for the first time. Increasing pessimism: 'What I had discerned during the pre-war period could be summed up as follows: human beings are swine. All the prattle about ethics is a swindle, intended for the stupid. There is no point to life other than the drive to satisfy one's hunger for food and women. The soul does not exist' (ibid.).

1914

In the Reichstag the Socialists join all other parties in voting unanimously for the declaration of war. On 11 November Grosz volunteers for the army.

1915

Bread rationing in Germany. In February Grosz is hospitalised with a severe sinus infection. On 11 March, after an operation, he is released as unfit for service. 'It is so wonderful, so holy, to live in Germany now; look, the whole world hates us... and to see all those magnificent well-fed men in their smart uniforms – oh, how I love uniform!... and as I write this I grow so sad because I had to lay my weapons down... Wonderful Prussia, splendid unified Germany with thy magnificent military! Thou alone hast been called to dribble the semen of culture into all the barbaric nations... (undated letter to Robert Bell, 1915, Knust, p. 30).

Meets Wieland Herzfelde in Ludwig Meidner's studio. Publishes a drawing and a poem in the pacifist, republican weekly *Die Aktion*.

1916

June-November, Battle of the Somme. Meat rationing in Germany. Changes the spelling of his name to 'George Grosz'. Poems and full-page drawings appear in the monthly *Neue Jugend*, published and edited by Wieland Herzfelde. Regularly visits the Café des Westens, the central watering place of the artistic avant-garde, where he gets to know the poetess Elsa Lasker-Schüler and the writer and critic Theodor Däubler who publishes an enthusiastic article in *Die Weissen Blätter*, a leading literary journal. Begins work on the important painting *Metropolis* (Thyssen-Bornemisza Collection).

'It is true, I am against the war... against every system which coerces and constrains *me*... The hero's death of every German on the field of honour (how nice!) delights me. To be German always means to be tasteless, stupid, ugly, fat, unelastic... a reactionary of the worst sort... only one in a hundred washes his body all over' (letter of 1916/17 to Robert Bell, Knust, p. 44).

Meets Eva Peter, his future wife, a fellow student at the School of Arts and Crafts.

1917

Military reverses at the front and increasing privation at home. In Berlin the 'turnip winter', so-called because the only food and drink available – bread, cakes, beer, etc. – is made from swedes. In November (the Russian October) Bolshevik Revolution. Grosz is recalled to the army on 4 January but is hospitalised a day later, seemingly having had a nervous breakdown. 'Everything around me is dark... my hatred of humanity has grown to gigantic proportions... I feel as though I will slowly go mad with melancholy... I am going through sheer hell' (letter of 18 January 1917 to Otto Schmalhausen, Knust, p. 46).

On 23 February admission to an army clinic for nervous disorders. In March declared permanently unfit for service and released. 'This time my nerves shattered before I saw the front, decomposing corpses and barbed wire. Before that I was made harmless, interned, under special observation to see whether I was unfit for the military... disgust, abhorrence!' (letter of 15 March 1917 to Otto Schmalhausen, Knust, p. 48).

Works with John Heartfield on an animated propaganda film for the military pictorial agency. Begins the important oil painting *Widmung an Oskar Panizza* (Dedicated to Oskar Panizza, Staatsgalerie, Stuttgart). Publication by the Malik Press of *Erste George-Grosz Mappe* (First George Grosz Portfolio) and *Kleine Grosz Mappe* (Little Grosz Portfolio). 'The movement in which I was caught up influenced me strongly, so that I considered any art pointless if it did not put itself at the disposal of the political struggle... my art was to be a gun and sword. I considered any drawing nib that did not contribute to the fight for freedom to be an empty straw' (*Autobiography*, p. 115).

1918

In October naval mutiny in Kiel spreads to Berlin. In November Soldiers' and Workers' Councils established on the Soviet model. The Spartacists, an extreme left-wing group of former Social Democrats, call for revolution. On 9 November the Kaiser goes into exile in Holland. On the same day a democratic republic is proclaimed by the Social Democrats (who form a provisional government) and, hours later, a German Soviet Republic is proclaimed by Karl Liebknecht, leader of the Spartacists. On 11 November Germany signs armistice at Compiègne. On 29 November the Kaiser, already in Holland, abdicates. Inflation begins to mount. Uprisings and street fighting in Berlin and other major cities. The former Austrian private and failed painter Adolf Hitler joins the German Workers' Party as one of about 40 members.

First sales of Grosz's paintings; exclusive contract with the Munich dealer Hans Goltz (who represents Grosz until 1922.) Leaves Südende for the more central area of Wilmersdorf where he rents a garden flat with studio. Executes the modern satirical history painting *Deutschland, ein Wintermärchen* (Germany, a Winter's Tale, present whereabouts unknown). With Raoul Hausmann and Richard Huelsenbeck takes part in the first Dada 'lecture evening'. Makes Dadaistic collages, some of them in collaboration with John Heartfield.

What did the Dadaists do? They said this: huff and puff as much as you like – recite a sonnet by Petrarch or Rilke – or gild the heels of your boots or carve Madonnas – the shooting goes on, the usury goes on, the starving goes on and the lying goes on. What earthly good is art? Was it not the highest form of swindle imaginable when art was conjuring up spiritual values before our eyes? Was it not totally ridiculous when art took itself seriously but no one else did? Hands off holy art!, screamed the opponents of Dadaism. Why did the same gentlemen forget to scream when their artistic monuments were shot at and their colleagues raped and murdered?
(*Abwicklung*, pp. 85-6)

Joins radical 'November Group' of artists; joins German Communist Party. 'Rosa Luxemburg... gave out the first party cards. During the founding party conference. That was on 31 December 1918. And we put our names down as members. My brother and Grosz' (GDR TV interview with Wieland Herzfelde, 19 June 1975, quoted after Fischer, p. 58).

1919

Second revolution in Berlin begins on 6 January. Election of a national constituent assembly which, because of the unrest, meets not in the capital but in the quieter city of Weimar. Acting under the orders of the Social Democratic Minister for War, Gustav Noske, private militia of demobbed soldiers and civilians, the so-called Freikorps, are covertly given weapons by the army and, together with the army itself, bloodily put the uprising down. On 15 January Liebknecht and Luxemburg are murdered. Under the Treaty of Versailles, signed on 29 June, Germany is forced to accept humiliating and economically ruinous terms. In August the new constitution passes into law. Weimar gives its name to the new republic. During the revolution soldiers force their way into Grosz's studio with a warrant for his arrest. Using false identity papers, Grosz escapes and goes into hiding. Draws political cartoons for, and helps edit the satirical papers *Die Pleite* (Bankruptcy), *Der Gegner* (The Opponent) and *Der blutige Ernst* (Bloody Earnest).

1920
Supported by units of the *Freikorps*, Dr Wolfgang Kapp, a right-wing radical, briefly overthrows the government which, having fled to Dresden, calls on the army to restore order. The commander, General Hans von Seeckt, holds his troops back. The putsch collapses after a general strike, and because of Kapp's ineptitude. German Workers' Party renamed National Socialist German Workers' Party (NSDAP). In April Grosz has first one-man show in Munich where he sees reproductions of Italian metaphysical painting in the journal *Valori plastici*. They make an immediate, thoroughgoing but brief impact on his work. On 22 May marries Eva Peter who has been his girlfriend since 1916. Helps organise and contributes to the 'First International Dada Fair' which results in legal action for bringing the army into disrepute. Grosz is one of the defendants. The trial ends in 1921 with a fine. 'All the strange creations, collages, montages, really shocked visitors and public opinion. Modern artists were especially annoyed since nothing was taken seriously here or respected. Even the avant-garde was mocked' (*Autobiography*, p. 132). Publication by Malik Press of the portfolio *Gott mit Uns* (May God be with Us).

1921
Deutschland über alles becomes the national anthem. Hitler elected leader of the still insignificant Nazi Party. One-man show at the Kestner-Gesellschaft, Hanover. Sends a hundred prints for exhibition to the Soviet Union. They are 'mislaid' and never returned. Some are said to have later resurfaced in Ilya Ehrenburg's private collection. Publication by Malik Press of the portfolio *Im Schatten* (In the Shadows) and the collection of drawings *Das Gesicht der Herrschenden Klasse* (The Face of the Ruling Class).

1922
In January one US dollar buys 192 marks, in June 74,750, and in November 4,210,500,000. The French occupy the Ruhr and are met by passive resistance. Rathenau, the German foreign minister, negotiates a friendship treaty with the Soviet Union and is subsequently murdered by members of the Freikorps. Mussolini marches on Rome and establishes a Fascist government. Grosz spends six months travelling to and within Russia. His companion is the Danish Communist writer Martin Andersen-Nexø who has been commissioned to write a book about the journey, illustrated by Grosz. Meets Trotsky and Lenin. The latter fails to impress him: 'Once upon a time in Stolp . . . there was a little pharmacist, a certain Voelzke . . . a goatee beard well cared for . . . Sunday best . . . stiff bearing of the upright philistine. . . He had a little remedy for everything . . . Lenin!!! . . . A very small pharmacist!' (quoted after Mehring, 1958, pp. 85–6).

Growing disillusion with Communism and the Soviet Union. (Leaves the party in 1923.) Starts to publish drawings in *Der Querschnitt* (The Cross-Section), the political, upmarket magazine produced by the art dealer Alfred Flechtheim.

Publication by Malik Press of the portfolio *Die Räuber* (The Robbers) and the collection of watercolours and collages *Mit Pinsel und Schere. 7 Materialisationen* (With Brush and Scissors. 7 Materialisations).

1923
By September banks are refusing to honour cheques for less than 50 million marks. On 4 October 1 US dollar bought 440 million marks, on 20 November 4,200 billion. Gustav Stresemann becomes Chancellor. Communist uprising in Hamburg. Communists are already in coalition governments in the regional parliaments of Saxony and Thuringia. In November Hitler and General Ludendorff stage an unsuccessful putsch in Munich. Hitler is imprisoned for five years but given parole after six months. He has meanwhile dictated the text of *Mein Kampf*.

Publication by Malik Press as portfolio (drawings and watercolours) and book *Ecce Homo*, from which thirty-four reproductions are confiscated. The artist and his publisher, Wieland Herzfelde, are accused of pornography. The sensational and much reported trial ends in 1924 with a fine of 500 marks to be paid by each of the defendants. Signs a contract with the dealer Alfred Flechtheim who stages Grosz's first one-man show in Berlin. 'Flechtheim was an art dealer, art lover, patron, collector and speculator . . . world traveller, gourmet and gourmand, wine connoisseur and someone who encouraged the sport of boxing, newly introduced to Germany. . .' (*Autobiography*, p. 188). Publication by Malik Press of the collection of drawings *Abrechnung folgt! 57 politische Zeichnungen* (The Reckoning is Coming! 57 Political Drawings).

1924
Currency reform, renegotiated reparations and American aid finally introduce a period of economic stability and prosperity. A Zeppelin crosses the Atlantic for the first time. Elections in May result in an increase of Communist seats in the Reichstag from 4 to 62; the Nazis, fighting a general election for the first time, win 32 seats. Lenin dies. In spite of having ceased to pay Communist party subscriptions, Grosz becomes chairman of the *Rote Gruppe* (Red Group), an association of Communist artists. Travels with Eva to Paris.

1925
Death of President Ebert. Stresemann signs Locarno Pact with the Western powers under which Germany's borders with France and Belgium are guaranteed. A survivor of Bismarck's Germany, Field Marshal Paul von Hindenburg, elected Ebert's successor. He is a 78-year-old reactionary. The Charleston arrives in Germany. Grosz takes up oil painting again after an interruption of several years. Participates in the *Neue Sachlichkeit* (New Objectivity) exhibition at the Kunsthalle, Mannheim. Publication be Carl Ressiner Verlag, Dresden, of the collection of drawings *Der Spiesser-Spiegel* (The Philistine's Mirror).

1926
Germany joins the League of Nations. Birth of Grosz's first son, Peter Michael. Completes the important satirical painting *Stützen der Gesellschaft* (Pillars of Society, Neue Nationalgalerie, Berlin).

1927
After exhibiting sixteen works in the spring show of the Prussian Academy of Arts, spends seven months on the French Riviera in order to distance himself from Berlin and develop a new style and new subjects. 'I am working here with mostly small formats. My plan (naturally with Flechtheim's investment) is to paint a series of . . . landscapes . . . which, because they cut out offensive subject-matter, are saleable. If I sell them I can go to work in the winter on the kind of big paintings I like, à la . . . "Pillars of Society" and suchlike. Courbet once did this too: he painted Lake Geneva several times for people who could pay' (letter of 27 May 1927 to Otto Schmalhausen, Knust, p. 101).

1928
Set and costume designs for Erwin Piscator's production of *The Adventures of the Good Soldier Schwejk*, dramatised by Brecht from Jaroslav Hasek's satirical novel. Seventeen drawings for the production are published by the Malik Press in a portfolio titled *Hintergrund* (Background). Three of the drawings are used as evidence in a trial for blasphemy against Grosz and Herzfelde which ends after many appeals only in 1931 with the defendents' acquittal. In September visits his friend Mark Neven DuMont in London. The city's charms elude him.

1929
The Young Plan reschedules German reparations to end in 1988 and Allied troops are withdrawn from the Rhineland. In October the New York stock market crash results in a world-wide recession and the withdrawal of loans to Germany where unemployment soars. Berlin plagued by insurrection and street skirmishes; members of the Social Democratic Party and the police are attacked by both Communists and Nazis.

1930

Thanks to emergency powers assumed by the Chancellor, Heinrich Brüning, the Weimar Republic ceases to function as a democracy. Between four and five million unemployed. In September elections the Nazis increase their representation in the Reichstag from 12 to 107, becoming the second largest party. First Nazi minister appointed to a regional government (Wilhelm Frick in Thuringia). Birth of Grosz's second son, Martin Oliver. 'What do you say about all the election uproar? The papers are again full of rumours about a putsch... The Nazis are putting on heavy anti-capitalist airs! Puzzling, beautiful Germany. The devil alone knows how things will turn out' (letter of 26 September 1930 to Eduard Plietzsch, Knust, p. 122).

Publication by Malik Press of the collections of drawings *Das neue Gesicht der herrschenden Klasse* (The New Face of the Ruling Class) and *Die Gezeichneten* (The Marked Men), and by the Bruno Cassirer Press, Berlin, of *Über alles die Liebe* (Love Above All).

1932

In January 6 million, in October 7.5 million unemployed. Hindenburg fires Brüning as Chancellor and appoints Franz von Papen. Hitler challenges Hindenburg for the Presidency. Supported by the Left, Hindenburg defeats him, but only in the second ballot. In July elections the Nazis secure 230 seats; Goering becomes President of the Reichstag whose Nazi members now customarily wear uniform. In November elections Nazis lose 34 seats. Franz von Papen resigns as Chancellor, succeeded by General Kurt von Schleicher after Hitler is rejected. Grosz, invited by the Art Students League of New York to become a guest teacher, arrives in New York on 3 June.

> Then went to Broadway... Great street. Between small, old houses, red on the outside with fire ladders, you suddenly see skyscrapers. All the façades are covered with advertisements, lit up even by day ... suddenly there's the elevated railway, old and filthy... In the middle of Broadway the street car with bronze seats reminiscent of a fairground... A negro with shoeshine box. Everywhere strangely nervous-looking, desperado-like men standing around in groups of dozens – every racial mixture. Half gangsters, half businessmen... Huge cigars in their gold-filled teeth... Here many people can't understand my romantic love of America (a few, the best, can: the others enthuse about Paris, Europe) (letter of 12 June 1932 to Eva Grosz, Knust, pp. 137–8).

Watercolour illustrations for *The New Yorker* and *Vanity Fair*. Gets to know James Thurber and George Gershwin. Returns to Germany, arriving on 17 October. 'I clearly saw that the floor was cracking, how this or that wall was beginning to shake. I saw how, overnight, the man who sold me cigars now had a swastika in the self-same buttonhole where before a red enamel hammer and sickle had always been' (*Autobiography*, p. 229).

1933

With Eva, Grosz leaves for New York on 12 January. In October they are followed by his two sons. On 30 January Hitler appointed German Chancellor by Hindenburg who intends him to be the figurehead of a largely non-Nazi (but right-wing) Cabinet. Burning of the Reichstag, probably by a Dutch Communist, used as a pretext by the Nazis to ban the Communist Party and call a general election. In the last free poll for 12 years the Nazis secure only a minority of 288 seats. On 23 March Hitler demands and is given dictatorial powers. Death of Hindenburg on 2 August. The offices of President, Chancellor and Supreme Commander of the Armed Forces are now merged and the army swears an oath of allegiance to Hitler personally. At Dachau on 20 March the first concentration camp opens. Boycott of Jewish firms. Gestapo founded. In May building of the *Autobahn* network begins. In March Grosz is deprived of German citizenship. 'Letters arrived from which I learned that people had been looking for me in my now empty Berlin flat and studio. I have good reason to doubt whether I would have escaped with my life' (*Autobiography*, pp. 230-31). 'I left because of Hitler. He is a painter too, you know, and there didn't seem to be room for both of us...' (from a CBS radio interview in 1942, quoted in Berlin 1994, p. 551).

Teaches full-time at the Art Students League (until 1936) and at a private school founded by Grosz with the American painter Maurice Sterne.

1934

Exhibition at the Mayor Gallery, London. 'I've painted around 350 watercolours, big ones. Some of them gloomy... I've also painted the Hitler man as a nightmare, between burning villages, bombers in the air – goyaesque, as a vision...' (letter to Wieland Herzfelde, 30 June 1934, Knust, p. 199).

1935

Visits Europe (Paris, Antwerp, Copenhagen, London and Amsterdam). Applies for US citizenship. 'Yesterday a friend sent me the *Kölnische Illustrierte*. There's an article in it entitled "Chamber of Horrors" which reproduces, among other things and next door to Dix, a painting by me. As a dreadfully horrifying and laughable example of what was possible under the Weimar regime and what was sold as "art". Well, I had to laugh heartily myself – it was indeed truly awful' (letter to Erwin Piscator, 23 August 1935, Knust, p. 221).

1936

Three battalions of German infantry enter the demilitarised zone on the left bank of the Rhine. Illustrations for *Esquire*. 'I got ... a job drawing postage stamps for *Esquire*, a beautiful magazine for college boys and bachelors. I don't mean that literally, just that my large-scale drawings were printed as small as stamps in the text, as so-called "spots". I therefore became an American illustrator, but was not allowed to do the large, beautiful, full-colour, sweet, attractive pictures for which I longed. Still, it was a good job' (*Autobiography*, p. 242).

Moves to Douglaston, Long Island and begins to paint in oils again. Exhibitions at the Leicester Galleries London and the Municipal University Omaha. Depression; excessive consumption of alcohol. Publication by The Black Sun Press, New York, of the collection of drawings *Interregnum*.

1937

Guggenheim grant for two years. Closes his private art school. Spends the summer at Cape Cod. Although not well off, Grosz supports several friends who have emigrated to the USA, among them Walter Mehring and Richard Huelsenbeck. In Germany Grosz's work is prominently represented in the 'Degenerate Art' exhibition; 285 of his paintings and drawings are confiscated from public collections, and many are destroyed. 'I do hardly any cartoons now... It's gone so far that I can scarcely draw "people" any more – I like to draw animals, birds, nature in all its forms, rocks, stones, plants, creepers and horizons with mountains and hills – moving clouds, too' (letter to Otto Schmalhausen, 5 December 1937, Knust, p. 266).

1938

Austria absorbed into the German Reich; the German-speaking Sudetenland occupied. 'Fine, your genius of a Führer gets what he wants, now he has got the thousand-year German Reich ... and a thousand years of peace; the Jews and freemasons have been destroyed... The next step, anticipated by us Hitler admirers, is a total understanding with Russia...' (letter to his aunt, Elisabeth Lindner, 5 October 1938, Knust, p. 275).

Grosz becomes US citizen. Exhibition at the Art Institute of Chicago.

1939

Non-aggression pact between Germany and the Soviet Union. Czechoslovakia occupied by Germany. German army marches into Poland; so, from the east, does the Red Army, thus partitioning the country. On 3 September Britain and France declare war.

1940

Teaches in the Fine Art Department of Columbia University (until 1942).

1941

Following the Japanese attack on Pearl Harbor, the USA declares war on Japan and her allies who include Germany. Retrospective at the Museum of Modern Art, New York which later tours to venues throughout the USA. Grosz teaches again at the Art Students League (until 1944). Grosz hates teaching but needs the money.

1943
Germany army surrenders at Stalingrad. German and Italian reverses in North Africa.

1944.
During a bombing raid on Berlin Grosz's mother is killed. 'When I was earlier attempting political and social satire I was always aware of its limits. In the satirical treatment of daily events . . . the artist is like a fiddler who scratches about on a violin that is too small. Great art has but little room for the mocking, teasing and allusions of the satirist' (*Über meine Zeichnungen*).

1945
On 30 April Hitler commits suicide. In May unconditional surrender.

1946
Publication of Grosz's autobiography, *A Little Yes and a Big No*, in New York. It omits a lengthy chapter about travels in the Soviet Union which is included in the original German typescript. Growing depression accompanied by increasing consumption of alcohol.

1947
Moves to Huntingdon, Long Island. Is offered a professorship at the Hochschule für Bildende Künste, Berlin.

1948
Berlin airlift. In spite of widespread critical recognition Grosz sells little work and has little money. Exhibition at the Associated American Artists Gallery in New York. 'Mehring (to whom I gave $20 at my show) told me he had eaten nothing for a week. . . I regretted the $20 – look, I'm not exactly rolling in money either, everyone takes me for secretly rich because I look so well ironed and pressed. . . In reality I've become very poor. . .' (letter to Otto Schmalhausen, 29 April 1948, Knust, p.410).

1949
Again teaches at the Art Students League (until 1955). 'In my class at the Art Students League there are two kinds of student: Picassoists and Miroists; then a third, the primitives. I am, as you know, not a moralist, not a pedant and defend no principles at all, so with the Picassoists I'm Picasso, with the Miroists Miró, primitive with the primitives' (letter to Rudolf Schlichter, 18 August 1949, Knust, p. 436).

1951
In Europe for the first time since the war. Entirely for financial reasons opens a private art school in his house on Long Island.

1954
Travels to Europe by air. Visits Hamburg, Berlin and South Germany where he visits Otto Dix. He is also in London where he designs sets for the film, based on Christopher Isherwood's Berlin stories, *I am a Camera*.

Exhibition at the Whitney Museum of American Art, New York.

1955
The West German Federal Republic gains sovereignty status and joins NATO. Publication of the original German version of Grosz's autobiography which, unlike the American edition, is unabridged.

1956
Teaches at the Skowhagen School of Painting and becomes guest lecturer at the Art Centre, Des Moines, Iowa.

1957
West Germany signs the Rome Treaty which establishes the European Common Market.

1958
In Berlin from September until December.

> Berlin W[est] is very exciting and, considered like a safari, worthwhile; nothing has changed; people still look out of their windows with cushions under their elbows, and you can still hear the happy beating of carpets in the courtyards as well as the usual fiddler (with 'last rose of summer' and so on). The same little wine lodges, green, snugly comfortable grottos. *Eisbein* with *sauerkraut* and puréed peas. . .
> (letter to Eugene and Marie Louise Garbaty, 5 December 1958, Knust, p. 522)

> I've given up making so-called satirical drawings completely, in any case it occupied only a brief period of my life . . . the only aspect of my satirical drawings that will perhaps stand the test of time – and I don't care one way or the other – is how they are done, their so-called artistic qualities. That is all. Apart from that I'm contented with life; no one can 'change' anything by drawing – I'm not an interpreter or enlightener any more either.
> (letter to Herr Hofner, 9 May 1958, Knust, pp. 515–16)

1959
Sells house, draws up his will and returns permanently to Berlin in June. 'In dark labyrinthine hours I battle, often unsuccessfully, with the demon alcohol . . . I don't drink like you, moderately and with enjoyment, but suicidally, wanting to escape from myself; but I can't get away from myself completely' (letter of 25 May 1957 to Herbert Fiedler, Knust, pp. 503–4).

In the early morning of 6 July collapses and is discovered in the entrance hall of his apartment block by a man delivering ice. Dies in his flat shortly after, asphyxiated by his own vomit.

It was a little after midnight when we left the restaurant and strolled the short distance to his home. Beneath a sky strewn with stars Grosz embraced us. Then he mounted the stairs, turned around once more, clicked his heels, raised his hat and, with the words 'Ladies and gentlemen', began a speech in which he praised the day and friendship, the night and the stars, Berlin and humanity in general. . . He held out his straw hat with its broad black band and waved with it. Then the key turned in the lock on the inside. We could still see his shadow as he went up the stairs. A few hours later George Grosz was dead.
(Martin G. Buttig, 'Der Tod des alten Dadaisten', *Der Monat*, vol. 12, no. 142, July 1960, p. 88)

Buried in the municipal cemetery, Trakehner Allee in the Charlottenburg district of Berlin.

SELECT BIBLIOGRAPHY

Frequently cited literature is abbreviated as follows:

Abwicklung
 Grosz, George, 'Abwicklung', in exhibition catalogue *George Grosz*, Galerie Flechtheim, Berlin, 1923; quoted after *George Grosz, Eintrittsbillett zu meinem Gehirnzirkus*, ed. Renate Hartleb, Leipzig and Weimar, 1988, pp. 81–5

Autobiography
 Grosz, George, *Ein kleines Ja und ein grosses Nein, sein Leben von ihm selbst erzählt*, Reinbek bei Hamburg, 1974

Bergius
 Bergius, Hanne, *Das Lachen Dadas*, Giessen, 1989

Berlin 1994
 Exhibition catalogue, *George Grosz: Berlin – New York*, Neue Nationalgalerie, Berlin, Kunstsammlung Nordrhein-Westfalen, Düsseldorf, 1994

Fischer
 Fischer, Lothar, *George Grosz in Selbstbildnissen und Bilddokumenten*, Reinbek bei Hamburg, 1976

Grosz, 1929
 Grosz, George, 'Jugenderinnerungen', *Das Kunstblatt*, Vol. 13, No. 6, 1929, pp. 166–9; quoted after *George Grosz. Eintrittsbillett zu meinem Gehirnzirkus*, ed. Renate Hartleb, Leipzig and Weimar, 1988, pp. 81–5

Huelsenbeck, 1964
 Huelsenbeck, Richard (ed.), *Dada, eine literarische Dokumentation*, Reinbek bei Hamburg, 1964, p. 265

Kessler
 Kessler, Harry, *Diaries of a Cosmopolitan, 1918–37*, trans. C. Kessler, London and New York, 1971

Knust
 Knust, Herbert (ed.), *George Grosz. Briefe 1913–1959*, Reinbek bei Hamburg, 1979

Mehring, 1958
 Walter Mehring, *Berlin Dada*, Zurich, 1958

Mehring, 1983
 Walter Mehring, *Verrufene Malerei*, Giessen, 1983

BIBLIOGRAPHIES

Bülow, Kjeld, *George Grosz. A bibliography and other check lists*, Copenhagen, 1993

Lang, Lothar, 'George Grosz-Bibliographie', *in Marginalien. Zeitschrift für Buchkunst und Bibliophilie*, Pirckheimer-Gesellschaft, Berlin, July 1968, No. 30, pp. 1–42

CATALOGUE RAISONNÉ

Dückers, Alexander, *George Grosz. Das druckgraphische Werk*, Frankfurt a.M., Berlin and Vienna, 1979

WRITINGS BY GROSZ

'Der Kunstlump' (with John Heartfield), *Der Gegner*, Vol. 1, Nos 10–12, 1920, pp. 48–56

'Statt einer Biografie', *Der Gegner*, Vol. 2, No. 3, 1920–21, pp. 68–70

'Zu meinen neuen Bildern', *Das Kunstblatt*, Vol. 5, No. 1, 1921, pp. 10–16

'Abwicklung', in exhibition catalogue *George Grosz*, Galerie Flechtheim, Berlin, 1923

'Kurzer Abriss', in *Situation 1924. Künstlerische und kulturelle Manifestationen*, Ulm, 1924, pp. 22–4

Die Kunst ist in Gefahr (with Wieland Herzfelde), Berlin, 1925

Foreword to *Der Spiesser-Spiegel*, Dresden, 1925, pp. 5–12

Foreword to *Über alles die Liebe*, Berlin, 1930

'Unter anderem ein Wort für deutsche Tradition', *Das Kunstblatt*, Vol. 15, No. 3, March 1931, pp. 79–84

'On My Drawings', *George Grosz Drawings*, New York, 1944

A Little Yes and a Big No. The Autobiography of George Grosz, tr. Lola Sachs Dorin, New York, 1949

Ein kleines Ja und ein grosses Nein, sein Leben von ihm selbst erzählt, Hamburg, 1955 (revised paperback ed. Reinbek bei Hamburg, 1974; 2nd ed. 1983)

George Grosz. Briefe 1913–1959, ed. Herbert Knust,

Reinbek bei Hamburg, 1979

Pass Auf! Hier kommt Grosz. Bilder, Rhythmen und Gesänge, 1915–1918, ed. Wieland Herzfelde and Hans Marquardt, Leipzig, 1981

The Autobiography of George Grosz. A small yes and a big no, tr. Arnold J. Pomerans, London and New York, 1982

George Grosz. An Autobiography, tr. Nora Hodges, New York, 1983

Ach knallige Welt, du Lunapark. Gesammelte Gedichte, ed. Klaus Peter Dencker, Munich, 1986

George Grosz. Eintrittsbillett zu meinem Gehirnzirkus. Erinnerungen, Schriften, Briefe, ed. Renate Hartleb, Leipzig and Weimar, 1988

Becher, Ulrich and Grosz, George, *Flaschenpost. Geschichte einer Freundschaft*, ed. Uwe Naumann and Michael Töteberg, Basle, 1989

George Grosz, *Teurer Makkaroni!, Briefe an Mark Neven DuMont 1929–1959*, ed. Karl Riha with Angela Merte, Berlin, 1992

So long mit Händedruck. Briefe und Dokumente, ed. Karl Riha, Hamburg, 1993

PORTFOLIOS AND COLLECTIONS OF DRAWINGS BY GROSZ

Erste George Grosz-Mappe, Berlin, 1917

Kleine Grosz Mappe, Berlin, 1917

Gott mit uns, Berlin, 1920

Im Schatten, Berlin, 1921

Das Gesicht der herrschenden Klasse, Berlin, 1921

George Grosz, Twelve Reproductions from his Original Lithographs, Chicago, 1921

Mit Pinsel und Schere. 7 Materialisationen, Berlin, 1922

Die Räuber, Berlin, 1922

Abrechnung folgt!, Berlin, 1923

Ecce Homo, Berlin, 1923

Der Spiesser-Spiegel, Dresden, 1925

Hintergrund, Berlin, 1928

Das neue Gesicht der herrschenden Klasse, Berlin, 1930

Die Gezeichneten, Berlin, 1930

Über alles die Liebe, Berlin, 1930

A Post-War Museum, London, 1931

Interregnum, New York, 1936

MONOGRAPHS

Anders, Günther, *George Grosz*, Zurich, 1961

Anon., *Grosz* (No.92 of *The Great Artists*), London, 1986

Bazalgette, Léon, *George Grosz, L'homme et l'oeuvre*, Paris, 1926

Becher, Ulrich, *Der grosse Grosz und eine grosse Zeit*, Reinbek bei Hamburg, 1962

Bittner, Herbert (ed.), *George Grosz*, New York, 1962; London, 1965

Deshong, Andrew Walter, *The Theatrical Designs of George Grosz*, Ann Arbor, MI, 1982

Fischer, Lothar, *George Grosz in Selbstzeugnissen und Bilddokumenten*, Reinbek bei Hamburg, 1976 (2nd revised ed. 1993)

Flavell, M. Kay, *George Grosz. A Biography*, New Haven and London, 1988

Hess, Hans, *George Grosz*, London, 1974

Hoffmann-Curtius, Kathrin, *'John der Frauenmörder' von George Grosz*, Stuttgart, 1993

Kranzfelder, Ivo, *George Grosz 1893–1959*, Cologne, 1993 (English ed., 1994)

Lang, Lothar, *George Grosz*, East Berlin, 1966

Lewis, Beth Irwin, *George Grosz, Art and Politics in the Weimar Republic*, Princeton, NJ, 1971

Neugebauer, Rosamunde Gräfin von der Schulenburg, *George Grosz – Macht und Ohnmacht satirischer Kunst*, Berlin, 1993

Ray, Marcel, *George Grosz*, Paris, 1927

Schneede, Uwe M., *George Grosz. Der Künstler in seiner Gesellschaft*, Cologne, 1975 (English ed. *George Grosz, Life and Work*, London and New York, 1979)

Wolfrat, Willi, *George Grosz*, Leipzig, 1921

ARTICLES

Behne, Adolf, 'George Grosz. Snob und Antisnob', *Die Weltbühne*, Vol. 20, 1924, p. 234

Coellen, Ludwig, 'Die Erste Grosz-Mappe', *Das Kunstblatt*, Vol. 1, 1917, pp. 348ff.

Däubler, Theodor, 'George Grosz', *Die Weissen Blätter*, Vol. 3, No. 11, 1916, pp. 167–70

Däubler, Theodor, 'George Grosz', *Das Kunstblatt*, Vol. 1, No. 3, March 1917, pp. 80–82

Herzfelde, Wieland, 'The Curious Merchant from Holland', *Harper's Magazine*, No. 187, 1943, pp. 569–76

Herzfelde, Wieland, 'George Grosz, John Heartfield und die Zwanziger Jahre', *Die Weltbühne*, 1 July 1964, pp. 846–9

Herzfelde, Wieland, 'John Heartfield und George Grosz. Zum 75. Geburtstag meines Bruders', *Die Weltbühne*, 15 June 1966, pp. 745–9

Herzfelde, Wieland, 'George Grosz, John Heartfield, Erwin Piscator, Dada und die Folgen oder die Macht der Freundschaft', *Zur Sache, geschrieben und gesprochen zwischen 18 und 80*, Berlin and Weimar, 1976, pp. 430–67

Jähner, Horst, 'Grosz contra Grosz', *Bildende Kunst*, Dresden, Vol. 3, No. 6, 1955, pp. 453f.

Lang, Lothar, 'Ein Künstler, der den Weg verfehlte. Gedanken über den Abstieg des grossen Talents', *Bildende Kunst*, Dresden, Vol. 11, 1958, pp. 768–71

Mehring, Walter, 'Gott contra Grosz', *Das Tagebuch*, Vol. 9, 14 April 1928, pp. 621–3

Melville, Robert, 'The Bastard from Berlin', *The Sunday Times*, 4 November 1973, pp. 58–72

Roditi, Eduard, 'George Grosz: An Embittered Romantic', *Arts Magazine*, Vol. 37, 1963, pp. 18–23

Scheffler, Karl, 'Der Künstler als Journalist. George Grosz', *Kunst und Künstler*, Vol. 24, 1926, pp. 354–8

Westheim, Paul, 'Erinnerungen an George Grosz', *Die Weltkunst*, Vol. 32, No. 15, 15 November 1962, pp. 16f.

Wilson, Edmund, 'A Little Yes and a Big No', *The New Yorker*, 4 January 1947

EXHIBITION CATALOGUES

1920, *Der Ararat, Erstes Sonderheft: George Grosz*, Galerie Neue Kunst/Hans Goltz, Munich

1926, *George Grosz*, Galerie Alfred Flechtheim, Berlin

1954, *George Grosz*, Whitney Museum of American Art, New York

1962, *George Grosz 1893–1959*, Akademie der Künste, Berlin (West)

1962, *Ohne Hemmung. Zeichnungen und farbige Blätter*, Galerie Meta Nierendorf, Berlin

1963, *George Grosz 1893–1959*, City Art Gallery, York and Arts Council Gallery, London

1965, *George Grosz 1893–1959*, Graphische Sammlung Albertina, Vienna

1966, *George Grosz. Zeichnungen und Druckgraphik*, Staatliche Kunstsammlungen Dresden, Kupferstichkabinett

1968, *George Grosz*, Marlborough Fine Art, London

1969, *George Grosz*, Württembergischer Kunstverein, Stuttgart

1971, *George Grosz*, Instituto di Storia dell'Arte, Università di Parma

1971, *George Grosz. Frühe Druckgrafik, Sammelwerke, Illustrierte Bücher*, Staatliche Museen Preussischer Kulturbesitz, Kupferstichkabinett, Berlin (West)

1973, *George Grosz. Theatrical Drawings and Watercolours*, Busch-Reisinger Museum, Harvard University, Cambridge, MA

1975, *George Grosz. Leben und Werk*, Kunstverein Hamburg

1977, *George Grosz. Works in Oil*, Heckscher Museum, Huntington, NY

1978, *George Grosz*, The Hirshhorn Museum and Sculpture Garden, Smithsonian Institution, Washington, DC

1980, *George Grosz, Porträt des Schriftstellers Max Herrmann-Neisse, 1925*, Mannheim Kunsthalle

1993, *The Sketchbooks of George Grosz*, ed. Peter Nisbet, Busch-Reisinger Museum, Harvard University Art Museums, Cambridge, MA

1993, *George Grosz. Die Berliner Jahre*, Städtische Galerie Rosenheim

1994-5, *George Grosz: Berlin – New York*, Neue

Nationalgalerie, Berlin, Kunstsammlung Nordrhein-Westfalen, Düsseldorf, Staatsgalerie Stuttgart

GENERAL STUDIES OF THE PERIOD

Bergius, Hanne, *Das Lachen Dadas*, Giessen, 1989

Catalogue, *George Grosz, John Heartfield and the Malik Verlag*, Ars Libri Ltd., Boston, MA, 1994

Eberle, Matthias, *World War I and the Weimar Artists. Dix, Grosz, Beckmann, Schlemmer*, New Haven and London, 1985

Exhibition catalogue, *Tendenzen der Zwanziger Jahre*, Neue Nationalgalerie (and other venues), Berlin, 1977

Exhibition catalogue, *Wem gehört die Welt – Kunst und Gesellschaft in der Weimarer Republik*, Neue Gesellschaft für bildende Kunst in der Staatlichen Kunsthalle, Berlin, 1977

Exhibition catalogue, *Paris–Berlin*, Centre Georges Pompidou, Paris, 1978

Exhibition catalogue, *Ich und die Stadt*, Berlinische Galerie, Berlin, 1987

Faure, Ulrich, *Im Knotenpunkt des Weltverkehrs. Herzfelde, Heartfield, Grosz und der Malik-Verlag, 1916–1947*, Berlin and Weimar, 1992

Gay, Peter, *Weimar Culture: The Outsider as Insider*, London, 1969

Haxthausen, Charles W. and Suhr, Heidrun, *Berlin. Culture and Metropolis*, Minneapolis and Oxford, 1990

Hermand, Jost and Trommler, Frank, *Die Kultur der Weimarer Republik*, Munich, 1978

Hermlin, Stefan and others, *Die wilden Zwanziger. Weimar und die Welt, 1919–33*, Reinbek bei Hamburg, 1988

Herzfelde, Wieland (ed.), *Der Malik-Verlag 1916–1947*, exhibition catalogue, Deutsche Akademie der Künste zu Berlin, Berlin (East), 1967

de Jonge, Alex, *The Weimar Chronicle. Prelude to Hitler*, New York and London, 1978

Kessler, Harry, *Diaries of a Cosmopolitan, 1918–37*, trans. C. Kessler, London and New York, 1971; exhibition catalogue, *Harry Graf Kessler, Tagebuch eines Weltmannes*, Deutsches Literaturarchiv im Schiller-Nationalmuseum, Marbach am Neckar, 1988

Laqueur, Walter, *Weimar. A Cultural History, 1918–33*, London, 1974

Roters, Eberhard, *Berlin 1910–1933. Die visuellen Künste*, Berlin, 1983

Schneede, Uwe M., *Die Zwanziger Jahre. Manifeste und Dokumente deutscher Künstler*, Cologne, 1979

Schrader, Bärbel and Schebera, Jürgen, *Die 'Goldenen' Zwanziger Jahre. Kunst und Kultur der Weimarer Republik*, Leipzig, 1987 (English ed., 1989)

Schrader, Bärbel und Schebera, Jürgen, *Kunstmetropole Berlin, 1918–1933. Dokumente und Selbstzeugnisse*, Berlin and Weimar, 1987

Tatar, Maria, *Lustmord. Sexual Murder in Weimar Germany*, Princeton, NJ, 1995

Von Eckardt, Wolf and Gilman, Sander L., *Bertolt Brecht's Berlin*, New York, 1975; London, 1976

Willett, John, *The New Sobriety. Art and Politics in the Weimar Period, 1917–1933*, London, 1978

Willett, John, *The Weimar Years. A Culture Cut Short*, London, 1984

INDEX

Numbers in bold refer to pages of catalogue entries of works exhibited. Figures are indicated by (fig.) after page number

Abrechnung folgt! (The Reckoning is Coming!; cat.147), anthology of drawings, 13, 145, 186, **188**, 199; 'United Front', 138
Abwicklung (Winding Up: autobiographical sketch), 36–8, 80, 95, 154, 198
Acrobats (cat.22) **61**
Die Affäre Mielzynski (The Mielzynski Case: cat.9), **48**
Akademie der Künste (Academy of Arts), Berlin, 18, 19
Die Aktion, journal, 6, 22, 25, 51, 145, 198
Alexander, Gertrud, 10, 25
Altdorfer, Albrecht, 39
Am Tempelhofer Feld (Tempelhof Field; cat.4), **44**
Am Tisch (At Table; cat.87), **126**
Among Other Things a Word in Favour of German Tradition *see Unter anderem ein Wort für Deutsche Tradition*
An der Grenze (On the Verge; cat.91), **131**
An Eva, meine Freundin (To Eva, My Girlfriend; cat.61), **96**
An Heiliger Stätte (*In a Holy Place*) *see Sonntagnachmittag* (cat.139)
Andersen-Nexø, Martin, 13, 134, 199
Arbeiter (Workers; cat.6), **46**
Arbuckle, Fatty, 95
Arendt, Hannah, 13
Art is in Danger *see Die Kunst ist in Gefahr*
The Art Scab *see Der Kunstlump*
Art Students' League, New York, Grosz teaches at, 17, 200, 201
Association of German Communist Artists, 13
Atelier Colarossi, Paris, 45, 198
Auf dem Weg zur Arbeit see Blauer Morgen
Auf der Pirsch (On the Hunt; cat.66), **102**
Auf der Strasse (On the Street; cat.124), 164, **165**
Aufruhr (Uproar; cat.50), **86**
Aus dem Zyklus Parasiten (*From the Cycle Parasites*; cat.62), **98**
Aus der Jugendzeit (*Youth Remembered*; cat.102), **142**
Autobiography, 24, 26, 49, 60, 82, 137, 180, 195, 198, 199, 200, 201
Avalov-Bermondt, General, 106

Baader, Johannes, 3, 10
Baltikumer (cat.70), **106**
Barnum and Bailey circus, 44, 90
Bateman, H.M., 185
Bavarian Soviet Republic, 110
Beardsley, Aubrey, 30
Becher, Johannes, R., 32
Becker, Ulrich, 52
Beckmann, Max, The Disappointed, 23 (fig.)
Bei Simsen (At Simsen's; cat.23), **62**
Beim Frühstück (At Breakfast), 168
Belebte Strassenszene (Lively Street Scene; cat.56), **92**
Bell, Robert, 68, 92, 198
Berlin Dada *see* Dada
Berlin School of Arts and Crafts, 4, 5, 10, 42, 57, 96, 122, 195–6

Berliner Illustrierte, 24
Berliner Strassenszene (Berlin Street Scene; cat.81), **119**
Berlin – Friedrichstrasse (cat.52), **88**
Bertolt Brecht (cat.128), **169**
Der Besessene Forstadjunkt (*The Possessed Forestry Assistant*; cat.48), **84**
Die Besitzröten (The Toads of Possession; cat.89), **128**, 146
Betrachtung (Scrutiny; cat.38), **75**
Bibergeil (Wanton as a Beaver by Edgar Firn; cat.146), 186, **188**
Bildnis Anna Peter (Portrait of Anna Peter; cat.112), **154**
Black Sun Press, 18, 200
Blaue Reiter, 102
Blauer Morgen (Blue Morning; cat.2), **42**
Blumenfeld, Erwin, 28; *Postcard to* (cat.141), **182**
Der Blumenverkäufer (The Flower Seller; cat.136), **176**
Der Blutiger Ernst (Bloody Earnest; cat.153), journal, 9, 186, **193**, 199
books and magazines, illustrations in, 185–94
Bosch, Hieronymus, 18, 39
The Boxer, 11
The Boxer Max Schmeling, 15, 15 (fig.)
Braque, Georges, 14
Brecht, Bertolt/Bert, 12–13, 19, 47, 118, 128, 169, 172, 199; *Die drei Soldaten*, 169; Grosz's caricature of (cat.128), 169; *Die Legende des toten Soldaten*, 72; *Threepenny Opera*, 180
Breker, Arno, 19
Briesemeister, Dr Otto, 182
Brillantenschieber im Café Kaiserhof (Diamond Profiteers in the Café Kaiserhof; cat.82), **120**
Brooke, Rupert, The Old Vicarage, Granchester, 5
Die Brücke, 195
Bruegel, Pieter, 18, 39
Brüning, Reich Chancellor Heinrich, 200
Buhnenbildentwurf zu G.B. Shaw 'Caesar und Cleopatra' (Stage set design for G.B. Shaw's 'Caesar and Cleopatra'; cat.79), **117**
Burchard, Otto, 10
By the Canal, Suburb, 23

Café (1918; cat.60), **96**
Café (1918–19; cat.159), **195**
Café (1926; cat.110), **152**, 174
Café am Rhein (Café on the Rhine; cat.65), **101**
Café des Westens, Berlin, 5, 92, 198
Café Kaiserhof, Brillantenschieber im (cat.82), **120**
Café 'Verlorenes Glück' (The Lost Happiness Café; cat.1), **42**
cafés, 1, 5, 78, 88, 89, 92, 96, 101, 120, 130, 152
Carrà, Carlo, 11, 36, 120
Cassirer, Bruno, 166
Cassirer Press, Berlin, 200
Cézanne, Paul, 34
Chagall, Marc, 19
Chaplin, Charlie, 95, 118

Chez Emile Hasenbohler (cat.123), **164**
Chirico, Giorgio de, 11, 31
Christus mit der Gasmaske (Christ with a Gasmask; cat.132), **173**
Christus mit der Gasmaske; Maul halten and weiter dienen (Christ with a Gasmask; Shut up and do your duty; cat.131), **172–3**
Circe (cat.134), 152, **174**
Clark, Christopher, 124
collages, 35, 120, 122, 186, 189, 198, 199
Communism, 9, 10, 12, 13, 17, 21, 22, 23, 25–6, 107, 108, 110, 134, 138, 156, 168, 169, 172, 198, 199, 200
Constructivism, 11, 38
Cooper, James Fenimore, 3, 68
Corinth, Lovis, 9, 59
Corot, Camille, 12
Courbet, Gustave, 16, 199
Courths-Mahler, Hedwig, 140
Cranach, Lucas, 14
Cubism, 38
Cycling and Weightlifting, 11 (fig.)

Dada, 2, 3, 8–10, 19, 22, 23, 25, 27, 29, 37, 59, 95, 114, 116, 168, 182, 191, 198; First International Fair (1920), 9 (fig.), 9–10, 96, 120, 122, 199
Dada Siegt! (Dada Triumphs!), Grosz's illustrations for (cat.148), 186, **189**
Dada Soirées, 191
Dadaco (anthology), 114
Dada-Zeichnung 'Mann mit Messer, Flasche und Mond (Dada drawing 'Man with knife, Bottle and Moon'; cat.47), **84**
Dämmerung (Dusk) see *Ecce Homo* (cat.75)
Däubler, Theodor, 80, 87, 92, 102, 198; *Nordlicht*, 92
Daum marries her pedantic automaton 'George' in May 1920. John Heartfield is very glad of it; (cat.83), **122**
Daumier, Honoré, 9, 37, 185
'Degenerate Art' exhibition, Germany (1937), 200
Delacroix, Eugène, 39
Deutsche Typen (German Types; cat.84), 112, **124**
Deutsches Lied, Deutsches Wein (German Song, German Wine; cat.76), **114**
Deutschland, ein Wintermärchen (Germany, A Winter's Tale), 7, 7 (fig.), 10, 15, 198
Die von der Liebe Leben (Those Who Live from Love; cat.125), **166**
Dix, Otto, 10, 195, 201
Döhmann, Dr, 122
Dolchstoss von Rechts (Stab in the Back from the Right; cat.99), **138**
Doppelbild (Double Image; cat.40), **77**
Dr Billig am Ende (Huelsenbeck), Grosz's illustration for (cat.78), **116**, 186
Drei Männer (Three Men; cat.74), **112**, 124
Dresden Academy of Art, 32; Grosz's studies at, 4, 42, 195
Duchamp, Marcel, *The Bride Stripped Bare by her Bachelors Even*, 122
Dücker, Alexander, 76, 137
DuMont, Mark Neven, 15, 82, 199
Dürer, Albrecht, 14

Ebert, Reich President Friedrich, 9, 21, 22, 24, 199; Portrait of (*Ebert der Präsident*; cat.108), **148**
Ecce Homo (1919–20; cat.75), **113**
Ecce Homo (portfolio of drawings), 13, 14, 26, 54, 66, 80, 84, 87, 88, 98, 113, 119, 124, 131, 137, 199
Edison, Thomas, 2, 29
Ehepaar (Married Couple; cat.143), **185**
Das Ende des Weges (The End of the Road; cat.17), **56**
Erinnerung an New York (Memory of New York), 68
Erinnerung an Rosa Luxemburg and Karl Liebknecht (In Memory of Rosa Luxemburg and Karl Liebknecht; cat.72), **108**
Ernst, Max, 10

Erste George Grosz-Mappe (First George Grosz Portfolio), 7, 23, 68, 76, 198
Erzberger, Matthias, 24
essays, Grosz's theoretical, 11, 12, 16–17, 24–5, 32–40
Ewers, Hanns Heinz, 5, 48
Expressionism, 2, 5, 6, 12, 22, 23, 24, 25, 26, 32, 48, 50, 51, 64, 145, 195, 198
Eymery, Marguerite (pseudonym: Rachilde), 64

The Face of the Ruling Class see *Das Gesicht der herrschenden Klasse*
Fahrendes Volk (Travelling People; cat.54), **90**
Fehrenbach, Chancellor Konstantin, 24
Der Feier (Celebration; cat.64), **100**
Feierabend (End of the Day's Work), 24
Firn, Edgar, *Bibergeil. Pedantische Liebeslieder*, Grosz's illustrations for (cat.146), 186, **188**
First International Dada Fair (Burchard Gallery, Berlin, 1920), 9 (fig.), 9–10, 96, 120, 122, 199
First World War, 1914–18: 5–9, 50–86, 198
Flaxman, John, 38
Flechtheim, Alfred, 14, 16, 26, 160, 174, 199
Flechtheim Gallery, Berlin, 36
Ford, Henry, 2
Freikorps, 9, 22, 23, 24, 25, 150, 199
French Riviera, Grosz's stay in (1927), 16, 164, 199
Früh um 5 Uhr (Five in the Morning), 25
Frick, Wilhelm, 200
Frühlingsanfang (The Beginning of Spring; cat.138), **178**
Führer durch das lasterhafte Berlin (Guide to Dissolute Berlin), 1, 180
Futurism, 2, 5, 7, 38, 51, 75, 77, 88, 89, 95, 113, 198

Galerie Neue Kunst, Munich, Grosz's first one-man show at (1920), 10
Ganoven an der Theke (Rogues at the Bar; cat.101), **140**
Gefangenen (Prisoners; cat.14), **52**
Gegensätze (Contrasts; cat.37), **74**
Der Gegner (The Opponent), journal, 9, 24, 32, 34, 134, 186, 199
Genelli, 38
George Grosz, The Clown of New York, 19, 19 (fig.)
German Communist Party (KPD), 9, 10, 12, 13, 21, 22, 23, 25, 26, 32, 107, 108, 110, 148, 168, 172, 198, 199, 200
Germanentag (Day of the Huns; cat.156), **194**
Gershwin, George, 200
Das Gesicht der herrschenden Klasse (The Face of the Ruling Class, political drawings; cat.149), 12–13, 24, 72, 128, 166, 168, 185, **189**, 199; 'God-willed Dependence', 25 (fig.); 'Oh Marburg, Oh Marburg...', 112; 'Post-War Idyll', 110; 'The Voice of the People is the Voice of God', 24 (fig.); '... where they go', 23 (fig.)
Die Gesundbeter (The Faith-Healers or Fit For Active Service; cat.36), **72**
Die Gezeichneten (The Marked Men), portfolio of drawings, 72, 128, 137, 200
Gillray, James, 185
Goethe, Johann von, 7
Goldgräber (Gold Diggers; cat.31), **68**
Goltz, Hans, 10, 198
The Good Soldier Schwejk (Hasek), Grosz's stage designs for, 152, 169, 172, 199
Gott mit uns (God Be With Us; political album), 10, 24, 72, 199
Gottes sichtbarer Segen ist bei mir (The Blessing of Heaven is Visibly upon Me; cat.155), **194**
Goya, Francisco de, 37
Grauer Tag (Grey Day), 11 (fig.), 12
Griebel, Otto, 31
Grossstadtstrasse mit Kutsche (Big City Street with Coach; cat.57), **93**
Grosz, George, childhood, 3–4; death (1958), 19–20, 201; with Eva Peter in the studio (c. 1920), xii (fig.);

identities/role-playing, 2–3; marriage to Eva Peter (1920), 10, 15, 96, 122; return to Berlin (1958), 18–20, 201; theoretical essays, 11, 12, 16–17, 24–5, 32–40; trial for blasphemy (1931), 169, 173, 199
Grosz, Martin Oliver (son), 200
Grosz, Peter Michael (son), 14, 42, 199
Grünewald, Mathias, 34
Grüss aus Sachsen (Greetings from Saxony; cat.100), **140**, 186
Grützner, Eduard, 3, 4
Gumperz, Julian, 14
Die Guten Jahre (The Good Years; cat.93), **132**
The Gymnast, 11

Haifische (Sharks; cat.88), **128**
Halbakt (Nude Torso; cat.26), **64**
Harig, Fritz, 63
Hasek, Jaroslav, 169, *The Good Soldier Schwejk*, 152, 169, 172, 199
Hausmann, Raoul, 3, 9, 10, 191, 198
Haussuchung (House Search; cat.95), **134**
Heartfield, John (Helmut Herzfelde), 8, 8(fig.), 9, 10, 12, 19, 24–5, 29, 110, 118, 122, 168, 186, 189, 191, 198; *Der Kunstlump* (with Grosz), 12, 24–5, 32–4; Portrait of (cat.127), **168**
Heartfield, Tom, 168, 186
Heine, Heinrich, 7, 128
Heligoland (cat.5), **45**
Hermann-Neisse, Max, 25, 92; Portrait of, 15, 15 fig.)
Herzfelde, Helmut see Heartfield, John
Herzfelde, Wieland, 6, 7, 8, 9, 10, 14, 16, 19, 23, 24, 28, 29–30, 51, 96, 118, 122, 168, 173, 186, 191, 198, 199, 200; Grosz's cover design for *Sulamith* by (cat.145), 186; Grosz's illustrations for *Tragigrotesken der Nacht* by (cat.150), 186, 190, 194; Grosz's portrait of, 15; *Die Kunst ist in Gefahr* (with Grosz), 38–9
Hindenburg, President Paul von, 15–16, 24, 199, 200
Hintergrund (Background; collection of drawings, 1928), 16, 169, 172–3, 199
Hitler, Adolf, 17, 26, 146, 198, 199, 200, 201; *Mein Kampf*, 146, 199
Hoech, Hannah, 3, 9, 10, 57; *Cut with the Cake-Knife*, 10
Hogarth, William, 16, 30, 37, 185; *Gin Lane*, 7
Huber, Wolf, 39
Huelsenbeck, Dr Richard, 8, 22, 30, 114, 122, 198, 200; Grosz's illustrations for: *Dada Siegt!* (cat.148), 186, **189**; *Dr Billig am Ende* (cat.78), **116**, 186; *Phantastische Gebete* (cat.144), 186

I am a Camera (film), 1, 20n
Ich will alles um mich her ausrotten, was mich einschränkt (I Will Root Up from my Path...; cat.106), **146**
Illustrierte Blatt, magazine, 14
Im Lokal (In the Pub; cat.41), **78**
Im Schatten (In the Shadows; collection of lithographs), 12, 113, 199
Impressionists, 38
In den Besten Jahren (In the Best Years; cat.121), **162**, 178
In the Robbers' Den (1908), 3 (fig.)
Der Indianerhäuptling (The Indian Chief; cat.98), **138**
Inflation (cat.86), **126**
Ingres, Jean-Auguste, 12, 38, 40, 63
Instead of an Autobiography see *Statt einer Biographie*
Interregnum (collection of prints), 18, 173, 200
Isherwood, Christopher, 1, 20n, 201

Jack the Ripper, 67
January uprising (1919), 2, 23
Jedermann sein eigner Fussball, journal, 9, 23
John Heartfield der Rote Regissör (John Heartfield the Red Director; cat.127), **168**
Jugendstil, 42
Jung, Franz, 9; *The rote Woche*, 134

206   Index

Kabarettszene (Cabaret Scene; cat.18), **57**
Kandinsky, Vassily, 38
Kanehl, Oskar, 145; Grosz's illustrations for *Die Schande* (Infamy; cat.105), 145, 186; *Strasse Frei*, 150
Kapp Putsch (1920), 32, 138, 199
Kautsky, Karl, 148
Keilerei II (Brawl II; cat.8), **48**
Kerr, Alfred, 142
Kessler, County Harry, 82, 186; *The Diaries of a Cosmopolitan*, 29, 30–1, 59, 63
Klapper, Dr Heinrich, 122
Klee, Paul, 38
Kleine Grosz Mappe (Little Grosz Portfolio), 7, 8, 54, 70, 198; advertisement for (1917), 8, 8 (fig.)
Kleines Café (Small Café; cat.90), **130**
Klink, Fanny, 63
Knödelessen (Eating Dumplings; cat.68), **104**
Der Knüppel (The Cudgel; cat.154), journal, 9, 25, 186, **193**
Kokoschka, Oskar, 12, 32, 33, 60, 64
Die Kommunisten fallen und die Devisen steigen (The Communists Fall and the Foreign Exchange Rises; cat.71), **107**
Kraft und Anmut (Strength and Grace; cat.103), **142**
Krawall der Irren (Lunatics Riot; cat.16), **55**, 66
Krupp von Bohlen und Hallbach, Gustav, 180
Ku Klux Klan (cat.80), **118**
Kubin, Alfred, 48
Die Kunst ist in Gefahr (Art is in Danger; Grosz and Herzfelde), 38–9; Jacket of 38 (fig.)
Das Kunstblatt, art journal, 35, 39, 90, 95
Der Kunstlump (The Art Scab: Grosz and Heartfield), essay, 12, 24–5, 32–4

Landscape near Point Rouge, Marseille, 16 (fig.)
Lappe and Vorratshaus (Laplander and Storage Shed; cat.94), **134**
Lasker-Schüler, Else, 5, 92, 198
The Latest Hit (cat.133), **174**
League of Nations, 110
Léger, Fernand, 14
Lenin, V.I., 13, 199
Letzte Flasche (Last Bottle; cat.120), **162**
Leviné, Eugen, 110
Liebermann, Max, 63
Der Liebesturm (The Tower of Love; cat.27), **64**
Liebknecht, Karl, 21, 22, 108, 198, 199
Liegende Akt (Reclining Nude; cat.24), **62**
Ludendorff, General Erich von, 24, 146, 199
Luftangriff (Aerial Attack; cat.12), **51**
Lunacharsky, Anatoliy Vasilevich, 24
Lustmord in der Ackerstrasse (Sex Murder in Acker Street; cat.30), 66, **67**
Luxemburg, Rosa ('Junius'), 21, 22, 23, 108, 198, 199; *Die Krise der Socialdemokratie*, 107

Macke, August, 102
Mädchen und ihre Liebhaber (Girl and Her Lovers; cat.33), **70**
Makart, Hans, 35
Mäleskircher, 39
Malik Press (Malik Verlag), 9, 13, 23, 38, 118, 166, 172, 186, 198, 199, 200; signet for, 37 (fig.)
Mammen, Jeanne, 1
Mann, die Haare kämmend, mit Frau (Man Combing Hair with Woman; cat.130), **171**
Mannheim Kunsthalle, *Die neue Sachlichkeit* ('The New Objectivity') exhibition (1925), 15, 154, 199
Marburg, 110
May, Karl, 3, 68, 195
Mayakovsky, Vladimir, 25
Mayor Gallery, London, Grosz's exhibition (1934), 200
M.E., The Wire-Puller (Nazi poster), 25 (fig.)

Mehring, Walter, 9, 20, 96, 191, 199, 200; Berlin Dada, 28; Grosz's portrait of, 15
Meidner, Ludwig, 28, 51, 198
Meissner, Otto, 180
Mein Deutschland (My Germany; cat.77), **114**
Menschen im Café (People in a Café; cat.53), **89**
Menzel, Adolf, 39, 63
Metropolis, 198
Meyrinck, Gustav, 5, 48
military mental asylum, Grosz admitted to (1917), 6, 82
Military Pictorial Office (now UFA), 29
Miró, Joan, 201
Mit Pinsel und Schere (With Brush and Scissors), 120, 199
Mondnacht (Moonlit Night; cat.39), **76**
Mondnacht (poem), 76
Mord (Murder), 54
Moreck, Curt, 'Guide to Dissolute Berlin', 1, 180
Mühsam, Erich, 18
Multscher, Hans, 39

Nachtkaffeehaus (Café at Night; cat.42), **78**
Nachwuchs (Next Generation; cat.97), **137**
National Gallery, Germany, 18
Nazis (NSDAP), 17, 39, 146, 150, 167, 199, 200
Neo-Pointillists, 38
Das neue Gesicht der herrschenden Klasse (The New Face of the Ruling Class, 1930), 26, 150, 153, 174, 180, 200
Die neue Jugend (New Youth), journal, 7, 8, 76, 198
Die neue Sachlichkeit (The New Objectivity) exhibition (1925), 15, 154, 199
Neugebauer, Rosamunde, 32
Neumann, Israel Ber, 17
Neumann gallery, J.B., 22
The New Face of the Ruling Class see *Das neue Gesicht der herrschenden Klasse*
The New Man, 9 (fig.), 11
New York, Grosz in, 17, 18, 200
New York Harbour 18 (fig.)
Niederkunft (Childbirth; cat.44), **80**
Noske, Gustav, 22, 23, 24, 150, 198–7
November Group (1918), 22, 198
'November Revolution' (1918), 7, 21–2

Olympiakino, Berlin (Olympia Cinema, Berlin; cat.55), 90–2
On My New Paintings see *Zu meinen neuen Bildern*
Eine Ordonnanz (An Orderly; cat.142), **183**
Orgie (Orgy; cat.67), **102**
Orlik, Emil, 57, 96, 195

Paar und Tanzende (Couple and Dancers; cat.158), **194**
Pandemonium, 22 (fig.), 24
Panizza, Oskar, 7, 20n, 198
Papen, Franz von, 180, 200
Paris (cat.117), **158**
Paris, Grosz in, 37, 45, 158, 164, 195, 198, 199
Paris als Kunststadt (Paris as City of the Arts; essay), 38
Paris Peace Conference (1919), 110
Pascin, Jules, 68, 198
Passantan (Pedestrians; cat.122), **164**
Passanten (Pedestrians; cat.126), **167**
Paul Whiteman Band, 14, 174
Peter, Anna (mother-in-law), *Portrait*, (cat.112) **154**
Peter, Eva ('Maud', 'Daum'), 17, 18, 19, 96, 198, 199, 200; Grosz's marriage to (1920), 10, 15, 96, 122, 199; with Grosz in the studio, xii (fig.)
Pfempfert, Franz, 22, 145
The Philistine's Mirror see *Der Spiesser-Spiegel*
photography, 36
photomontages, 2, 8, 9, 10, 19, 19 (fig.), 168
Picasso, Pablo, 34, 201
Pierre in Saint Nazarre (animated film), 29–30
Phantastische Gebete (Fantastical Prayers: Huelsenbeck; cat.144), **186**

Piscator, Erwin, 18, 152, 169, 172, 199, 200
The Pit, 18, 19
pittura metafisica (Italian Metaphysical painting), 11, 120, 122, 199
Die Pleite (Bankruptcy; cat.152), journal, 9, 22, (fig.), 23, 72, 128, 146, 150, 186, **193**, 199
Plietzsch, Eduard, 30, 200
Poe, Edgar Allan, 5, 48
Pointillists, 38
Pop Art, 19
pornography, 75, 80, 199
Portrait of the Writer Max Hermann-Neisse, 15, 15 (fig.)
Postcard to Erwin Blumenfeld (cat.141), 182
Poussin, Nicolas, 12, 38
Prost Noske! (Cheers Noske!), 22, (fig.), 23–4
prostitution, 1, 63, 90–2, 98, 169
Prussian Archangel (Heartfield and Schlichter), 10

Queen Bar (cat.140), **180**
Quergebäude Vier Treppen (Tenement, Four Flights Up; cat.28), **66**
Der Querschnitt (The Cross-Section), magazine, 14, 174, 199

Die Räuber (The Robbers), portfolio, 128, 146, 199
Rathenau, Walther, 199
Red Group, 25
Redslob, Edwin, 10
Reimann, Hans, 140; Grosz's illustrations for *Hedwig Courths-Mahler, Schlichte Geschichten fürs traute Heim*, 140
Reinhardt, Max, 169, 191
Reis, Bernard, 78
Reissner, Carl, 14
Republican Automata 11 (fig.), 12
Restaurant (cat.137), **178**
Rheidt, Celly de, 180
Richter, Hans, 31, 168
Rilke, Rainer Maria, 33, 37, 198
Rimbaud, Arthur, 152
Rockwell, Norman, 4
Die Rote Fahne (The Red Flag), Communist Party newspaper, 10, 12, 13, 25
Rote Gruppe, 169, 199
Rousseau, Henri Douanier, 34
Rowlandson, Thomas, 185
Royal Prussian Emperor Franz Grenadier Guard Regiment, Grosz's service in (1914), 52
Rubens, Sir Peter Paul, 25; *Bathsheba at the Well*, 32
Rudi Schlichter (cat.129), **170**

Sahl, Hans, 28–9
Schacht, Hjalmar, 180
Schad, Christian, 1
Schadow, Johann Gottfried, 63
Schall und Rauch (Noise and Smoke), cabaret, 29, 191
Schall und Rauch, journal, cover illustration (cat.151), **191**
Die Schande (Infamy by Kanehl; cat. 105), 145, 186
Schaufenster in Berlin (Shop Windows in Berlin; cat.118), **160**
Scheidemann, Philipp, 21, 24
Schiele, Egon, 64
Schiller, Friedrich, 146
Schlachtfeld (Battlefield; cat.13), **52**
Schlägerei (cat.10), **49**
Schleicher, General Kurt von, 180, 200
Schlichter, Rudolf, 10, 169, 170, 201; autobiography of, 170; Grosz's caricature of (cat.129), **170**
Schmalhausen, Charlotte (née Peter), 92
Schmalhausen, Otto ('Oz'), 16, 68, 75, 82, 92, 96, 174, 191, 198, 199, 200
Schmeling, Max, 15, 15 (fig.), 31
Schmidt, P.F., 10

Index 207

Schneede, Uwe M., 14
Scholz, Georg, 10
Schönheit, Dich will ich preisen! (Beauty, I wish to praise thee!; cat.63), **98**, **128**
Schönheitsabend in der Motzstrasse (Beauty Contest in Motz Street; cat.58), **94**
Schulze-Naumburg, Paul, 39; *Kunst and Rasse*, 39
Searle, Ronald, 185
Sechstagerennen (Six-Day Bicycle Race; cat.7), **47**
Seiwert, Franz, 'The Hole in Rubens's Ham', 25
Selbstbildnis (Self-Portrait; cat.45), **82**
Selbstbildnis (Self-Portrait; cat.46), **82**
Selbstbilnis mit Hund vor der Staffelei (Self-Portrait with Dog in Front of an Easel; cat.114), **156**
Selbstporträt (für Charlie Chaplin) (Self-Portrait; cat.59), **95**
self-portraits, 15, 18, 82, 95 102, 156
Shaw, George Bernard, 117
Siegfried Hitler (cat.107), **146**
Sinclair, Upton, 118; Grosz's illustrations for *100%*: 118, 186
Sind Wir nicht Volkerbundfähig? (Are we not eligible for the League of Nations; cat.73), **110**
Song of the Gold Diggers (poem), 68
Sonnenfinsternis (Eclipse of the Sun), 15, (fig.), 15–16
Sonniges Land (Sunny Country; cat.85), **124**
Sonniges Land (collage by Grosz and Heartfield), 189
Sonntagnachmittag (Sunday Afternoon; cat.139), **180**
Soviet Union, 9, 22, 128, 199; Grosz's trip to, 13, 134, 199, 201
Spartacists, 21, 22 (fig.), 23, 108, 198
Spaziergang (The Stroll; cat.135), **176**
SPD (Social Democrats), 21–2, 23, 108, 148, 200
Der Spiegel, news magazine, 18
Der Spiesser-Spiegel (The Philistine's Mirror; collection of drawings), 14, 16, 26, 198, 199
stage and costume designs, 16, 18, 20n, 117, 152, 169, 172, 183, 199, 201
Statt einer Biographie (Instead of an Autobiography), essay, 34–5, 38
Stehender Akt (Standing Nude; cat.25), **63**
Sternberg, 169
Sterne, Maurice, 17, 200
Stinnes, Hugo, 24, 167

Stinnes & Cie, 24
Stolp, Grosz's childhood in, 3–4, 195
Strasse in Berlin (Street in Berlin; cat.115), **156**
Strasse in Berlin (Street in Berlin; cat.119), **160**
Strassenszene mit Zeichner (Street Scene with Draftsman; cat.43), **80**
Streseman, Gustav, 199
Sturm gallery, Berlin, 5, 60, 198
Der Stürmer (Nazi paper), 124
Stützen der Gesellschaft (Pillars of Society), 15, 16, 18, 199
Südende, Berlin, 5, 29, 42, 195, 198
Sulamith (Herzfelde), Grosz's cover design for (cat. 145), 186

Tägliche Illustrierte, 24
techniques, Grosz's, 6, 15, 35, 36, 49, 50, 55, 77, 98, 102, 117, 152, 178, 185
Texasbild für meinen Freund Chingachgook (Texas Picture for My Friend Chingachgook; cat.32), **68**
Thälmann, Ernst, 26
Thomas, Dr William King, 2, 3, 11, 67
Thurber, James, 200
Der Tote Mann (The Dead Man; cat.15), **54**
Toulouse-Lautrec, Henri de, 39
Tragigrotesken der Nacht (Herzfelde), Grosz's illustrations for (cat.150), 186, **190**, 194
Trapeze Artists (cat.19), **58**
Traum Fantasia (Dream Fantasy; cat.34), **71**
Tucholsky, Kurt, 26, 31
Tumult (cat.35), **72**
Two Men in a Room (cat.29), **66**
Typenblatt (Standardised Types; cat.157), **194**

Über alles die Liebe (Love Above All), collection of drawings, 16, 162, 166, 200
Der Überfall (The Attack; cat.11), **50**
Ulk (*Berliner Tageblatt* comic supplement), 4, 195
United States, 68, 78, 118, 169; Grosz in, 1, 17, 18–19, 96, 200–9
Unter Anderem ein Wort für Deutsche Tradition (Among Other Things a Word in Favour of German Tradition), essay, 16–17, 39–40

Valetti, Rosa, 180
Van Eyck, Jan, 15
Varieté Tänzer (Variety Dancers; cat.21), **60**
Vera Truppe (The Vera Troupe; cat.20), **59**
Verlag Neue Jugend, 23
Verstimmte Flöte (Dissonant Flute; cat.104), **144**
Vier Menschen vor der Kirche (Four People in Front of a Church; cat.96), **136**
Vorstadt (Suburb; cat.49), **85**

Walden, Herwarth, 5, 92
watercolours, 1, 11 (fig.), 18 (fig.), 35, 98, 102, 113, 117, 120, 122, 124, 126, 130, 140, 160, 162, 164, 165, 174, 176, 178, 183, 185
Der Weg allen Fleisches, VI (The Way of All Flesh, VI; cat.111), **153**
Weimar Republic, 1, 9, 21–7, 124, 148, 199–8
Der Weisse General (The White General; cat.109), **150**
Werbung (Courtship; cat.92), **132**
Westheim, Paul, 29
Whisky (cat.51), **87**
Whitman, Walt, 3
Widmung an Oskar Panizza (Dedicated to Oskar Panizza), 7, 7(fig.), 15, 19, 198
Wilhelm II, Kaiser, 104
Winding Up see Abwicklung
Wolff, Kurt, 114

Zech, Paul, *Das trunkene Schiff*, 152
Zille, Heinrich, 5, 46; *Moving House with the Brown Sofa* 5 (fig.)
Zirkus (Circus; cat.3), **44**
Zola, Emile, 6
Zu meinen neuen Bildern (On My New Paintings), essay, 11, 12, 35–6, 120
Der Zuchthäusler (The Convict; cat.69), **104**
Zwei Männer (Two Men; cat.116), **158**
Zweig, Arnold, *Der Streit um den Sergeanten Grischa*, 183
Zweig, Stefan, 13–14

PHOTOGRAPHIC CREDITS

All works of art are reproduced by kind permission of the owner. Specific acknowledgements are as follows:

All works by George Grosz reproduced in this catalogue are © of the George Grosz Estate c/o DACS, London.

Anders, Jörg P., Berlin, cat. 16, fig. 1
Bartsch, Hans-Joachim, Berlin, cat. 117
Basel, Oeffentliche Kunstsammlung Basel, Martin Bühler, cat. 59
Berlin, Akademie der Künste, cats. 52, 71, 95, 99, 145, 148
Blanc, Ricardo, cats. 11, 102
März, Roman, cats. 70, 147, 149, 152, 153, 154, 280; fig. 8, 9
Riphe, Ilona, cats. 18, 77, 144, 151
Cambridge, © Fitzwilliam Museum, University of Cambridge, cat. 7
Düsseldorf, Studio K, cat. 68
Cambridge, MA., © President and Fellows Harvard College, Harvard University Art Museums, cats. 32, 106, 107, 108
Cologne, © Rheinisches Bildarchiv, cats. 90, 103
Freeman, K.G. (Photography), cats. 15, 19, 54

Gawryszewska, Elzbleta, cats. 115, 119
Hagadorn, Randall, New Jersey, cats. 1, 2, 3, 4, 5, 6, 8, 14, 20, 24, 26, 28, 31, 38, 39, 45, 48, 55, 61, 62, 69, 79, 80, 86, 88, 91, 92, 94, 97, 104, 105, 114, 118, 123, 124,
Herling, Michael, cat. 121
Hölzel, © Willi Hölzel, cat. 51
Lauri, Peter, cat. 109
Lehmann, Christel, fig. 3
Littkemann, © J. Littkemann, Berlin, cats. 50, 63, 82, 83
London, Prudence Cuming Ass. Ltd., cats. 13, 25, 29, 33, 58, 74, 78, 122
London, © The British Museum, cat. 53
London, © Christie's, cat. 132
London, © Tate Gallery, cat. 143
New York, © 2017 The Museum of Modern Art, cats. 12, 17, 36, 110, 112, 134, 142
Schälchi, Peter, cat. 139
Simak, Fritz, cat. 30
Stalsworth, Lee, cat. 161
Studio Patrick Goetelen, cats. 96, 129
Zóltowska-Huszcza, Tieresa, cat. 87

FRIENDS OF THE ROYAL ACADEMY

SPONSORS

Mrs Denise Adeane
Mr and Mrs Theodore Angelopoulos
Mr P.F.J. Bennett
Mr David Berman
Mr and Mrs George Bloch
Mrs J. Brice
Mr Jeremy Brown
Mr and Mrs P.H.G. Cadbury
Mrs L. Cantor
Mrs Denise Cohen
Mrs Elizabeth Corob
Mr and Mrs S. Fein
Mr and Mrs R. Gapper
Mr and Mrs Robert Gavron
Mr and Mrs Michael Godbee
Lady Gosling
Lady Grant
Mr and Mrs Allan B.V. Hughes
Mr Harold Joels
Mrs G. Jungels-Winkler
Mr J. Kirkman
Mr and Mrs Leonard S. Licht
Dr Abraham Marcus
Mrs Xanna De Mico
The Oakmoor Trust
Ocean Group p.l.c. (P.H. Holt Trust)
Mr and Mrs Godfrey Pilkington
Mr and Mrs G.A. Pitt-Rivers
Mr and Mrs David Shalit
Mrs Roama Spears
The Stanley Foundation
Mrs Paula Swift
Mr Robin Symes
Mrs Edna S. Weiss
Mrs Linda M. Williams
Sir Brian Wolfson

ASSOCIATE SPONSORS

Mr Richard B. Allan
Mr Richard Alston
Mr Ian F.C. Anstruther
Mrs Ann Appelbe
Mr John R. Asprey
Lady Attenborough
Mrs Susan Besser
Mrs Linda Blackstone
Mrs C.W.T. Blackwell
Mr Peter Boizot
C.T. Bowring (Charities Trust) Ltd
Mrs J.M. Bracegirdle
Mr Cornelius Broere
Lady Brown
Mr T.M. Bullman
Mr and Mrs James Burt
Mrs A. Cadbury
Mr and Mrs R. Cadbury
Mrs C.A. Cain
Miss E.M. Cassin
Mr R.A. Cernis
Mr. S. Chapman
Mr W.J. Chapman
Mr John Cleese
Mrs R. Cohen
Mrs N.S. Conrad
Mr and Mrs David Cooke
Mr C. Cotton
Mrs Saeda H. Dalloul
Mr and Mrs D. de Laszlo
Mr John Denham
The Marquess of Douro
Mr D.P. Duncan
Mr Kenneth Edwards
Mrs K.W. Feesey MSc
Dr G.-R. Flick
Mr J.G. Fogel
Mr Graham Gauld
Mr Stephen A. Geiger
Mrs R.H. Goddard
Mrs P. Goldsmith
Mr Gavin Graham
Mr and Mrs R.W. Gregson-Brown
Mrs O. Grogan
Mr B.R.H. Hall
Miss Julia Hazandras
Mr Malcolm Herring
Katherine Herzberg
Mrs. P. Heseltine
Mr R.J. Hoare
Mr Reginald Hoe
Mr Charles Howard
Mrs A. Howitt
Mr Norman J. Hyams
Mrs Manya Igel
Mr S. Isern-Feliu
The Rt. Hon. The Countess of Iveagh
Lady Jacobs
Mr and Mrs S.D. Kahan
Mr and Mrs J. Kessler
Mr D.H. Killick
Mr P.W. Kininmonth
Mrs L. Kosta
Mr and Mrs M.J. Langer
Mrs J.H. Lavender
Mr and Mrs Andrew D. Law
Mr J.R.A. Leighton
Mr Owen Luder
Mrs G.M.S. McIntosh
Mr Peter I. McMean
Ms R. Marek
The Hon. Simon Marks
Mr B.P. Marsh
Mr and Mrs J.B.H. Martin
Mr R.C. Martin
Mr and Mrs G. Mathieson
Mr J. Moores
Mrs A. Morgan
Mr A.H.J. Muir
Mr David H. Nelson
Mrs E.M. Oppenheim-Sandelson
Mr Brian R. Oury
Mr Michael Palin
Mrs J. Palmer
Mrs J. Pappworth
Mr J.H. Pattisson
Mrs M.C.S. Philip
Mrs Anne Phillips
Mr Ralph Picken
Mr G.B. Pincus
Mr W. Plapinger
Mrs J. Rich
Mr Clive and Mrs Sylvia Richards
Mr F.P. Robinson
Mr M. Robinson
Mr D. Rocklin
Mrs A. Rodman
Mr and Mrs O. Roux
The Hon. Sir Stephen Runciman CH
The Worshipful Company of Saddlers
Sir Robert Sainsbury
Mr G. Salmanowitz
Mr Anthony Salz
Lady Samuel
Mrs Bernice Sandelson
Mrs Charles H. Schneer in memory of B. Gerald Cantor
The Schuster Charitable Trust
Mrs Bernard L. Schwartz
Mr Mark Shelmerdine
Mr R.J. Simmons
Mr John H.M. Sims
Dr and Mrs M.L. Slotover
The Spencer Wills Trust
Professor and Mrs Philip Stott
Mr and Mrs J.G. Studholme
Mr J.A. Tackaberry
Mr N. Tarling
Mr G.C.A. Thom
Mrs Andrew Trollope
Mr A.J. Vines
Mrs C.H. Walton
Mr D.R. Walton Masters
Mr Neil Warren
Miss J. Waterous
Mrs Roger Waters
Mrs C. Weldon
Mr Frank S. Wenstrom
Mr Julyan Wickham
Mrs I. Wolstenholme
Mr W.M. Wood
Mr R.M. Woodhouse
Mr and Mrs F.S. Worms

Royal Academy Trust

BENEFACTORS

H.M. The Queen
Mr and Mrs Russell B. Aitken
American Airlines
The Annie Laurie Aitken Charitable Trust
American Associates of the Royal Academy Trust
American Express Company
Mrs John W. Anderson II
The Andor Family
The Hon. and Mrs Walter H. Annenberg
Mr Walter Archibald
Marilyn B. Arison
The Hon. Anne and Mr Tobin Armstrong
Asprey
AT & T
AT & T (UK) Ltd
Barclays Bank plc
Mr and Mrs Sid R. Bass
Mr Tom Bendhem
Benihana Group
Mrs Brenda Benwell-Lejeune
Mr David Berman
In Memoriam: Ida Rose Biggs
Charlotte Bonham-Carter Charitable Trust
Denise and Francis Booth
British Airways, North America
British Gas plc
The British Petroleum Company plc
BP America
British Steel plc
Mr Keith Bromley
The Brown Foundation Inc.
BT
BUNZL plc
Iris and B. Gerald Cantor
Sir Richard Carew Pole
The Rt. Hon. the Lord Carrington
The Trustees of the Clore Foundation
The Cohen Family Charitable Trust
The John S. Cohen Foundation
The Ernest Cook Trust
Mrs John A. Cook
Crabtree & Evelyn
The Hon. and Mrs C. Douglas Dillon
Sir Harry and Lady Djanogly
In Memoriam: Miss W.A. Donner
The Dulverton Trust
Alfred Dunhill Limited
Miss Jayne Edwardes
The John Ellerman Foundation
Mr E.A. Emerson

209

English Heritage
The Eranda Foundation
The Esmée Fairbairn Charitable Trust
Esso UK PLC
Lord and Lady Faringdon
Mr and Mrs Eugene V. Fife
Mr and Mrs Donald R. Findlay
Mr Walter Fitch III
Mrs Henry Ford II
The Henry Ford II Fund
The Foundation for Sport and the Arts
The Late John Frye Bourne
The Garfield Weston Foundation
Gartmore plc
The Gatsby Foundation
The Getty Grant Program
The J. Paul Getty Jr Trust
The Lady Gibson
Glaxo Wellcome plc
The Jack Goldhill Charitable Trust
Maurice and Laurence Goldman
The Horace W. Goldsmith Foundation
The Worshipful Company of Goldsmiths
The Greentree Foundation
Mr and Mrs Lewis Grinnan Jr
The Worshipful Company of Grocers
The Worshipful Company of Haberdashers
The Paul Hamlyn Foundation
The Late Dr and Mrs Armand Hammer
Mrs Sue Hammerson
Mr and Mrs Jocelin Harris
Philip and Pauline Harris Charitable Trust
Mr and Mrs Gustave Hauser
The Hayward Foundation
Mr and Mrs Randolph Hearst
Klaus and Belinda Hebben
The Hedley Foundation
Mrs Henry J. Heinz II
The Henry J. and Drue Heinz Foundation
Drue Heinz Trust
The Heritage of London Trust
The Howser Foundation
The Idlewild Trust
The J.P. Jacobs Charitable Trust
Jerwood Foundation
Mr and Mrs Donald P. Kahn
The Kresge Foundation
The Kress Foundation
Mr and Mrs Sol Kroll
Ladbroke Group Plc
Mr D.E. Laing
The Kirby Laing Foundation
The Maurice Laing Foundation
The Landmark Hotel
The Landmark Trust
The Lankelly Foundation
Mr John S. Latsis
The Leche Trust
The Leverhulme Trust
Mr Leon Levy and Ms Shelby White
Lex Service Plc
The Linbury Trust
The Ruth and Stuart Lipton Charitable Trust
Sir Sydney and Lady Lipworth
Mr John Madejski
Mrs T.S. Mallinson
The Manifold Trust
The Stella and Alexander Margulies Charitable Trust
Mr and Mrs John L. Marion
Marks & Spencer
Mrs Jack C. Massey
M.J. Meehan & Company
Mr. Paul Mellon KBE
The Anthony and Elizabeth Mellows Charitable Trust
The Mercers' Company
The Monument Trust
Mr and Mrs Donald Moore
The Henry Moore Foundation

Museums and Galleries Improvement Fund
National Westminster Bank PLC
Diane A. Nixon
The Normanby Charitable Trust
Otemae College
The Peacock Charitable Trust
Mr and Mrs Frank Pearl
The Pennycress Trust
In Memoriam: Mrs Olive Petit
The P.F. Charitable Trust
The Pilgrim Trust
Mr A.N. Polhill
The Hon. and Mrs Leon B. Polsky
The Edith and Ferdinand Porjes Charitable Trust
Provident Financial plc
The Radcliffe Trust
The Rayne Foundation
Mr and Mrs Laurance S. Rockefeller
The Ronson Charitable Foundation
Mr and Mrs Leonard Rosoman
Rothmans UK Holdings Limited
The J. Rothschild Group Charitable Trust
Rothschilds Inc
Royal Mail International
The RTZ - CRA Group
The Late Dr Arthur M. Sackler
Mrs Arthur M. Sackler
Mrs Jean Sainsbury
Mrs Basil Samuel
Save & Prosper Educational Trust
Mrs Frances G. Scaife
Sea Containers Limited
Sheeran Lock
Shell UK Ltd
The Archie Sherman Charitable Trust
Mr and Mrs James C. Slaughter
The Late Mr Robert Slaughter
Pauline Denyer Smith and Paul Smith CBE
Sotheby's
The Spencer Charitable Trust
Miss K. Stalnaker
The Starr Foundation
The Steel Charitable Trust
Bernard Sunley Charitable Foundation
Lady Judith Swire
Mr and Mrs A. Alfred Taubman
Mr and Mrs Vernon Taylor Jr.
Texaco Inc
Time Out Magazine
G. Ware and Edythe Travelstead
Seiji Tsutsumi
The Douglas Turner Charitable Trust
The 29th May 1961 Charitable Trust
Unilever PLC
The Weldon UK Charitable Trust
Mr and Mrs Keith S. Wellin
The Welton Foundation
Westminster City Council
Mr and Mrs Garry H. Weston
The Hon. and Mrs John C. Whitehead
Mrs John Hay Whitney
Mr Frederick B. Whittemore
Mr and Mrs Wallace S. Wilson
Mr and Mrs A. Witkin
The Wolfson Foundation
The Late Mr Charles Wollaston
The Late Mr Ian Woodner
Mr and Mrs William Wood Prince

Corporate Membership Scheme

CORPORATE PATRONS

Arthur Andersen
Glaxo Wellcome plc
The Economist Group

CORPORATE MEMBERS

Alliance & Leicester Building Society
All Nippon Airways Co. Ltd.
Atlantic Plastics Limited
A.T. Kearney Limited
Bankers Trust
Bank Julius Baer & Co Ltd
Banque Indosuez
Barclays Bank plc
BAT Industries plc
BP Chemicals
British Aerospace PLC
British Airways
British Alcan Aluminium plc
British Gas plc
Bunzl plc
BUPA
Christie's
Chubb Insurance Company
Cookson Group plc
Coopers & Lybrand
Courage Limited
Credit Suisse First Boston Limited
The Daily Telegraph plc
Datastream International
The Diamond Trading Company
Dow Jones Telerate Ltd
Eaga Ltd
E.D.& F. Man Limited Charitable Trust
Gartmore Investment Management plc
Goldman Sachs International Limited
Grand Metropolitan plc
Guardian Royal Exchange plc
Guinness PLC
Hay Management Consultants Limited
Hillier Parker May & Rowden
IBM
ICI
Jaguar Cars Ltd
Kvaerner Construction Ltd
John Laing plc
Lloyds Private Banking Limited
M & G Group P.L.C.
Marks & Spencer
Merrill Lynch Europe PLC
Midland Bank plc
MoMart plc
Morgan Guaranty Trust Company, New York
Morgan Stanley International
Pearson plc
The Peninsular and Oriental Steam Navigation Company
Pentland Group plc
Price Waterhouse
The Reader's Digest Association
Reuters
Rothmans UK Holdings Limited
The Royal Bank of Scotland plc
The RTZ-CRA Group
Salomon Brothers International Limited
Saga Petroleum U.K. Limited
Sea Containers Ltd.
SmithKline Beecham
The Smith & Williamson Group
Société Générale, UK
Southern Water plc
TI Group plc
Unilever UK Limited

CORPORATE ASSOCIATES

ABL Group
Ashurst Morris Crisp
AT & T
Bass PLC
BHP Petroleum Ltd
BMP DDB Limited
BMW (GB) Limited

The BOC Group
Booker plc
Bovis Construction Limited
Charterhouse plc
CJA (Management Recruitment Consultants) Limited
Clifford Chance
Coutts & Co
Credit Lyonnais Laing
The Dai-Ichi Kangyo Bank, Ltd
Dalgleish & Co
De La Rue plc
Durrington Corporation Limited
Enterprise Oil plc
Fina plc
Foreign & Colonial Management Ltd
General Accident plc
The General Electric Company plc
H.J. Heinz Company Limited
John Lewis Partnership plc
Kleinwort Benson Charitable Trust
Lex Service PLC
Linklaters & Paines
Macfarlanes
Mars G.B. Limited
Nabarro Nathanson
NEC (UK) Ltd
Newton Investment Management Limited
Nortel Ltd
Ove Arup Partnership
The Rank Organisation Plc
Reliance National Insurance Company (UK) Ltd
Robert Fleming & Co. Limited
Royal Insurance Holdings plc
Sainsbury's PLC
Save & Prosper Foundation
Schroders plc
Sears plc
Sedgwick Group plc
Slough Estates plc
Smith System Engineering Limited
Sotheby's
Sun Life Assurance Society plc
Tate & Lyle Plc
Tomkins PLC
Toyota Motor Corporation
United Biscuits (UK) Limited

Sponsors of Past Exhibitions

The Council of the Royal Academy thanks sponsors of past exhibitions for their support. Sponsors of major exhibitions during the last ten years have included the following:

Alitalia
Italian Art in the 20th Century 1989

Allied Trust Bank
Africa: The Art of a Continent 1995*

Anglo American Corporation of South Africa
Africa: The Art of a Continent 1995*

The Banque Indosuez Group
Pissarro: The Impressionist and the City 1993

Banque Indosuez and W.I. Carr
Gauguin and The School of Pont-Aven: Prints and Paintings 1989

BBC Radio One
The Pop Art Show 1991

BMW (GB) Limited
Georges Rouault: The Early Years, 1903-1920 1993
David Hockney: A Drawing Retrospective 1995*

British Airways
Africa: The Art of a Continent 1995

British Petroleum Company plc
British Art in the 20th Century 1987

BT
Hokusai 1991

Cantor Fitzgerald
From Manet to Gauguin: Masterpieces from Swiss Private Collections 1995

The Capital Group Companies
Drawings from the J. Paul Getty Museum 1993

The Chase Manhattan Bank
Cézanne: the Early Years 1988

Chilstone Garden Ornaments
The Palladian Revival: Lord Burlington and his House and Garden at Chiswick 1995

Christie's
Frederic Leighton 1830-1896 1996

Classic FM
Goya: Truth and Fantasy, The Small Paintings 1994
The Glory of Venice: Art in the Eighteenth Century 1994

Corporation of London
Living Bridges 1996

The Dai-Ichi Kangyo Bank Limited
222nd Summer Exhibition 1990

The Daily Telegraph
American Art in the 20th Century 1993

De Beers
Africa: The Art of a Continent 1995

Deutsche Morgan Grenfell
Africa: The Art of a Continent 1995

Digital Equipment Corporation
Monet in the '90s: The Series Paintings 1990

The Drue Heinz Trust
The Palladian Revival: Lord Burlington and his House and Garden at Chiswick 1995
Denys Lasdun 1997

The Dupont Company
American Art in the 20th Century 1993

The Economist
Inigo Jones Architect 1989

Edwardian Hotels
The Edwardians and After: Paintings and Sculpture from the Royal Academy's Collection, 1900-1950 1990

Elf
Alfred Sisley 1992

Esso Petroleum Company Ltd
220th Summer Exhibition 1988

Fiat
Italian Art in the 20th Century 1989

Financial Times
Inigo Jones Architect 1989

Fondation Elf
Alfred Sisley 1992

Ford Motor Company Limited
The Fauve Landscape: Matisse, Derain, Braque and their Circle 1991

Gamlestaden
Royal Treasures of Sweden, 1550-1700 1989

Générale des Eaux Group
Living Bridges 1996

J. Paul Getty Jr Charitable Trust
The Age of Chivalry 1987

Glaxo Wellcome plc
From Byzantium to El Greco 1987
Great Impressionist and other Master Paintings from the Emil G. Bührle Collection, Zurich 1991
The Unknown Modigliani 1994

Goldman Sachs International
Alberto Giacometti 1901-1966 1996

The Guardian
The Unknown Modigliani 1994

Guinness PLC
Twentieth-Century Modern Masters: The Jacques and Natasha Gelman Collection 1990
223rd Summer Exhibition 1991
224th Summer Exhibition 1992
225th Summer Exhibition 1993
226th Summer Exhibition 1994
227th Summer Exhibition 1995
228th Summer Exhibition 1996

Guinness Peat Aviation
Alexander Calder 1992

Harpers & Queen
Georges Rouault: The Early Years, 1903-1920 1993
Sandra Blow 1994
David Hockney: A Drawing Retrospective 1995*
Roger de Grey 1996

The Headley Trust
Denys Lasdun 1997

The Henry Moore Foundation
Henry Moore 1988
Alexander Calder 1992
Africa: The Art of a Continent 1995

The Independent
The Art of Photography 1839-1989 1989
The Pop Art Show 1991
Living Bridges 1996

Industrial Bank of Japan, Limited
Hokusai 1991

Intercraft Designs Limited
Inigo Jones Architect 1989

Joannou & Paraske-Vaides (Overseas) Ltd
From Byzantium to El Greco 1987

The Kleinwort Benson Group
Inigo Jones Architect 1989

Land Securities PLC
Denys Lasdun 1997

Lloyds Bank
The Age of Chivalry 1987

Logica
The Art of Photography, 1839-1989 1989

The Mail on Sunday
Royal Academy Summer Season 1992
Royal Academy Summer Season 1993

Marks & Spencer
Royal Academy Schools Premiums 1994
Royal Academy Schools Final Year Show 1994*

Martini & Rossi Ltd
The Great Age of British Watercolours, 1750-1880 1993

Paul Mellon KBE
The Great Age of British Watercolours, 1750-1880 1993

Mercury Communications
The Pop Art Show 1991

Merrill Lynch
American Art in the 20th Century 1993*

Midland Bank plc
The Art of Photography 1839-1989 1989
RA Outreach Programme 1992-1996
Lessons in Life 1994

Minorco
Africa: The Art of a Continent 1995

Mitsubishi Estate Company UK Limited
Sir Christopher Wren and the Making of St Paul's 1991

Mobil
From Byzantium to El Greco 1987

Natwest Group
Reynolds 1986
Nicolas Poussin 1594-1665 1995

Olivetti
Andrea Mantegna 1992

Park Tower Realty Corporation
Sir Christopher Wren and the Making of St Paul's 1991

Premiercare (National Westminster Insurance Services)
Roger de Grey 1996*

Redab (UK) Ltd
Wisdom and Compassion: The Sacred Art of Tibet 1992

Reed International plc
Toulouse-Lautrec: The Graphic Works 1988
Sir Christopher Wren and the Making of St Paul's 1991

Republic National Bank of New York
Sickert: Paintings 1992

The Royal Bank of Scotland
The Royal Academy Schools Final Year Show 1996
Braque: The Late Works 1996*

Arthur M. Sackler Foundation
Jewels of the Ancients 1987

Salomon Brothers
Henry Moore 1988

The Sara Lee Foundation
Odilon Redon: Dreams and Visions 1995

Sea Containers Ltd
The Glory of Venice: Art in the Eighteenth Century 1994

Silhouette Eyewear
Egon Schiele and His Contemporaries: From the Leopold Collection, Vienna 1990
Wisdom and Compassion: The Sacred Art of Tibet 1992
Sandra Blow 1994
Africa: The Art of a Continent 1995

Société Générale, UK
Gustave Caillebotte: The Unknown Impressionist 1996*

Société Générale de Belgique
Impressionism to Symbolism: The Belgian Avant-Garde 1880-1900 1994

Spero Communications
The Royal Academy Schools Final Year Show 1992

Texaco
Selections from the Royal Academy's Private Collection 1991

Thames Water Plc
Thames Water Habitable Bridge Competition 1996

The Times
Old Master Paintings from the Thyssen-Bornemisza Collection 1988
Wisdom and Compassion: The Sacred Art of Tibet 1992
Drawings from the J. Paul Getty Museum 1993
Goya: Truth and Fantasy, The Small Paintings 1994
Africa: The Art of a Continent 1995

Tractabel
Impressionism to Symbolism: The Belgian Avant-Garde 1880-1900 1994

Unilever
Frans Hals 1990

Union Minière
Impressionism to Symbolism: The Belgian Avant-Garde 1880-1900 1994

Vistech International Ltd
Wisdom and Compassion: The Sacred Art of Tibet 1992

* Recipients of a Pairing Scheme Award, managed by ABSA (Association for Business Sponsorship of the Arts)

Other Sponsors

Sponsors of events, publications and other items in the past two years:

Academy Group Limited
Agnew's
Air Hong Kong
Mr and Mrs Martin Beisly
The Beit Trust
The Britto Foundation
The Brown Foundation
Bvlgari
James Butler RA
The Calouste Gulbenkian Foundation (Lisbon)
Christopher Wood Gallery
Mr and Mrs Terence Cole
Columbus Communications
Condé Nast Publications
Continental Airlines
Mrs Shimona Cowan
David Linley Furniture Ltd
Hamish Dewar
Jennifer Dickson RA
Sir Harry and Lady Djanogly
D.W. Viewboxes Ltd
The Elephant Trust
Brenda Evans
Sebastian de Ferranti
Finnair
FORBES Magazine, New York
The Four Seasons Hotels
Isabel Goldsmith
Ivor Gordon
Lady Gosling
Grand Hotel, Stockholm

Hammerson UK Properties plc
Julian Hartnoll
Ken Howard RA
IBM UK Limited
Inter-Continental Hotels
John Lewis Partnership plc
Count and Countess Labia
The Landmark Hotel
The Leading Hotels of the World
The Leger Galleries, London
The A.G. Leventis Foundation
Mr and Mrs J.H.J. Lewis
London Borough of Southwark
The Maas Gallery
Mandarin Oriental Hotel Group
Michael Hue-Williams Fine Art Limited
The Nigerian Friends of africa95
Richard Ormond
Mr and Mrs James Phelps
Stuart Pivar
Price Waterhouse
The Private Bank & Trust Company Limited
Ralph Lauren
The Robina Group
The Rockefeller Foundation
N. Roditi & Co.
Mrs Basil Samuel
The Savoy Group
Sears Plc
Simon Dickinson Ltd
Peyton Skipwith
Swan Hellenic Ltd
John Ward RA
W S Yeates plc
Mrs George Zakhem
ZFL